July-1985

THE LIBERATORS

THE LIBERATORS

My Life
in the Soviet Army

VIKTOR SUVOROV

There is on earth no sadder ditty
Than the tale of the Central Committee!
—Russian Folk Song

W • W • NORTON & COMPANY
New York   London

Library of Congress Cataloging in Publication Data
Suvorov, Viktor.
    The liberators.
    1. Suvorov, Viktor.   2. Soviet Union.   Armia—
Biography.   3. Soviet Union. Armia—Military life.
4. Czechoslovakia—History—Intervention, 1968–
I. Title.
U55.S82A34   1983   355′.0092′4 [B]   83–2202

ISBN 0-393-01759-1

W.W. Norton & Company, Inc., 500 Fifth Avenue, New York, N.Y. 10110
W.W. Norton & Company Ltd., 37 Great Russell Street, London WC1B 3NU

2 3 4 5 6 7 8 9 0

CONTENTS

Preface: How I became a Liberator   1

Kiev Tank-Technology School Check Point. 25 March, 1966   11

Kiev Garrison Detention Centre. 29 March, 1966   25

Kiev Garrison Detention Centre. 31 March, 1966   42

April 1967. The final days before graduation from the Kharkov
Guards Tank Commanders' School   48

Kharkov 1967. Theatre   55

Summer 1967. The Ukraine. Operation 'Dnieper'   61

1967. Moscow – The Ukraine. Operation 'Bridge'   86

Oster, the Ukraine. October 1967. Training   92

Oster, the Ukraine. March 1968   94

Headquarters, Leningrad Military District. Early 1969   101

The Ukraine, 1967   107

The all-army conference of young officers. The Kremlin.
26 November, 1969   114

The Group of Soviet Troops in Germany. Spring 1970   116

A training division, Oster. Early 1967. Durov's Way   118

Impressions of the Soviet combat air force   127

The Ukraine. Beginning of summer 1968   135

Liberators   146

The Western Ukraine. August 1968   153

The final stop before the state frontier   158

Invasion   161

The centre of Prague. August 1968   164

First days of September 1968. Counter-revolution   182

Koshitse. Early September 1968. Flight   185

Koshitse – Prague. September 1968. Farewell to the Liberators   189

The Soviet Army after the liberation   193
The Western Ukraine, 12 October, 1968   198
Postscript   201

vi

How I Became a Liberator

The Party is our helmsman – *Popular song*

The General Secretary of the Party set a task: there must be a sharp rise in agricultural output. So the whole country reflected on how best to achieve this magnificent aim. The Secretary of our Regional Party Committee thought about it, as did all his advisers, consultants and researchers.

To tell the truth, it was a ridiculously easy task: the climate of our Region is similar to that of France – there is plenty of sun and warmth and water. And our soil is splendid. The black earth is nearly a metre thick and rich enough to spread on a slice of bread. There are also plenty of technicians and specialists. The only misfortune is that the people themselves have no interest in work because, however much a peasant works, the reward for him, personally, will be just the same, since to pay for a peasant's labour according to results is, of course, quite impossible. Just imagine what would happen! Your hard-working peasant would soon be rich while layabouts would remain beggars. A rift would appear and then inequality would creep in. And all this would be contrary to the ideals of socialism.

So the First Secretary of the Regional Party Committee and all his advisers gave much thought as to how to increase agricultural output without infringing the principle of common material equality. And at last it dawned on them what to do. They could achieve the desired increase by using fertilizers.

A vast meeting, thousands strong, complete with brass bands, speeches, placards and banners, was urgently called at the local Chemical Combine. To a man, they shouted slogans, applauded, chanted patriotic songs. After that meeting, a competitive economy drive was launched at the Chemical Combine to harvest raw materials and energy resources. It lasted throughout the winter and, in the spring, on Lenin's birthday, all the workers reported at the Combine and laboured all day, without wages, using up the raw materials which had been saved. During the course of this day, they produced several thousand tons of liquid nitrogen fertilizer and, in accordance with the meeting's resolution, they decided to hand over all this fertilizer, free of charge, to the Region's collective farms.

It was a real red letter day for labour, and not only the newspaper correspondents of the local and republican press but also those of the central newspapers came in person to the Combine. In the evening, both the All-Union radio and the Central Television programmes reported this remarkable feat. The Central Committee of the Party officially commended the initiative of our chemical workers and appealed to all Chemical Combines, throughout the country, to launch competitions aimed at economising on raw materials which would later be used to produce additional amounts of fertilizer, to be handed over, in turn, free of charge, to neighbouring collective farms. Let our country bloom! Let it blossom forth like a vernal garden!

When the labour fête-day ended, the labour daily grind began.

The next morning, the Director of the Chemical Combine telephoned to the Regional Committee and said that, if the collective farms did not, during the next twenty-four hours, collect the free fertilizer presented to them, the Chemical Combine would come to a standstill: all its tanks were full to overflowing with excess fertilizer production and there was nowhere to put current production.

There followed a series of insistent calls from the Regional Committee to all the small District Committees, and from them to all collective farms. Each of the fifty regional collectives had immediately to take away the 150 tons of the fertilizer presented by the Combine. The news that our own collective had been given such an amount of fertilizer free of charge did not please our Chairman. Our collective farm owned seventeen lorries, but only three of these had tanks. One was used for milk, another for water, the third for petrol. Those used for milk and water could not possibly be used for liquid fertilizer. There remained only the one used for petrol. The lorry was old and battered beyond recall. The capacity of its tank was one and a half tons of liquid. The distance from our collective farm to town was seventy-three kilometres; taking into consideration the state of our road, that meant five hours there and five hours back. I was the driver of this lorry.

'Now look here,' said the Chairman, 'if you do not sleep for twenty-four hours, if your battery does not pack up, if your radiator does not melt with the heat, if your gear-box does not jam, if your lorry does not get stuck in the mud, you can do two trips in twenty-four hours, and bring back three tons of this bloody fertilizer. But you have to do, not two, but a hundred trips!'

'Right,' I said.

'That is not all,' he said. 'We are short of petrol. Of course I will give you petrol for three trips but, for the remaining ninety-seven, do the best you can. Push your lorry with your arse if you have to!'

2

'Right,' I said.

'You are our only hope. If you cannot do a hundred trips, you know only too well I will be dismissed from the chairmanship.'

I knew it. I knew also that, although our chairman was not to everyone's liking, nevertheless his replacement was a bloody sight worse.

'Any questions?'

'Yes. Even if I do a hundred trips – without petrol – where shall I put all this fertilizer?'

The Chairman glanced anxiously round the broad farmyard and scratched the back of his head. Where indeed? 150 tons of liquid, poisonous, stinking matter? Lenin's birthday is in April, worse luck, but the fertilizer only goes on the soil in June. So where to keep the fertilizer until June?

'Look here,' he said. 'Don't start nattering on about it. Get yourself to town as soon as possible. All the region's farms are busy with the same problem. Somebody may have some bright idea. You just watch what the others do and then you do the same. Get a move on! And don't return unless you've succeeded.'

I sighed, spat on my palms like a boxer before a fight, then got into my wretched lorry and set off to town over the bumps, pot-holes and huge puddles, which the spring sun had not yet dried up.

There was a long queue of trucks of different makes, dimensions and colours standing outside the Chemical Combine. But the queue was moving fast. I soon discovered that lorries, which had only a moment before been loaded, were already returning and taking up new places in the queue. Every one of these lorries ostensibly needed many hours to deliver its valuable load to its destination and then to return. But they rejoined the queue in a matter of minutes. Then came my turn. My tanks were rapidly filled with the foul-smelling liquid and the man in charge marked down on his list that my native kolkhoz had just received the first one and a half tons of fertilizer. I drove my lorry out through the Combine's gates and followed the group of lorries which had loaded up before mine. All of them, as if at a word of command, turned off the road and descended a steep slope towards the bank of the river Dnieper. I did the same. In no time at all, they had emptied their tanks. I did the same. Over the smooth surface of the great river, the cradle of the Russian civilisation, slowly spread a huge poisonous, yellow, stinking stain.

Having emptied my tank, I headed again for the Combine and another one and a half tons of fertilizer were marked off for our kolkhoz. And so it went on. The work proceeded vigorously and noisily. Tens of lorries, hundreds of trips, thousands of tons! Never in my life have I seen so many fish. And I would never have believed that

3

there were so many fish in the Dnieper. The whole surface of the river, from one side to the other, was crammed with the dead bodies of pike, bream and other fish. And still the lorries came, in a never-ending stream. And every driver knew that, if we did not succeed in emptying the gigantic reservoirs of that huge Combine, it would grind to a halt – and this would be a crime for which our unfortunate Chairman would have to bear responsibility.

The militia appeared suddenly at noon. The whole region was cordoned off: we were all detained. The representatives from the Combine also appeared, and then a young adviser from the Regional Committee turned up in a black Volga car. With an expression of disgust, he examined the place of work. He put a small white handker-chief to his little nose: the stench was unbearable. After a short chat with the Combine's representatives and with one of the detailed drivers, he got back into his car and drove off. After him disappeared both the militia and the Combine's representatives. We were ordered to proceed. Clearly, having acquainted himself with the situation on the ground and understanding all the implications, the adviser found our solution the best one.

And what other kind of solution could possibly be found? Donate all this excess production to the State? But where would the State find the reservoirs to store such a huge amount of liquid? The kolkhozes had nowhere to store it and nothing to transport it in. Should it be recorded as the work quota? But, in that case, what to do with the still unprocessed raw material arriving at the Combine in an endless stream? If this production was taken as part of the work quota, the inspectors would of course sense that something was wrong and ask where so much excess production had come from. There would be investigations etcetera. So it was better to let things go on as they were.

Towards evening, we finished the job. Everyone took delivery of his final load of liquid, but this time no one carried it off to the river, but instead to his own kolkhoz. It was then relayed to Moscow that everything was going well and that this year's harvest would be a record, thanks to the Regional Committee's First Secretary. Moscow promptly replied with a congratulatory telegram to the First Secretary and to all workers of the Region. And that was that.

Late that night, I delivered one and a half tons of the fertilizer to the kolkhoz and reported to the Chairman that I had fulfilled the task ahead of time. He thanked me but did not go into detail. Everything had been clear to him from the very beginning. He had long been accustomed to the fact that, whenever the Communist Party issues instructions, these invariably end in a way no one wishes to remember.

'Where shall I put this one and a half tons?' I asked.

'Keep them yourself! If necessary, I could produce record harvests without fertilizers. But what's the point?'

And that was that. I poured the liquid over my own tiny private plot. It proved an unpardonable mistake. Apparently, there was too much fertilizer for my tiny area of ground and I applied it at the wrong time. In May, when all the neighbouring kitchen gardens were producing strong shoots mine was barren. I was horrified. What would I eat during the winter? I was not going to become a soldier until the following spring: so how was I to live until then? The money I would receive for my work at the kolkhoz would be hardly enough for two months of very frugal existence. The peasant's only hope is his private plot which is not much bigger than the palm of his hand. And if nothing grows on that – what then?

I had to make some urgent decisions. But what? I could not run away from the kolkhoz: under socialism a peasant has no right to a passport, although everybody else has an internal passport. As a result of this simple restriction, a peasant cannot live in a town, cannot marry a town girl or stay in a hotel. Travelling on a plane is also forbidden. Who will let you board an aircraft without a passport? Maybe you are a criminal?

Don't think it is just a Soviet communist caprice, either. It is a vital necessity. If you are trying to establish material equality among the inhabitants of any country, you must introduce similar measures against the peasants. If you make all people equal, there will be mass migration of peasants into towns, where the working day is limited, where one need not work on rest days and holidays, and where one can have a holiday in summer. But, if all the peasants go to live in towns, your state of universal equality will perish from hunger. And, in order to prevent that state of affairs, you will be obliged to revert to the free market system, that is to capitalism, or else keep the peasants in their villages by force, by barbed wire, guard-dogs, threats and the introduction of special anti-peasant legislation.

I was a convinced supporter of the material equality of all mankind and therefore was prepared to spend all my life without an internal passport, which means never flying in an aircraft, never staying at an hotel and never marrying a town girl. But, in compensation, we would have equality. There would be no exploitation of man by man and we would have no rich and no poor!

That bloody fertilizer which ruined my harvest also ruined all my plans and forced me to look for some new way of life. The choice was not great: I could land up in jail, where the food is free, or I could become an officer, where the food is also free. Taking into consideration the fact that it is not difficult to land in jail, I decided to exploit this possibility only if I did not succeed in becoming an officer. And that didn't turn out to be particularly simple!

In order to become an officer, I had to become a citizen of my country, in other words somehow or other obtain a passport. They say that, in the USSR, the acquisition of a passport for going abroad is so difficult that it sometimes takes a man's whole life to achieve. But, for anyone not entitled to receive one, to obtain an internal passport is an altogether more difficult task. If you have an internal passport and are trying to obtain one allowing you to go abroad, theoretically the law is on your side. You can protest, go on hunger-strike or write letters to Brezhnev. In the end, if you persist, you may well be successful. But how to obtain an internal passport if you are not entitled to one by law? If you are just a Soviet peasant and if the law is against you and if you live in a country but are not considered a citizen of that country but only its peasant? If you have no right to any form of defence? If you are born simply to work, simply as an integral part of the agricultural work force, then what do you do? What can one do if one does not represent a legal entity, just like for instance, a horse or a pig, which also has no right to an internal passport (let alone one for going abroad) and which is similarly forbidden to stay in hotels or to travel by air?

To all intents I, like any other Soviet peasant, was an outlaw. And yet, in spite of everything, I managed to get a passport. It is a very long story indeed which I take no pleasure in recalling. I had to blackmail the kolkhoz Chairman, deceive the Chairman of the village Soviet, bribe a village Soviet Secretary as well as an employee of the Military Commissariat: there was no other way.

And, after all that, my passport was still not quite legal. At any moment, it could have been proved that, even though I had been born in the USSR of Soviet parents, whose ancestors down several hundred years had never crossed any frontier or had any contact whatsoever with foreigners, I had illegally appropriated the name of a USSR citizen. So, as a matter of urgency, I had to change my half-legal passport for another officially-issued document in my name. And, to achieve that, I entered the Kharkov Guards Tank Command School. They took my passport and I was given a new red 'military Card' in its place. Now nobody on earth could send me back to the kolkhoz. There is no way back from the Soviet Army.

While still a trainee, I participated in some of the biggest ever training exercises by Soviet troops on Soviet Army training grounds, each of which could accommodate on its territory several completely sovereign states. So, I had the opportunity of seeing from the inside the life of the most famous Soviet divisions, such as the 120th Guards Rogachevsky Motor-Rifle Division, the 2nd Guards Taman and the 41st Guards Berlin Division. Even at that time, I was staggered by the fact that each one of them was living a double life: one for show to the outside world, while the other inner reality was something quite apart and completely different.

In 1967 I was to become an officer. I served in the 287th Novograd-Volynsk Training Motor-Rifle Division of the Kiev Military District. At the time of the events in Czechoslovakia, I commanded a motor-rifle company of the 24th Samaro-Ulyanovsk Iron Motor-Rifle Division. Later I served on the Staff of the Leningrad Military District, and in diversionary troops, and after graduating from the Military Academy I served on the 10th Chief Directorate of the General Staff.

During my Staff service, I took part in many important training exercises like, for instance, that of the 3rd Shock Army of the Group of Soviet Troops in Germany.

The story related in this book starts from the moment when, while still a trainee at the Kharkov Guards School, I arrived in Kiev together with a group of my comrades to hand over battle equipment to the Kiev Tank Technical School. The hand-over dragged on for several days and, in order to save us from boredom, they entertained us with various studies and with service at the control check-points and other control points.

After a sleepless night, each member of a control check-point team was allowed to sleep, without undressing, in the small room beside the control point. When the story starts, I was asleep.

Part One

The Glasshouse

'Soldier! Boy!'

'Well?'

'What do you mean, well? Fucking well get up, I tell you, we're all on a charge!'

Shielding myself from the blinding sun with my arm, I tried to postpone the moment of awakening.

'I was on guard duty all night so even under regulations I am entitled to sleep three hours . . .'

'All you're entitled to is your cock in your pocket! Get up, I tell you, we're all on a charge.'

The news of our arrest made no impression on me at all. The only thing I realised clearly was that a good one and a half hours' compensation for a sleepless night was lost beyond recall. I sat up on the hard bench and rubbed my forehead and eyes with my fist. My head was cracking from lack of sleep. I yawned, stretched until my joints creaked, then sighed deeply to disperse any remaining sleep, and twisted my head about a bit in order to relieve a stiff neck.

'How much did we get?'

'Five for you – you were lucky, Viktor. But Sashka and I've been clobbered with ten days each while Vitya, the sergeant, got all of fifteen!'

What a bloody life our poor old sergeants have at Military School! You are paid five roubles extra for the job but they take twenty-five roubles' worth away from you.

'Where's my automatic?' I exclaimed.

'Everything's back at Company HQ – automatics, cartridge belts and bayonets. The Sergeant-Major will bring the equipment and food vouchers in a few moments, and then a bath, a haircut and off we go.'

In the main room of the Pass Check Point, the officer cadets of the first course, who had been precipitately removed from their usual occupations, were being handed documents and were counting the instruction files. Their sergeant was a very understanding fellow and was listening to us in a businesslike way, and nodding his head concernedly.

11

'I never took my eyes off him, and shouted the command as loudly as I could, and my lads opened the gate at once and, like lions, they devoured him with their eyes. And there you are: I didn't do a bloody thing and he clobbered me with fifteen, and my lads got ten each.'

'Okay, Kolya, never mind, get on with it!'

The other lads from the guard came in after us and, under their escorts, we all went for a haircut and a cold bath.

The cleanliness in the 'Reception Room' of the Kiev Garrison glasshouse was blinding.

'Comrade First Lieutenant, Guards Officer Cadet Suvorov presents himself at the Garrison Prison to serve his sentence.'

'How many?'

'Five days' arrest.'

'What for?'

'Bugger it,' flashed through my mind, 'What was it really for anyway? Why *was* I on a charge?'

The First Lieutenant, who had an unusually broad face and tiny feet, drilled into me with his small leaden eyes.

'What for?' he asked again.

'I don't know.'

'Who arrested you?'

'I don't know.'

'You'll soon find out here,' the First Lieutenant promised.

'Next.'

In came my sergeant.

'Comrade First Lieutenant, Guards Sergeant Makeyev for . . .'

'How many?' ugly mug cut in.

'Fifteen days.'

'Who sentenced you?'

'The Deputy Commander of the Military District, Colonel General Chizh.'

'What for?'

'We are guarding the School Check Point.'

'Ah-hah,' the First Lieutenant smiled understandingly.

He, of course, knew – indeed all three armies of the district knew – this habit of Colonel General Chizh, invariably to arrest the guard on duty at the Pass Check Point. It was an established fact that he arrested only those guarding the Check Point, but he did it without fail, on every visit to any school, regiment, battalion, division, at any training ground, firing range or depot. He did it anywhere and everywhere. Whenever he was passing through the Check Point, he arrested all those on duty and he meted out standard punishments. Fifteen days to the head of the party, ten days to those actually on duty, and five days to those resting and awaiting their turn on duty. It had been going on for many years. All three armies and many separate units, sub-units, military establishments and other organisations, all suspected that the Deputy Commander was striving to establish for himself some special kind of reception ceremony, not provided for under regulations, but what exactly he really wanted no one could actually guess throughout all the years that he held this high office.

Two savage-looking lance-corporals appeared on the threshold of the 'Reception Room' and the reception had officially begun.

'Ten seconds . . . UNDRESS!'

Boots, belts, caps, coats, everything was instantly thrown on to the floor. Now, stark naked, we all stood in front of ugly mug.

'About turn! Bend forward! Open up!'

At this point a First Lieutenant of the Soviet Army examined our arses. Smoking in the glasshouse is forbidden, so sometimes heavy smokers try to smuggle in little pieces of cigarettes, by wrapping them in paper and pushing them into their anal passages. This trick is well known to the glasshouse authorities and is dealt with mercilessly.

Meanwhile, the savage-looking lance-corporals had been carrying out a brief but thorough examination of our clothes and boots which were lying on the floor.

'Fifteen seconds . . . GET DRESSED!'

If you are arrested not in town, but in a unit or while at a military school, and if you are well prepared and have your food vouchers ready and have had a bath, try to find an extra five minutes to change your boots for larger ones. Anyone who knows what is in store for you will willingly give you his. Wearing your smaller size, he will suffer no less than you, but he will wait patiently for your return. Large-size boots spell salvation in the glasshouse. If your boots are difficult to put on, then the few seconds given you for 'Get Dressed' or 'Undress', would not be long enough and five days on a charge could easily become ten or even fifteen.

'Documents on the table!'

'Lance-Corporal, collect all the belts!'

While in the glasshouse, no inmate is allowed a belt, in case he tries to commit suicide. The history of the Kiev glasshouse does, however, know of one enterprising and inventive chap who, while in solitary confinement, with nothing but a stool screwed to the floor, still managed, by tearing away the lower hem of his shirt, to make for himself a short, thin, but very strong rope. All this was achieved with the utmost caution, under the almost constant supervision of the escort sentries who, day and night, patrol corridors. After having made a small loop, the end of which he tied to the stool's leg, he rolled on the floor, tightening the loop, for about ten long minutes. In the end, and in spite of every obstacle, he just managed to strangle himself.

'Money . . . watches?'

'No.'

One never takes such valuables to the glasshouse, as they will be taken away and old and broken ones will be returned in their place. And there is nowhere to go to protest!

'Flashes and badges?'

'And what are you bloody well doing with Guards badges? Do you think you're going to a carnival?'

'Comrade First Lieutenant, we are officer cadets of the Kharkov Guards Tank High Command School.'

'But what the hell are you doing lolling about in Kiev?'

'We brought over some equipment for the Kiev Tank School. The hand-over of the equipment was delayed and, so that we shouldn't be idle, we were given different duties – some in the kitchens, others at the Control Point, and our lot were sent to the Pass Check Point.'

'Lance-Corporal Alekseyev?'

'Here.'

'First of all, send all these guardsmen on firewood duties.'

'Right, Comrade First Lieutenant!'

Across the asphalted, incredibly clean courtyard, we were taken to another small inner courtyard surrounded by a very high brick wall. The first thing which surprised me was the glaring orderliness of it all. All the sawn logs were arranged in such an accurate pile that their ends formed a polished wall. Every log had to be cut to a standard size of exactly twenty-eight centimetres and an error of one or two centimetres was severely punished. All these logs were destined for the stove, and such exactness in sawing them was completely pointless, but order is order.

The logs, which we were to cut with the same exactness, had been brought in one to two days earlier, and they were not just thrown down in a heap, but arranged with indescribable love and even, one would say, artistry. First of all, they were sorted according to thickness, with the thickest underneath and the thinnest ones on the very top. But whoever had built up this stack of logs apparently possessed an even finer artistic taste, as they had also taken the colour of the logs into consideration. Those at the right-hand end were darkest in colour, while to the left they gradually changed in colour, ending with completely white blocks. It fell to us to demolish this artistic creation and to cut the wood to the standard size and then build it up again into a pile.

14

Here too, in the same yard, lay the stump and roots of an entire tree of absolutely unimaginable form, resembling anything you wished, except a tree. It was a fantastic intertwining of immense cables and ropes, or maybe of something else, but in any case the image was very flexible. The intertwined sections were of such a complicated form that it was hard to believe that nature could manage to create such a wonder. But in spite of the complexity of these knots, looking for all the world like a coiled snake, this immense block nevertheless retained very great solidity in all its elements, and had been lying there most probably for more than a decade, judging by the thousands of old and new notches made in it by a saw.

All those who did not realise fully where they had landed and who still manifested any obstinacy were given the task of 'cutting some wood', that is to say of sawing this particular block. After one hour, somebody from the glasshouse authorities would come to see how things were going and he always feigned surprise that nothing had yet been accomplished; punishment inevitably followed. This particular task was always allotted to only one man at a time and never to two. And this one man was always supplied with a long, supple but absolutely blunt saw, which could be operated only by two men.

When we entered the yard, a dark-haired soldier was trying vainly to succeed in making at least a single cut. After twenty minutes, he was taken off and accused of shirking. And then, depending on the mood of the management at the time, the behaviour of the unlucky wood-cutter would be appraised as they saw fit, from shirking and insubordination (if he tried to prove that the task was impossible) to economic sabotage and refusal to obey orders. And, after such an accusation, the Chief of the glasshouse or his deputy could do just as he wished with the poor wretch. That wooden block is destined to have a long life. I, for one, am quite sure that it still lies there to this day in the very same place and that some unfortunate is still trying vainly to saw it up. He bites his lip, there are tears in his eyes, and his face registers total desperation . . . but time runs out . . .

Once we had started to saw the logs to the standard twenty-eight-centimetre size, we learned another very interesting fact. We intended first to saw them and then to arrange them according to their thickness and colour, and, only after that, to sweep up the sawdust.

'Oh, no, that won't do, it isn't done like that here. Here, there must always be order!'

So then, after having sawn only one log, we started to gather up all the sawdust by hand, down to the smallest speck. There was no broom and, after the second log and been sawn, the same process began again, and so on . . .

In the meantime, the glasshouse escort was wheeling in one poor wretch after another to saw up that unique block.

'What about sawing some wood, brother?'

Towards seven o'clock, the glasshouse yard became increasingly noisy. Lorries started to arrive, bringing back those on charges who had spent the whole frosty day working on countless different projects. Some had been moving tank tracks at a tank-repair works. Others had been unloading batches of artillery shells. They were all frozen, wet, starving and tired to death. And still they were all ordered to form up upon arrival, because after work, without any break, a three-hour training exercise was the order of the day. We also were ordered to form up, and that was exactly the moment when the count of time served by each inmate officially started – the whole working day up to this moment had just been loosening up.

Kiev glasshouse knows only two sorts of training – drill and tactics. I make no mention here of political training because this does not take place every day, but only twice a week for two hours each time, and not in the evening but in the morning, before work. I will tell of this later but for the moment I will concentrate on drill and tactics. One and a half hours are spent on drill and it is a pulverising business. Approximately a hundred inmates, in single file, move along the perimeter of the yard. They don't walk but they just slash along, marching to attention, lifting their legs to an unthinkable height. There is no one in the yard except the inmates – no superiors, no escort – but the yard shudders from their mighty tread. Only sometimes, one of the savage lance-corporals emerges from the porch:

'Hey, you! . . . with the big ears. No, no, not you – you. Did you see that film called *Ordinary Fascism*? There you are now, that's real marching for you . . . So why can't you, my little pigeon, achieve the same excellence in marching as the men in the film? Now then, practise marking time.'

The man with the big ears goes to the centre of the yard and, marking time, lifts his knees as high as his chest. All the others marching round the yard redouble their own efforts. The fact of the matter is that the asphalt in the centre of the yard is slightly lower than that at the perimeter, a bizarre arrangement engineered on the personal initiative of Comrade Grechko, when he was still only Chief of the Kiev Military District. The idea is one of simple genius. During rain or melting snow, there is always a big puddle in the centre of the yard. Even during summer, when there is no rain, water is still pumped there under the pretext of watering the yard. So those who find themselves sent to the centre have to march round in the puddle. If there are about five men there at a time they will not only soak themselves up to the ears, but they will also drench the others marching round the yard by the splashes they produce. There is no way of drying oneself in the glasshouse, as it is heated only during the day when the inmates are out working and, towards the evening, when the inmates return to their wards, the stoves are already cold, and there are no radiators at all. I myself experienced 'Grechko's bowl' on my own skin in March when the snow melted by day and there was a biting frost at night.

Drill training takes place every single day, regardless of weather or temperature, as do all the other 'measures'. One and a half hours of drill at our standard speed of sixty steps per minute makes 5,400 steps in all, each with the maximum raising of the legs, and an intolerable downward stretching of the instep, because no one wants to be sent into the middle of the yard. This is why drill training is called 'individual practice' and is then followed by 'collective practice' or tactics.

Tactics, as distinct from drill training, are not based on the personal fear of each man, but on socialist competition among the collective as a whole, and this is why it is so much more exhausting than drill.

All tactics boil down to one tactical skill – crawling *Plastun**-fashion, with your head and whole body as close as possible to the ground, in our case to the asphalt. Hands and legs must move with the maximum agility and the body must twist and flex like that of a lizard. So now it's crawling. Every ward has now become an infantry section.

'Landmark – the birch tree! Section, towards the landmark, *Plastuny!* FORWARD!'

The stop-watch is turned off when the last man of the section reaches the birch tree and, if the time spent by the section as a whole proves unsatisfactory, then the last man home will be beaten in the ward during the night, because in the socialist world only beating ensures a conscientious approach.

'Well, your time wasn't bad' – and the filthy, wet with perspiration and suffocating members of the section sigh with relief – 'but your speed will not be taken into consideration, as this handsome fellow here had his arse sticking up all the time and was trying to move forward on all fours instead of crawling.' So the handsome fellow is sure of a beating, as he has let down the whole collective in Socialist Competition.

'Now then, let's try once more. Section to the departure point – at the double.'

---

*Plastuny were former Cossack infantry battalions, manned by poor Cossacks who could not afford the price of a horse. They were renowned for their skill in crawling on their stomachs like Red Indians. The word *plastun* is a derivative of *plast*, meaning 'layer'.

'MARCH! Landmark the birch tree. Section towards the landmark, PLASTUNY – FORWARD!'

'Ah! . . . This time your speed was worse! Well, never mind, we will soon train you!'

At the end of the training session, the glasshouse Chief or his deputy sums up. First, the worst ward is told the name of the man whose fault it is that they are all going to have to undergo another trial, and then follows the order: 'Landmark – Oak tree.'

'Oak tree' means that they must crawl straight through the centre of the yard, straight through the icy water and straight over the water obstacle invented by that most ingenious and brilliant leader. He was a clever one for inventions, Comrade Grechko was, until the withering disease eventually caught up with him!

Food in the Soviet Army is worse than that for any other soldiers in the whole world. Nevertheless, on the first day in the glasshouse, after having spent all day hungry and cold, and after unthinkable burdens, a soldier, already accustomed to any privation, still cannot overcome disgust at what is called 'supper' in the glasshouse. The first evening he cannot touch what is called 'food' at all. He is still incapable of accepting the fact that he must eat, not from his own private dish, albeit a dog's dish, but from a communal pan, containing some kind of mess faintly smelling of soup or even of sour cabbage soup. And, while the senses of hunger and disgust are still fighting each other, the short sharp order is given: 'Stand up! Form up outside!' After that wretched episode called supper, comes the evening check.

Under the corridor ceiling, in the frosty haze, the yellowish lamps glimmer dimly. The inmates stand in formation, there is not the slightest movement. This is the evening check. All wait for the order. After a quick roll-call the order is given.

'Ten seconds . . . GET UNDRESSED!'

Hell! Where did that bloody burst of speed come from? It is simply astonishing. But ten seconds were quite enough for a hundred men to undress fully. To tell the truth, everyone was carefully and secretly getting themselves ready for this order. Even during supper, each man had secretly unbuttoned one button on each sleeve in order to have only one button on his sleeve to deal with when the order came. All the buttons of his tunic collar seemed to be buttoned up, but in fact a small part of each was already slightly pushed inside the buttonhole, and he had only to pull at his collar to have all five buttons open at once. Experience is a great thing and every soldier knows about ten such tricks.

'First rank, three steps forward, MARCH! Second rank, ABOUT TURN!'

Both ranks are now facing opposite corridor walls. Everyone is naked. The wind drives a few snowflakes along the concrete floor.

And, while those savage lance-corporals are on the floor rummaging among our tunics, our trousers and our dirty leggings, creating a scene like a Soviet customs post, Captain Martyanov, Chief of the glasshouse, or his deputy, First Lieutenant Kirichek, is performing that sacred ritual: the inspection of our anal passages. It is a very responsible job. Maybe somebody has found a nail while working outside and brought it in, in his anus, and will let his blood out at night as he lies on the plank-bed. In the daytime he is watched by the escort, but at night, although the wards are permanently illuminated by a blinding light, nevertheless trouble always lurks nearby; perhaps somebody had a cigarette hidden in his anus and will have a secret smoke during the night. This operation requires special skills and, as we have seen, mere lance-corporals are not capable of performing it. So, let them rummage in our dirty linen. But, with the other operation, only a Soviet Army officer is qualified to cope.

'Fifteen seconds . . . GET DRESSED.'

All the inmates go to their wards and 'jobs time' has arrived. The glasshouse is not like a jail. The *parasha** has no place in the glasshouse. There is a big difference between the glasshouse and a civilian jail. The jail authorities have plenty of time to influence a prisoner. The time available to the glasshouse authorities is limited and, naturally, they try to 'enrich the programme' to the maximum by exploiting any, or even all, of a man's physical needs to the full 'for educational purposes'. The exercise of one's physical needs is here elevated to the rank of their educational influence and is carried out under the vigilant eyes of the administration.

After the inmates are settled in their wards, the escort and the rest of the administration, sometimes including the Chief of the glasshouse himself, take up their posts and the procedure begins. Clanking the locks loudly, a lance-corporal and two members of the escort enter the ward. The prisoners are formed up, at attention, as if on parade. The lance-corporal then lazily pokes his dirty fingers at the chest of the first inmate:

'Off you go!'

The inmate rushes along the corridors and staircases. Another member of the escort is posted at every corner and shouts out:

'Faster!'

'Faster!'

'Faster!'

But the inmate needs no encouragement because he knows full well

---

*Originally a girl's name, this has come to mean the communal bucket used as a latrine at night.

that at any moment, under the pretext of insufficient speed, he may be sent back, sometimes after having nearly reached the cherished door.

'It looks very much as if you, my little pigeon, did not really want very much "to go" at all. Now then – about turn. Back to your ward!'

But, coming towards you, there is already another inmate belting up and down the staircases, showing a clean pair of heels. Having finished with one ward, the lance-corporal and the escort lock the door and go on to another one. Often, the lance-corporal may 'forget' to send one or two of the inmates to the toilet at all, and sometimes he may even 'omit' a whole ward altogether. However, there is nobody to complain to in any case. Everything here is being done without any breach of Soviet laws.

I here affirm categorically that not a single letter of the law is being infringed in any Soviet glasshouse. Let us take, for instance, 'jobs time'. That most democratic constitution in the world – the Soviet Constitution – ensures, for all citizens, the right to work. Now where else, if not in the glasshouse, can you indulge this right to your heart's content? Or, let us take the right to education. Whether you want it, or whether you don't, you must give three hours a day to drill and tactical training, plus political training twice a week. Is that not education? Or, for instance, the right to rest. Every day they take you to and from work, so use this time for resting, or at night on that plank-bed take your rest, then right up to reveille, at 0530 hours – if, of course, you were not arrested during the night in accordance with the regulations concerning the right to work. But neither in the Constitution nor in any other law is any mention made about the exercise of one's physical needs. So don't go and demand anything over and above what is stipulated in the constitution! Or, are you setting yourself up in opposition to our Soviet rule of law?

'Over here – Escort to me!'

At long last, after 'jobs time', follows what the inmates have been dreaming of all day from the very moment of awakening – retreat!

Once again the lock clanks, and once again the lance-corporal with the escort appear in the ward. The inmates are all standing to attention, and the senior prisoner in the ward reports to the all-powerful one about general preparedness for retreat. A hardly audible order is made with only a feeble movement of the lips which can really be interpreted any way you wish. But the ward does understand. Behind our backs, at a distance of approximately one metre, is the edge of our plank-bed. At this order, which we have seen rather than heard, all ten of us, just as we have been standing, backs to the communal plank-bed, we all perform a most prodigious feat – a single jump backwards on to the plank-bed. There is neither time nor room to plan or even to move our hands: we have all been standing in one rank, tightly pressed together and, from this position, we perform a jump backwards into complete uncertainty. Who the hell really knows what our heads will crack down on? Will it be the edge of the plank-bed if I drop short, or will it be the brick wall if I overshoot the target, or will it be the ribs, elbows and skull of my nearest neighbour if the jump is right on target? In addition – and the most unpleasant aspect of all – there is the complete impossibility of swinging round and facing the bare planks, and therefore the absolute impossibility of softening the blow, which is always violently sudden.

There is the noise of crashing heads, a suppressed shriek, but everyone freezes in the pose in which they hit the plank-bed. One feels a terrible pain in the shoulder and a completely unbearable pain in the knee. One's head has at least not been split open – that's one good thing. The dead silence is suddenly shattered in another ward, which means that the neighbouring ward is being given some training. You see, the lance-corporal did not much care for their first retreat. Will we be for it today or not?

'Get up.' The order is given in an extremely quiet voice and the whole ward is immediately transformed from a horizontal to a vertical position. In less time than it takes to say it, we all stand to attention, in ranks, ready to fulfil any party or government order. It looks as if it is all because of that fat soldier in Airforce uniform that they have dragged us up. He is one of the staff clerks, those dregs of humanity, but we'll show him when night-time comes. He'll soon learn how to fulfil orders!

'Retreat!'

Again, there is the sound of crashing bodies and suppressed groans. Again, the whole ward freezes as ten bodies hit the plank-bed. What a shame! The fat clerk has missed! He made a terrific jump, but his body was too fat for a soldier. He came a cropper sideways on the edge of the boards, and froze motionless, with his hands at his sides, his body on the planks but his legs hanging over the edge. His face is a picture of horror and suffering. 'You fat pig, you'll pay for that tonight. The worst is still in store for you.'

The legs of the fat clerk start slowly slipping lower and lower, getting nearer and nearer to the brick floor. He gathers every shred of his strength in order, without moving, to attempt to transfer the weight of his body on to the planks. The lance-corporal patiently awaits the result of his balancing act. All the blood rushes to the face of the fat fellow, he stretches his neck and the whole of his body, trying surreptitiously to raise his legs. It seems momentarily that his body, stretched out like a ruler, will succeed in overbalancing his slightly bent legs, but the very next moment his legs start slipping down again and, in the end, the sole of his foot gently touches the floor.

'Get up . . . What's up, brother? Don't you want to sleep? You get the order to retreat, everybody else lies down like normal people and you apparently don't feel like sleep. Everybody has to go into training because of you. Well, okay. Off we go! I'll soon find some entertainment for you . . . Retreat!'

The order is given quietly and suddenly, counting on our having stopped paying attention, but we have learned to expect such tricks. You can't catch us like that! Nine men make a terrific jump, there is a crash and all movement freezes.

The lock creaks and I fall asleep immediately with my cheek resting on the unplaned boards, polished by the thousands of bodies of my predecessors. In the glasshouse there are no dreams, only complete oblivion, as one's whole organism is switched off. There is a blinding light in the wards throughout the night. The boards are bare, the spaces between the planks are three fingers wide, it is cold. There is only one's greatcoat for cover and it is permitted to put it under one's head and side. The coat is wet, one's legs too are wet. There is no feeling of hunger because, you see, only the first day has elapsed.

The glasshouse is not a prison. In prison, there is a collective of sorts, but it is still a collective for all that. Secondly, in prison, one finds people who have revolted, if only once, against laws, against society, against the regime. In the glasshouse, one finds only frightened soldiers mixed in with officer cadets. And cadets are people who voluntarily offer themselves as members of that social grouping totally deprived of all rights: junior Soviet Army officers. You can do what you like with them. Everyone who has been there in the glasshouse, and with whom I had an opportunity later to discuss all that I saw there, is unanimous that conditions in any one of the thousands of Soviet glasshouses could be made much more severe without the slightest risk of any organised opposition on the part of the inmates, particularly in large towns where officer cadets form the majority of all glasshouse inmates.

I woke up in the middle of the night, not from cold and not from the unendurable stench of nine dirty bodies compressed into a single, small, unventilated ward. No, I woke up because of an unbearable desire to visit the toilet. This happens when it is cold. Half the ward was awake, jumping up and down and generally dancing around. Through the peephole, the optimists, in the lowest possible whisper, were begging the escort to have pity on them, and take them to the lavatory. But there is no *parasha* in the glasshouse. It's not a civilian jail but a military establishment. Top brass visit this place and, in order to please them, there is no *parasha*.

Theoretically, the escort (as the very name implies) should, sometimes, at night, escort inmates, one at a time, to the lavatory. But this could completely undermine the educational impact of such an important measure as 'jobs time'. That is why the attempts of any liberal escorts (themselves officer-cadets, who are changed every day) to acquiese to the inmates' entreaties are rigidly suppressed. It is quite a different matter with the wards of those under investigation, or of the accused, or of the condemned; they are escorted off there at their very first request. And those in solitary confinement cells, where the position is worse, even they are sometimes taken out during the night, probably because they are usually psychopaths prepared to do any kind of damage; but, in general, where normal men are concerned, it is very bad indeed. They are never taken to the toilet during the night, because the escort knows that the ward as a whole, fearful of common punishment, would never allow anybody to relieve himself inside the ward.

The heavy bolt suddenly clanked, signifying either an incomprehensible favour on the part of the escort, or his anger at persistent demands. All those who had been dancing about only a moment ago in the ward, promptly jumped as noiselessly as tom-cats on to the plank-bed and feigned sleep. But it was only the fat clerk being pushed into the ward, having cleaned out the lavatories during the night after 'jobs time', and the door slammed shut with a bang. The fat clerk was completely exhausted, and his eyes were red from lack of sleep. One could see his tears and his plump cheeks were trembling. Groaning, he crawled on to the plank-bed, and putting his dirty cheek on to the hard planks he was instantly out for the count.

Meanwhile, the ward had come to life again, and I, like all the others, had started to dance about in anticipation.

'Staff shit!' said the tall dark-haired CW soldier. 'He went and pissed in the lavatory and now he's sleeping soundly. He's just like any other fat cow, who's never really done its turn and yet's now set up better than anyone else.' All those who were already awake wanted sleep more than life itself, because only sleep can conserve any remaining strength. But he was the only one who was sleeping at that moment, and that is why hatred towards him particularly welled up in all the rest of us simultaneously. The tall CW soldier takes off his coat and covers the head of the sleeping man. We all rush towards him, I jump on to the plank-bed and kick his stomach as if it were a football. Quite unable to shout, he only whimpers softly. Because of the noise we all produce, the footsteps of the escort slowly approach the ward doors. His indifferent eye surveys what is going on, and his steps slowly move off again with the same indifference. The escort is a brother officer-cadet, most probably he himself has been under arrest on more than one occasion. He understands us and is completely on our side. He would not have minded coming into the ward and putting in the boot himself – but that is not allowed, the escort must not resort to violence. It is forbidden.

By this time it is probably already five o'clock in the morning. There are about thirty minutes left before reveille. This is the most difficult time of all. Oh, I can't stand it any more. Probably all those who performed badly during tactical training, or at work or during the evening check, or during retreat, are now being beaten in all the other wards.

I have never run so fast in all my life as at the first morning 'jobs time' in the glasshouse. Walls, floors, staircases and the faces of the escorts flashed past, and the only thought in my head was, 'I hope I arrive in time!' Nothing whatsoever could distract me from this thought, not even a familiar face, and those black tank corps shoulder-straps which rushed towards me. It was only later, after returning to my ward and getting my breath back, that I realised that I had seen a fellow cadet running from the lavatory just as I was. This officer cadet was a first-year cadet who had replaced us at the Check Point after we had been arrested, and this could mean only one thing: Colonel General Vladimir Filipovich Chizh, the Deputy District Commander, had arrested us upon entering our school and, in just one hour, upon leaving the school, he had arrested those who had replaced us. The Colonel General was a hard man indeed, and it is greatly to be regretted that he was only interested in one thing – the reception accorded him personally – and in nothing else whatsoever.

Return from Communism

Of all the billions of people who inhabit our sinful planet, I am one of the few who have lived under real communism and, thanks be to God, have returned from it, safe and sound to tell the tale. This is how it happened.

In the glasshouse, during the morning posting of inmates, Lance-Corporal Alekseyev made the following quick-fire announcement while poking our greasy tunics:

'You, you and you – project No. 8', which meant the tank factory, to load worn-out tank tracks, completely exhausting work with totally unattainable norms.

'You, you, and those ten there – project No. 27', which meant the railway station, unloading trucks of artillery shells, which was even worse.

The escort immediately collected together its detail of inmates and embarked them on a lorry.

'You, you, you and those over there – project No.110.' That was the worst of all, it was the oil refinery, and meant cleaning out the insides of immense reservoirs. There, one absorbed such a stench of petrol, paraffin, and other foul substances that it was quite impossible to eat or sleep. There was no issue of special clothing, and one was not supposed to wash either. But, for today anyway, it looked as if we had escaped.

The lance-corporal approaches.

And where are we going today?

'You, you and those three there – project No. 12.'

Where is that?

The escort took us aside, wrote down our names and gave us the usual ten seconds to get ourselves on to the jeep. Light and agile as greyhounds, we leapt under the tarpaulin roof of the new GAZ jeep.

While the escort was signing for our souls, I nudged the puny officer cadet with the artillery flashes with my elbow. Apparently, he was the most experienced of our number, and upon hearing the figure 12 he had visibly quaked.

'Where is that?'

25

'To communism, to Saltychikha* herself,' he whispered and in the same breath swore foully and inventively.

I swore too, for everyone knows that there is nothing on earth worse than communism. I had already heard much about communism and Saltychikha, what I did not know was that it was called project No. 12. Our escort, with a clatter of his automatic rifle, jumped in over the side of the GAZ jeep, which sneezed a couple of times, jerked once for the sake of order and sped off along the smooth pre-revolutionary cobbled road straight on to communism.

Communism is located on the south-western outskirts of that ancient Slavonic capital – the mother of all Russian towns – the thousand-year-old city of Kiev.

And, though it occupies a large slice of Ukrainian soil, it is simply impossible for the uninitiated just to catch sight of it or even of its four-metre-high boundary walls. Communism is hidden in a dense pine forest, surrounded on all sides by military bases, depots and stores. And, in order just to glimpse the walls of communism, one has to penetrate a military base which is defended by ever-wakeful guards armed with machine-guns and by fierce guard-dogs.

Our GAZ jeep was speeding on down the Brest–Litovsk highway and, after passing the last few houses, it dived smartly into an insignificant passage between two green fences, marked 'Entry Forbidden'. After about five minutes, the jeep stopped in front of grey, wooden, unpainted gates which in no way resembled the entrance to a shining bright tomorrow. The gates opened and, after having allowed us entry, instantly slammed tightly shut. We were in a mousetrap. On both sides there were walls about five metres high – behind us were some wooden, but clearly very solid gates, while those in front of us were metal and obviously more solid still.

From somewhere a lieutenant and two soldiers armed with sub-machine guns sprang forward to meet us; they quickly counted us, looked inside the jeep, into its engine and even beneath the jeep, and they checked the documents of both the driver and the escort. The green steel wall in front of us quivered momentarily, and then smoothly slid off to the left, opening out before our eyes the panoramic view of a pine forest, bisected by a broad and flat road resembling an airport runway. Beyond those steel gates, I had expected to see anything you like, but not a dense forest.

Meanwhile the jeep was still speeding on along the concrete road. On

*Saltychikha was a Tsarist landowner, notorious for cruelty to her serfs. The story goes that these same serfs later walled her up in one of the stone columns of her own mansion. This mansion eventually became a school for the daughters of the privileged, and the girls used to whisper to each other at night, in terror of the fate of the original owner.

both right and left, among the pine trees, one could distinguish the huge concrete structures of depots and stores completely covered over by earth and overgrown with prickly bushes. After some minutes we stopped again in front of an unbelievably high concrete fence. The previous procedure was repeated: the first gates, then the concrete trap, the check on papers, the second gates and then beyond that a straight level road into the forest, although this time the depots and stores were missing.

Finally, we stopped at a striped control barrier, guarded by two sentries. On either side of this barrier, stretching out into the forest, were wire fences, attached to which were grey watch-dogs straining at their leashes. I have seen all manner of dogs in my time but these particular ones immediately struck me as being somehow unusual. Only much later, I realised that every other chained dog barks furiously as it strains at the leash, while these enraged creatures were quite mute. They did not bark, but only growled, choking themselves with their own saliva and their furious rage. Being real watchdogs, they barked only in accordance with instructions.

Having overcome this last obstacle, the jeep stopped in front of a huge red placard, about six to seven metres high, on which prominent golden letters proclaimed: 'THE PARTY SOLEMNLY PROMISES THAT THE PRESENT GENERATION OF SOVIET PEOPLE WILL LIVE UNDER COMMUNISM!' And a bit lower in brackets was written: 'Extract from the Programme of the Communist Party of the Soviet Union, agreed at the XXII Congress of the CPSU.'

The escort yelled, 'Ten seconds!' – and, like little grey sparrows, we all flitted out from the jeep's interior and formed up at its rear side. Ten seconds – one could manage that, there were only five of us and to jump out of a jeep is easier than to clamber on to it over ice-covered sides; oh yes, and, in addition, we had grown much lighter these last few days.

A crude-faced lance-corporal with lordly manners appeared before us wearing officer's boots. He was one of the place's regular retinue. He explained something briefly to the escort, who then yelled, 'Hands behind backs! Follow the lance-corporal in single file!'

'Quick march!'

We moved singly along a paved path cleared of snow and, after rounding a beautiful plantation of young fir trees, we all suddenly stopped dead in our tracks without any order being given, we were so staggered by the unprecedented picture before us.

In a woodland clearing, surrounded by the young fir trees, buildings of amazing beauty were scattered about in picturesque disorder. Never before nor since, either in any fairy tale film, nor any exhibition of

27

foreign architecture, have I ever met such a turbulent, passionate and rapturous fantasy of colours, such an amazing intermingling of nature, in light, colour, elegance, taste, simplicity and originality. I am no writer and it is beyond my powers to describe adequately the sheer beauty of that place to which fate saw fit to transport me, once upon a time.

Not only I, but our escort too, all of us, open-mouthed, admired the view. The lance-corporal, apparently accustomed to such a reaction among strangers, shouted at the escort to bring him to his senses; the latter, still spellbound, straightened the strap of his automatic, first cursed us and then our mothers, and we began to straggle our way along a footpath paved with grey granite, past frozen waterfalls and ponds, past Chinese bridges, arching their cat-like backs over canals, past marble summer-houses and pools covered with coloured glass.

Having passed through this delightful little town, we found ourselves once more in a young fir-tree plantation. The lance-corporal stopped in a small clearing surrounded by trees and ordered us to rake away the snow, under which was revealed a trap-door. Five of us lifted its cast-iron lid and threw it to one side. A monstrous stench issued from the bowels of the earth. Holding his nose, the lance-corporal jumped back into the snow. We did not follow him of course, as by doing so we could easily have got a short sharp burst between our shoulder-blades. We merely clamped our noses tightly shut as we drew back from the cesspool.

The lance-corporal took a gulp of clean forest air and gave the order: 'The pump and hand barrows are there, and the orchard is – way – over there. By 1800 hours, the cleaning of the cesspool must be completed and the trees must be manured!' And then away he went.

This heavenly place where we had landed was called the 'Country-house of the High Command of the Warsaw Treaty Army', otherwise known as 'Project No. 12'. This country house was kept in case any member of the Warsaw Treaty High Command suddenly felt the urge to have a rest on the outskirts of ancient Kiev, Russia's former capital city. But the heads of the Warsaw Treaty organisation were more inclined to spend their rest periods on the Black Sea coast of the Caucasus. And so, the country house remained empty. If the Defence Minister or the Chief of the General Staff ever came to Kiev, there was yet another country house, officially named the 'Country House for Senior Officials of the Defence Ministry', or 'Project No. 23'. But, as the Minister of Defence and his First Deputies do not come to Kiev even once every ten years, this country house also remains empty. In the event of the arrival in Kiev of any Soviet Party or Government leaders, there were many other 'Projects' at the disposal of the Kiev Town Party or Executive Committees; yet others, more imposing still, at the disposal of the Kiev Regional Party Committee or the Regional Executive Committee; and, the most impressive of all, better by far than any of our military houses, which were of course entirely at the disposal of the Central Committee of the Ukrainian Communist Party, the Ukrainian Council of Ministers and the Ukrainian Supreme Soviet. Since there was really plenty of room to accommodate any cherished guests, Country House No. 12 was permanently empty. Neither the Commander of Kiev Military District nor his deputies ever used it for the simple reason that they were all entitled to have their own personal country houses. Therefore, No. 12 came to be occupied by the Military District Commander's wife. In country house No. 23 resided his only daughter, while the Commander himself lived with whores in his personal country house. (The organisation supplying leading personnel with prostitutes is officially named 'The Song and Dance Ensemble of Kiev Military District'. Such organisations are in existence for all military districts, fleets, groups of troops, as well as for all other organisations of high standing.)

The staff that waits upon the wife of Yakubovskiy is huge. And every day, to help the countless cooks, servants, maids, gardeners and others, five to eight or, sometimes, up to twenty glasshouse inmates are brought here to perform the dirtiest work. Today is no exception to the rule.

Among the inmates themselves, the Warsaw country house was known by that one very bad word, 'Communism'. It is difficult to say why it had been so christened – perhaps it was owing to the placard at the entrance, or maybe owing to the fairy-tale beauty and charm of the natural surroundings. Then again, perhaps it was because, here, mystery and fascination were so tightly interlaced with the daily humiliation of people, or else it was simply because, organically speaking, beauty and shit are so very closely related! And, when it came to shit, there was enough here for anyone.

'Is the cesspool deep?' asks an Uzbek military engineer.

'It reaches to the centre of the earth.'

'But it could easily be connected to the town sewerage system by a pipe!'

'You fool, do you really believe that an Army General would defecate in the same sewer as you! You are still not old enough to have that honour. This system has been devised for the sake of safety, otherwise some secret paper could fall in, and what then? The enemy is ever watchful and uses all possible channels open to him. That is why a closed circuit has been devised here, to avoid the drain of information!'

'So, according to you, this self-same drain of information occurs through the generals' arses?'

'You don't understand a bloody thing,' the puny fellow from the artillery said, 'this system was invented simply in order to conserve generals' excrement, which, unlike ours, is full of calories. The quality of the shit is exactly proportionate to the quality of the food consumed, and if someone like Michurin had been given this much prime quality excrement, he would have glorified our motherland for centuries with the richness of the harvests he achieved!'

At this point our discussion was interrupted by our escort. It is of course an advantage if one's escort hails from the tank corps like oneself. Then, life is quite different, even though the escort knows full well that if he is too lenient towards prisoners, after his own stint of duty he, too, will find himself confined to the glasshouse, along with those same prisoners he was escorting only a little while earlier. But, all the same, a brother tank corps man is much to be preferred to a man from the infantry or the artillery. It is also not too bad when the escort, even if not one of the lads, is nevertheless an experienced third or fourth officer cadet. For, even though not from the same squad, they have probably been in the glasshouse at least once themselves: so they really do know what is what. The worst of all is when the escort consists of a bunch of young wet noses and strangers to boot. First year cadets are always the most stupid and the most strict. They go by the book. And it is one of these that we have been landed today.

He is tall with a big ugly face and, judging by his behaviour alone, he is obviously a first year man. Besides, everything he has on is new – coat, cap, boots – and such a thing would be quite impossible for an old-timer. The fellow's a rookie, and his badges are those of a signals unit, which in Kiev could only mean that he belongs to the Kiev Higher Engineering Radio Technical School or KVIRTU for short. In Kiev, these chaps are only referred to as 'Kvirtanutyy'. This particular Kvirtanutyy looks as if he is getting angry. So it must be time to start work.

And so our first working day under communism has begun. One fellow pumps up the shit, the remaining four carry the stinking sludge into the general's garden. My partner turned out to be that same puny artillery officer cadet who looked the most experienced of our number. The work was clearly beyond his powers. And, as we carried away our loaded hand barrows, he turned red in the face, groaned and generally looked as if he was going to collapse at any moment. I could not help him at all as I myself could hardly hold the handles on my own side. We could not sneak off with a lighter load either, as the other pair promptly started to protest: whereupon the escort threatened to report us to the powers-that-be.

But the poor fellow clearly had to have some support from somewhere, if not in deed then at least in word. With a loaded container, this was quite impossible, but on the return trip it was quite an easy matter as our journey took us about three hundred metres away from the stinking cesspool and from the escort so that we could get into conversation.

'Now then, artillery, how much longer are you in for?' I began when we had dumped our first load beneath a spreading apple tree.

'I have already served out my time,' he answered languidly, 'that is if we manage not to get "extra rations" today.'

'Lucky chap,' said I, sincerely envying him. 'Tell me, O God of War, how far are you off getting your golden shoulder-straps?'

'It's all been done already.'

'How so?' I just did not understand.

'Well, that's how it is. It's three days since the order reached Moscow. If the Minister signs it today – there you are – golden shoulder-straps, but he may only sign it tomorrow!'

I envied him once more. I had another year to wait. One more year at the Guards Tank School – a year is such a long time, unlike my comrades, I had not yet started counting in hours and minutes, but I counted only the days.

'You lucky bastard, artillery, you'll go straight from the glasshouse for a bath and then on to a graduation party. Some people certainly have all the luck.'

'If we don't get "extra rations",' he interrupted gloomily.

'There is an amnesty in that case.'

He did not answer, maybe because we were getting near to the ugly-faced escort.

The second trip proved considerably more difficult than the first for the artillery man, and he hardly managed to drag himself to the first trees. While I was tipping up the barrow, he rested all his weight upon the gnarled trunk of a tree nearby. I had to support the poor chap. I had already wasted two trump cards as neither the thought of his imminent graduation from military school nor his early release from the glass-house had cheered him up even a little bit. My only hope was to boost his morale to the required level. This approach simply could not fail. So I decided to toss him the idea of the bright future in store for us, of communism, so to speak.

'Do you hear what I say, God of War?'

'What's up with you now?'

'Listen, artillery, life is hard for us now, but the time will come when we too will live in a paradise, like this – under communism. That will be life! Eh?'

'How do you mean? With our hands full of shit?'

'Oh, no, I don't mean that', I said, grieved by such lack of vision. 'What I am saying is that the time will come when we too will live in such heavenly gardens, in the same beautiful little towns with lakes, surrounded by hundred-year-old pine trees, and apple orchards or, better still, cherry orchards. See how much poetry there is in it . . . Cherry orchards! Well?'

'You are a fool,' he answered wearily. 'A real fool, even if you are a tank corps man.'

'Why am I a fool?' I asked indignantly. 'Now wait a bit, you. Why am I a fool?'

'And who, in your view, will carry the shit under communism? And now shut up, we are getting near.'

The question was so simple and it was put in such a mocking tone, it was like being pole-axed. At the beginning, it did not seem to be insoluble, but it was the first time in my life that any question about communism had ever arisen to which I could not find an immediate answer. Before, everything had been absolutely clear: everyone works as he wants, as much as he wants, according to his ability, and receives whatever he wants and as much as he wants, i.e. according to his needs. It was absolutely clear that, say, supposing one man wants to be a steel founder, right then, work for the common good and for your own, of course, because you are an equal member of society. You want to be a teacher? Right then, every kind of work is honoured in our society. You want to be a wheat farmer? What work can be more honourable than to provide people with bread? You want to become a diplomat – the way is open! But who will be busy in the sewers? Is it possible that there will be anybody who will say, 'Yes, this is my vocation, this is my place, I am not fit for anything better?' On the island of Utopia, it was prisoners who did such work as we are doing now, but under communism there will be neither crime, nor prisons, nor glasshouses, and no prisoners, because there will be no necessity for crime – everything will be free of charge. Take what you like – it is not a crime, but a necessity, and everybody will take according to his needs, that is the basic principle of communism.

We tipped up the third barrow and I exclaimed triumphantly,

'Everyone will clean up after himself! And, in addition, there will be machines!'

He looked at me with pity.

'Did you read Marx?'

'Indeed I did,' I said passionately.

'Do you remember the example of the pins? If one man is producing them, there will be three per day, but if production is divided between three men, one cuts the wire, another sharpens the ends and the third attaches the heads, then there will be three hundred pins per day – one hundred per man. This is called division of labour. The higher the division of labour in a society, the higher is its productivity. But there has to be a master, a virtuoso, in every business, not just an amateur or dilettante. Now take Kiev, for instance, and see how each of its one and a half million inhabitants arranges his own sewerage system, in his free time, and cleans it and maintains it in good order. As for machines, Marx prophesied the victory of communism at the end of the nineteenth century, but at that time such machines did not exist, which means that at that time communism was impossible. Is that not so? These machines still do not exist, which means that communism is still impossible. Am I right or not? ... And, so long as these machines are missing, somebody must rummage in somebody else's shit, and this, with your kind permission, is not communism. Let's assume that some day such machines will be invented, but even then somebody will still have to look after them and clean them, and that, too, will not be very pleasant work either. It's hard to believe that anybody will really ever want to do nothing but that throughout his whole life. Do you support Marxist theory about the division of labour, or aren't you a Marxist?'

'Of course I'm a Marxist,' I mumbled.

'The time is fast approaching and so there are additional questions which demand independent study. Who, under communism will bury the corpses? Will it be self-service or will amateurs carry out the work in their spare time? Generally speaking, there is plenty of dirty work in society and everyone is not a diplomat or a general. Who will carve up the pig carcasses? Have you ever been in a fish-filleting outfit? The fish arrives and must be dealt with immediately and there's no bloody mechanisation either. So, what then? And who will sweep the streets and cart off the rubbish? To cart off rubbish nowadays, one needs qualifications and not low ones either, and dilettantism is no bloody good either. And will there be any waiters under communism? For the time being it's certainly a profitable business, but when money is liquidated, what will it be like then? And finally, for someone who at present has not the slightest idea about how to set about shit-cleaning, like Comrade Yakubovskiy himself for instance, has he any personal interest at all in the arrival of that day, when he will have to clean up his own shit all by himself? So just think it over! And now, we are getting near to the escort again, so shut up!'

'You chatter too much, you should be working!'

'Look here, artillery, do you mean that in your opinion communism will never come at all?'

At this, he stopped dead in his tracks, thunderstruck by the very outrageousness of my question.

'Of course not!'

'But why not? You counter-revolutionary bastard, how have you managed to avoid the chop? You're a dirty anti-Soviet swine.' And, with all my might, I heaved that very heavy hand barrow down on to the ground and a stinking golden mass spilled out over the blindingly white snow and over the granite pathway.

'Damn your bloody balls,' the artillery man spat out in utter rage. 'Now we'll each get an extra five days – like nobody's business, you just see if we don't! But, no . . . it looks as if no one has noticed; let's cover it with snow.' And feverishly, we started to throw snow on to the dirty patch. But our escort was already running towards us.

'You idle bastards! What have you done now? You're chattering again, are you? But I'm answerable for you and I'll soon make you dance for it.'

'Wait! . . . Don't make a noise, we'll soon cover it with snow and no one will see anything. It's a very heavy carrier and it just fell out of our hands. It's good for the garden anyway. The snow will melt in a week and wash away all traces.'

However, the ugly-faced escort did not relent.

'You should work instead of chattering! But I'll make you dance for your pains.'

Then the artilleryman changed his tone.

'You complete fool! First serve for as long as we have and then you'll have something to shout about. Report us and you'll be punished along with us for not noticing in time.' I supported these remarks.

'You are still young and silly and haven't experienced any real difficulties in your life. As for this man here, a report has already been sent and, in three days' time, he will be made an officer – but you are still a snotty boy . . .'

'Who are you calling a snotty boy? Right you are!'

He shouldered his automatic and shouted:

'Back – to – work! Step lively! I'll teach you to show your paces.'

The artilleryman looked indifferently in the escort's direction and calmly said to me: 'Let's go . . . It's no use trying to reason with a sheep . . . He's going to be arrested today . . . You can take my word for it.'

And off we strolled in the direction of the trap door.

'He'll report us for sure,' said the artilleryman confidently.

'No,' I said, 'he'll only play the fool a bit and then recover towards the evening.'

'Okay, but you'll see!'

'Don't be mournful, my friend, and don't sigh. Take life as a horse by its bridle.'

'Tell everyone to piss off, at the very least. So that they don't tell you first to fuck off!'

'That, artillery, is one of my firm convictions.'

'And mine too!'

Two kindred souls . . . in the General's sewer!

'Look here, you counter-revolutionary. Why do you claim that communism will never come?'

'Because . . . But don't throw down your shit-carrier again . . . Because neither our Party nor its Leninist Central Committee has the slightest need of communism.'

'You're nothing but a counter-revolutionary liar!'

'Blow your nose with both nostrils, you miserable idiot. Quieten down and stop yelling, it's impossible to talk here. Have patience and in a minute, when we have unloaded, I'll teach you all.' We unloaded.

'Okay. Just you imagine that communism arrives tomorrow morning.'

'No, that's impossible,' I interrupted. 'The material technical base has to be built first.'

'Just imagine that the year 1980 has arrived and that the Party, as it promised, has built this base. So, what exactly does our ordinary run-of-the-mill Secretary of a District Party Committee stand to gain from this communism? Eh? Plenty of caviare? But he's got so much caviare already that he can even eat it through his arse if he wishes. A car? But he has two personal Volga cars and one private one as well, in reserve. Medical care? Food, women, a country house? But he already has all of these things. So our dear Secretary of the most Godforsaken District Party Committee stands to gain bugger-all from communism! And what will he lose? He will lose everything. At the moment, he's warming his belly at the best health resort on the Black Sea coast, but under communism all men are equal as they are in a bath-house, and there won't be enough room for everybody on that beach. Or, let's assume that there's an abundance of products, just take whatever you like and as much as you like in any shop. Also let's assume that there's not even a queue. There will still be inconveniences, and you will still have to go and collect things. But what good is that to him, if the local yokels already bring him everything he needs? Why would he prefer tomorrow if today is even better? He will lose everything under communism – his country house, his personal physicians, his hirelings and his guards.

'So, even at District Committee Secretary level, nobody is interested in communism's arrival tomorrow, or the day after for that matter. And when it comes to the Yakubovskiys and Grechkos of this world, communism has long since ceased to be of any interest to them at all. Did you see how they jumped on China because of the so-called levelling process there, when everyone was wearing identical trousers, so to speak. And what about us, how will we live under communism? Will there be any fashions, or will we all be wearing prisoners' jackets? The Party says not – but if that is true, how can everybody be provided with fashionable clothes, if they are free and everyone takes as many as he wants? And where will you get all the fox and polar bear fur for all the women's coats? Yakubovskiy's wife wears a different ermine coat every day. If communism suddenly came tomorrow, would you be able to convince the milkmaid, Marusya, that her thighs are any less desirable than those of Yakubovskiy's wife or that her status in society is less honourable? Marusya is a young woman and she also wants ermine and gold, and diamonds. But do you believe that the old stoat, Yakubovskaya, will give up her furs and diamonds without a fight? Fuck off with you! This is why they don't want communism to come tomorrow, and that's all there is to it. And that is why an historical period is invented. Did you ever read Lenin? When did he promise us communism? In ten to fifteen years! Wasn't that so? And Stalin? Also in ten to fifteen years, though sometimes it was even twenty. And Nikita Sergeyevich*? In twenty years, and the whole Party swore to the people that this time there would be no deception. Do you really believe that in the year 1980 communism will finally come? Not bloody likely: and do you think anybody will ask the Party to explain this lie? No, there will not be a single questioning voice.

'And did you ever reflect my dear tankman, on why all our rulers mention ten to fifteen years? It's to give them time for their own "dolce vita" and yet still not destroy other people's hopes. And, incidentally, also time for all those promises to be long forgotten. Who remembers now what Lenin promised, once upon a time? And when 1980 does arrive, precisely no one will recall that the promised year has, at last, arrived. It is certainly about time for an answer. The time is almost ripe for the Party to give an account of itself.'

'Are you really a communist at all?'

'I am not a communist, but I am a Party member and it's about time you saw the difference!'

He became silent, and we did not speak any more until the evening.

Towards evening, we had finally succeeded in cleaning out the pit to its very bottom. We had scooped out everything when there suddenly

*Nikita Sergeyevich Khrushchev, the Soviet Party leader subsequently deposed by Brezhnev.

appeared on the path a skinny, wrinkled woman, wearing an ermine fur coat and accompanied by the lance-corporal, whose face had by now lost its lordly expression and was wearing that of a country yokel instead.

'Now look,' warned the artilleryman, 'if Saltychikha sentences us to extra days in the glasshouse – don't you go kicking up a fuss. She's only a mere woman but she'll have you up in front of the tribunal, quick as look at you, if you don't watch out.'

The lance-corporal inspected the cesspool and the garden, and reported in oily tones, 'They have done it all. I kept them at it all day.'

She smiled faintly, approached the cesspool and looked down into its depths.

'They did not work badly, all day I . . .' the lance-corporal continued unctuously.

'But they dirtied the path and covered up the dirt with snow,' observed our escort.

The lance-corporal cast a stealthy look of utter hatred at the escort.

'Which path was that?' enquired the skinny woman almost tenderly.

'Well, just let's go over here, let's go and I'll show you,' and he began to stride off along the path with the skinny woman tripping along behind him.

Night was falling and it was getting frosty and the escort had some difficulty in kicking away the lump of frozen show which covered the dirty spot.

'Here it is, they covered it with snow and thought I wouldn't notice it. But I see everything!'

'Who is responsible?' shrieked the old hag.

'Those two there . . . they thought they would get away with it and pass unnoticed . . . But we notice everything . . .'

'Five days . . . each,' hissed the old hag. 'As for you, Fedor . . . as for you . . .' and, her face distorted by rage and without even finishing the sentence, she wrapped her fur coat more tightly around her and swept off in the direction of the fairy-tale small town. The lance-corporal's face twisted in a grimace and he turned towards our escort who, apparently, had not yet realised that he had accidentally dropped the all-powerful Fedor right in it.

'Take your rabble away then! I won't let you forget this, you bastard!'

The puzzled escort looked at the lance-corporal:

'I was only doing my best . . .'

'Get out of here, you scum. I'll get even with you one day!'

We stamped off past the wonderful little town, which in the darkness managed to become still more entrancing. Children splashed about in a pool, separated from the frost only by a greenish, transparent wall. A

tall woman, in a severe blue frock and white apron, busied herself with
them.

First Lieutenant Kirichek, the Deputy Chief of the Kiev Garrison
glasshouse, had already been informed of the 'extra rations' handed out
to us as he awaited our return from communism. The first lieutenant
opened a thick ledger.

'Five days each. So . . . we write down . . . Five . . . days . . . arrest . . .
From the Commander of the Military District . . . for . . . bre . . . ach of
military discipline . . . – Oh, hell,' he exclaimed suddenly, 'the Commander has flown to Moscow for a Party congress. How can I . . .?' He
looked at the book, and then, on second thoughts, inserted the word
'Deputy' before the word 'Commander.' Now everything was in order.
'So, Suvorov, your first five days were given to you by the Deputy
Commander and so were the second five days. Now, let's see who'll
give you the third lot.' Amused by his own joke, he gave a sort of
neighing laugh.

'Escort!'

'Yes, comrade First Lieutenant!'

'Put these two pigeons in 26. Let them sit there for one or two hours
to learn that extra rations is not just extra time to serve, but something
with rather more bite.'

Ward 26 in the Kiev glasshouse is known by the title of 'Revolutionary', because once, before the Revolution, a famous petty criminal
called Grigoriy Kotovskiy, on trial for rape, had escaped from it. Later,
in 1918, Kotovskiy and his gang joined the Bolsheviks and, for
invaluable services of a criminal nature, were later officially renamed
revolutionaries instead of pickpockets on the personal instructions of
Lenin himself. But the experience gained from this famous revolutionary's escape was exploited to the full, and there were no further
departures from the notorious ward.

There is neither plank-bed nor bench in this ward, only a spittoon in
one corner. And it is not just standing there by chance, it is filled to the
very brim with chlorine. The window through which that hero of the
Revolution escaped has long ago been bricked up, and the ward itself is
so small, and there is so much chlorine, that to remain there longer
than five minutes seems a complete impossibility. Tears stream from
one's eyes, one chokes for breath, saliva fills one's mouth and one's
chest feels like bursting from the pain of it.

As soon as we were pushed into the ward, the experienced artilleryman, though himself already coughing and choking, still managed to
push me away from the door which I was going to kick. Bowing to his
experience, I gave up the attempt. Much later, I discovered that, as

usual, he was quite right. It emerged that, just opposite our ward 26, there was ward 25, expressly intended for those who could not stand being in ward 26. After a sojourn in ward 25, anyone and everyone calmed down and returned meekly to ward 26.

Meanwhile, a third person had been pushed into our ward. I couldn't have cared less who he was and did not even try to discern his features through my tears, but the artilleryman had been awaiting his arrival. Nudging me (it was absolutely impossible to speak), he gestured with his hand towards the third man. And, after I had rubbed my eyes, I recognised our very own escort.

Usually, a period under arrest does not start with wards 21, 25 or 26. Only those given 'extra rations' pass through one of these wards and, sometimes, even through all three of them. Our first-year 'Kvirtanutyy' had started his particular epic in ward 26. Was this because the all-powerful lance-corporal had complained to the ADC or to the deputy commander, or was it because our escort had protested when, after surrendering his automatic and cartridges, he had suddenly learnt that his platoon was actually returning home but that he, for some unknown reason, was to remain here, on a charge, for ten days. Or maybe the first lieutenant had decided to put him with us just for the fun of it, knowing in advance what our reaction was bound to be.

In the whitish haze of chlorine fumes, the new inmate choked in his first fit of coughing. His eyes filled with tears. Helplessly, he groped in the void, trying to find a wall. We were no three musketeers, and the two of us had not the slightest inclination to forgive. It might be said that it is wrong to beat a helpless and temporarily blind man, especially at the moment when he least expects any assault. This may very well be true for anyone who has never seen the inside of this ward. But we construed the appearance of our escort as a gift of fate, for the one and only time when we could beat him up was when he was quite helpless. At any other time, he would have made us scatter like cats, he was much too powerful. I write all this exactly as it happened. I, personally, showed no finer feeling at all, and have not the least intention of falsely attributing to myself any high ideals. But those who have been there will understand, and those who have not can never be my judges.

The artilleryman made a sign and, as the tall escort straightened himself between fits of coughing, I kicked him hard in the crotch. He let out an inhuman scream and bent over double in agony. At this same moment, the artilleryman kicked him as hard as he could on the left knee-cap. And, as the escort writhed on the floor, the artilleryman kicked him again, twice, in the stomach. As a result of all this exertion, we had swallowed a lot of chlorine. I vomited, the artilleryman choked. Meanwhile, the escort was lying prostrate on the floor, and we could not have cared less. I vomited again and felt quite certain that I was not long for this world. I had no wish for anything, not even for fresh air. The walls shook and started to rotate around me. From afar, I heard the clank of the door being opened but I was totally indifferent.

Apparently, I regained consciousness quite soon. The escort, still unconscious, was carried past me along the corridor. And, suddenly, I felt unbearably sorry that, when he regained consciousness on the plank-bed, he would still not understand what had happened to him in ward 26. Immediately, I decided to put matters right and to finish him off while there was still time. I strained with all my strength to get up from the concrete floor but all the effort dissolved into a pitiful attempt to move my head.

'He's come to,' said somebody from somewhere above my head.

'Let him have another whiff.'

The artilleryman was still on his feet and now he was vomiting. Somebody quite close to me said, 'On the orders of the Defence Minister, he's already an officer!'

'The Minister's order came today, but it was signed yesterday,' objected another voice. 'That means the amnesty covered only the time served yesterday. But, today, after becoming an officer, he was put on another charge by the Deputy Commander of the District and therefore this period is not covered by the ministerial amnesty.'

'Bugger it, can't we approach the Deputy Commander personally in connection with this case since it's so exceptional?'

'But the Deputy Commander has never set eyes upon your newly-fledged lieutenant. It was done on the orders of Himself's wife. Himself has gone to the Party conference. You do not propose to ask Herself, do you?'

'Too right!' agreed the second voice.

'And we can't set him free under the amnesty either! Otherwise, what will happen if she comes tomorrow to check up? Then all our heads will roll!'

'Quite right!'

And so it happened that, while our artilleryman was cleaning the sewers, the Minister of Defence had signed the orders, promoting him and, with him, another two hundred fortunate officer cadets to the rank of lieutenant. In such cases, the ministerial order is normally an absolution. But, while this order was on its way from Moscow, our artilleryman had been put on a further charge purporting to emanate from the Deputy Commander of the Kiev Military District. And no one could do anything about it.

But, even so, he had officially become an officer, and his place was in the officers' quarters which were separated from those of the common herd by a high wall. So, we embraced like brothers, like two men who are very close and yet who are destined to part from each other for ever. He smiled wanly at me and, just as he was, filthy from the excrement of the wife of the future Commander-in-Chief of the Combined Armed Forces of the Warsaw Treaty Powers, Marshal of the Soviet Union Yakubovskiy, but now at long last without any escort, he went towards the iron gates leading to the officers' quarters.

On that very day, in the capital of our Motherland, in that most heroic city of Moscow, to the accompaniment of the thunderous applause of thousands of delegates and of our numerous brothers, assembled from all the corners of the earth, in the Kremlin Palace of Congresses, the work of the XXIII Congress of the Communist Party of the Soviet Union began. It was an historic occasion. From that day forward, the Party promised the present generation of Soviet people . . . nothing at all!

Risk

It may be argued that political training in the glasshouse is the very best time of all. Just sit there on a stool for an hour and a half, just nod off and do absolutely nothing. It would seem hard to invent any better form of relaxation. Any such thought is pure imagination and could only enter the head of one who has never seen the inside of a glasshouse or of someone who has not been warned in advance how to behave during a spell of training there. For the inexperienced inmate, the seeming simplicity of it all can turn out to be a load of trouble. The inmate is pleased beyond bounds by his first attendance at a political training session but he has only to let himself be distracted for a single moment, to forget for a single second where he is and what he is there for, and misfortune will instantly strike.

Exhausted by lack of sleep and the terrible cold, by damp and hunger, by punishing work, by constant humiliations and insults and, what is worse, by the expectation of still more terrible things to come, after one has calmed down a little and got warm, one's organism does finally relax for a moment or two.

And if one slackens, even momentarily, this steel spring, taut from the very first moment of being in the glasshouse, gets instantly out of hand and unwinds spontaneously in a flash . . . and one loses all control.

Exactly that is happening nearby to a little soldier who, most probably, has never been in the glasshouse before – his eyes are glazed, his eyelids stick together, he is going to fall asleep . . . any moment now he will bury his head in the dirty, hunched-up back of that weedy sailor who came to Kiev on leave and was picked up by a patrol at the railway station. It looks as if the sailor will also drop off to sleep at any moment. I am sorry for the soldier, for the sailor, and for myself too . . . but my feet are getting warm . . . and my head feels intoxicated. I can hear the ringing of little bells . . . they sound so sweet . . . my head droops on to my chest . . . but my neck seems to be made of cotton wool, it will never bear the weight of my head . . . it will surely break . . . I must relax my neck.

And there you are, my little one, you are done for and, instead of a nice warm plank-bed, a stinking lavatory awaits you at night, and the kitchen awaits you too, which is still worse. And, when you have served your time, you will be given an extra three days, just to teach you not to dream of a nice little slice of black bread, or of dry socks, but, instead, of the policies of our beloved Party, which open before us such bright new horizons. And that is how it goes.

It was not the first time for me – not in the Kiev glasshouse, it is true, but in Kharkov. And there is no real way of distinguishing which of the two is better. Of course, 'communism' in Kharkov is not the same, but a rather more modest affair. But the tank factory is a good deal bigger than that in Kiev and every day half of all the glasshouse inmates are raked in there and it's no picnic. But, when it comes to political training, I have known the ropes for a long time and you won't ever catch me on that score.

At first, I did not think about sleep because I was much too hungry, but I also tried not to think about food either as such dreams made my stomach ache. And there was another thing which had been bothering me from the very start of political training and that was how to change my socks. Those I was wearing had been wet through for six whole days and it made no difference how you put them on. Outside, frost and slush alternate. It's cold to the feet, it's wet . . . I wish I could change my socks . . . Stop! That's a very dangerous thought. One must not think about dry socks! Such thought is pure provocation! It must be promptly driven out, otherwise, one is in very deep water indeed. Now, it seems to me that my feet are completely dry . . . that I had put them on the radiator during the night, although there are no radiators in the glasshouse . . . and that they have dried out during the night. They are so dry now that they won't even bend . . . and now my feet are so warm . . . STOP IT! I'm not asleep! Two hefty lance-corporals, charging through the room, are bearing down on me. Fuck your mother, you bastards, I wasn't asleep! . . . The lance-corporal angrily heaves me aside and continues to carve his way through those seated behind me. Involuntarily, I turn my head to watch him and, the very next moment, realising the danger, I turn it back again. But one moment is enough to take in the faces of those seated behind. All, without exception, were the faces of men crushed by fear. Sheer animal terror and supplication registered in about fifty pairs of eyes. Only one thought registered on all their faces. 'Oh, please don't let it be me!' Probably the same expression had been on my own face a moment before, when I thought the lance-corporals were homing in on me. God, how easy it is to frighten us! How pitiful is a frightened man! To what depths will he sink to save his skin!

Meanwhile, the lance-corporals have caught hold of a pilot officer cadet who sits slouched right in the very corner. This future ace, like a heavy wooden doll with strings instead of joints, wasn't sleeping, he had just switched off completely and was out for the count. And, while the lance-corporals carry this defender of the motherland out along the passage, his head hangs loose like some trinket on a chain. You are wrong, O Air Ace, you should not lose control of yourself! That will not do, little falcon! You weakened and, now, they will put you in number 26 revolutionary ward for a whiff of chlorine and you will soon come to and then you'll go into 25 and, only after all that, they will give you another five days, it's as easy as falling off a log! Hell! Just how long will the first lieutenant go droning on about our beloved Party? No bloody watch, no nothing! Seems like five hours we've been sitting here already and still he can't get it over with! If only I could change my socks, it would be easier to go on sitting here. I can't stand it any more. My head gets heavier by the minute, as if a pair of huge cast-iron dumb-bells had been placed inside it. Only . . . my feet are cold. If only new socks . . . Or even if the lance-corporals would carry away those who have passed out more often – it would make a change, it would relieve the monotony and I might manage to see it through. It would be good to get out into the frost now, or to the petrol refinery, or to the tank works. If only my feet were comfortable.

'ANY QUESTIONS?'

A resounding 'NO' explodes from a hundred throats. It's salvation! It's the end of political training! It's over . . .

Now comes the order! 'Form up for relief . . . you've got one minute and a half.' This means that I must rush, with all the combined might of my body and soul, with all my wish to live, straight for the exit, straight into a doorway choked with the stinking bodies of other dirty inmates like me and, then, heaving them all aside, break out into the corridor. It is very important not to stumble – one would be trampled underfoot since, naturally, everyone wants to live! Racing upstairs seven steps at a time, I must get to the second floor and grab my coat and cap. It is most important to find one's own coat quickly since if, later on, somebody gets yours, which is too small for him he will not be able to get it on and you will soon be caught and get five days for stealing, and the other big ninny will be put in the same ward as you for his sluggishness, and then both of you will have time to find out who is right and who is wrong and whose fists are stronger. Then, with coat and cap in hand, one must crash straight through the upward-rushing stream of inmates desperate to get their own coats and caps, and rush back down. There's already a pile-up at the exit and the lance-corporals are on the look-out for the stragglers. So just launch yourself into the crowd like an ice-breaker – smash, break and crunch. One and a half

44

minutes have nearly expired but you still haven't formed up, you are still not properly dressed, your red star is not yet lined up with your nose, and your cap is still not sitting precisely two fingers above your eyebrows . . . it's no good . . .

The order 'Form up to receive orders' will be given at any moment. Everybody stands tense, ready for a superhuman effort, ready to rush and crash headlong into others, to carry out the order . . . but the first lieutenant hangs back on purpose . . . to test our readiness to be standing to attention in one and a half minutes . . . Is everyone imbued with the importance of the moment? Has everyone screwed himself up into a tight ball? Is everyone so strained that he is ready to gnaw at his neighbours with his teeth? But the first lieutenant's gaze strays off somewhere into a corner, and no one dares to turn his head to find out what could possibly have attracted the attention of the Deputy Commander of the Kiev Garrison glasshouse at such a moment as this. It is a hand which has attracted the first lieutenant's attention, a dirty hand which has been cleaning lavatories for the last two weeks and which has not been washed once in all that time. And at that very moment when the first lieutenant asked the traditional question 'Any questions?' – the answer to which is always, as loudly as possible, 'NO QUESTIONS' – this hand was raised in a distant corner. Now, no one ever asks any questions in the glasshouse; so much is clear from the very first moment. And here you are! Just fancy, somebody now wants to ask a question!

The first lieutenant knows absolutely all the answers to all possible questions. In addition, he is so mighty and all-powerful that he can destroy anyone who presumes to disturb his peace with such impertinence. Even after the report of some First Secretary of a District Party Committee, no one dares to ask any questions. And here we have a member of the lower orders trying to disturb the peace of the Deputy Chief of the Kiev Garrison glasshouse himself!

The first lieutenant is clearly very interested by this phenomenon, the more so since he sees that it is not the inmate's first day in the glasshouse and that he must fully realise the degree of risk to which he is exposing himself and all those who, like himself, are under arrest.

The first lieutenant is a psychologist and he certainly realises full well why this officer-cadet with the hollow eyes, an expert in electronics, is taking such a risk: clearly he has only one or two days left to serve in the glasshouse but, if he is then sent to the tank factory, of course he will not be able to fulfil his norms and will surely be given another five days, which could transform him permanently into an oppressed, humiliated, intimidated semi-idiot. It is conceivable that his service and his career will even be furthered by such an ineluctable process, but this is not what the officer-cadet wants nor what he is ready to take any risk to avoid. He has obviously decided to ask his question simply in order to flatter the first lieutenant and thus to secure for himself a timely discharge. But it is not an easy matter to flatter the omnipotent! And if that flattery is taken exception to as being crude flattery . . .? So then, the flattery, in the form of a question, must clearly combine within itself something very original and must even verge upon the permissive . . . And well we all knew it!

'What do you want?' the first lieutenant enquired politely, thus emphasising his respect for the bravery on display.

'Officer-cadet Antonov, arrested for fifteen days and thirteen of them already served,' he reported efficiently. 'Comrade First Lieutenant, I have a question!' A sinister silence descended upon the room. We had all been waiting for this moment, but the unusual impertinence of it struck us all very forcefully. It was as if a fly, after having warmed itself on the hot stove, were to dive down on us from the ceiling with the thunderous boom of a strategic bomber. We shuddered and hid our heads in our shoulders, as if trying to soften the blow, if sheer unadulterated rage descended upon any head in that room.

'Put your question . . .' – and then, as an afterthought, the first lieutenant added, 'Please.'

'Comrade First Lieutenant, tell me, please . . . will there be any glasshouses under communism?'

My shoulders cringed, and my head sank down even lower. I was not the only one who expected a pole-axe in the neck. Only the man who had asked the question stood there, proud and straight, his sunken breast thrust forward and looking, with those intelligent grey eyes of his, straight into the eyes of the omnipotent one. The latter was thoughtful for a while, then his thick lips parted in an almost childlike smile. He obviously enjoyed the question. Mischievous lights caught fire in his eyes and he pronounced the words with complete conviction and faith! 'There will always be a glasshouse!' Whereupon, he burst out laughing. The omnipotent one looked once more at the electronics expert and then added heartily, 'Good lad! And now . . . and now . . . at the double . . . to the lavatories, and see to it that before evening comes they shine like a cat's testicles!' Hundreds of throats sighed with envy at the very thought. 'Right you are, Comrade,' he responded joyfully.

And can anything better than that ever be invented. It is true that, after morning high-speed 'jobs time', the lavatory is a pretty filthy place but, in two or three hours, it can easily be licked clean enough to be proud of it. And then . . . and then, throughout the whole day, just pretend that you are improving on what has already been done. After all, it is not that bottomless, stinking pit of communism itself! Oh, no!

46

Not that! This is only a lavatory when all is said and done. It's only at night that it's not very pleasant to clean it, because that's instead of sleeping, but during the day, in the warmth and in comfort . . .

'Form up for duty detail, you've got one minute and a half!'

With the weight of my whole body I lurched forward.

That was a wonderful day, and I was lucky for, as one of a small group of inmates, I found myself in the regional Military Hospital lugging about bales of dirty linen. Our escort was a fourth-year artilleryman who had obviously been in the glasshouse himself more than once. And when, late in the evening, he gave us a ten-minute break and we sat about on ice-covered logs of wood leaning our weary backs up against the warm walls of the furnace, and a tender-hearted, sprightly nurse from the skin-venereal department brought us a whole box of chewed scraps of wonderful white bread, we ate them with delight. I am quite incapable of describing the ecstasy of that unforgettable day. But I, for one, am sure that each of us, in that moment, thought only of that brave officer-cadet, about the risk he had taken upon himself, about the exactness of the psychological calculation he had made and, in general, about the limitless possibilities of the human mind.

April 1967. The final days before graduation from the Kharkov Guards Tank Commanders' School.

Ever Ready!

The boots shone so that you could have used them as shaving mirrors and the trousers were so well pressed that, if a fly had brushed against the crease, it would have been sliced in two. We were to take over as town patrol and our outward appearance was checked personally by Colonel Yeremeyev, the Military Commandant of Kharkov. And he didn't like jokes! The smallest fault in one's uniform meant ten days under arrest. Everyone had long been acquainted with this as being the accepted norm. And now the Colonel was giving his briefing. 'In conclusion, the productivity norms: railway station – 150 convictions; town part – 120; airport – 80; the remainder – 60 each.' The Colonel here omitted to mention the main point, but there was no need, as everybody knew that those guilty of under-fulfilment were not relieved at 2400 hours, as prescribed, but were sent out on the 'bigger round', that is to say on all-night duty; and if, towards morning, the patrol did not get another thirty convictions, then it was the glasshouse for them all and yesterday's patrol would find itself in the same wards where the earlier victims of this very same patrol were already sitting. All this was well known and there was no need to remind anyone of the facts. Norms are scientifically based, and are verified in practice over many years' experience. Well then, our objectives were clear! Our tasks had been clearly defined! So now, get to work, Comrades!

Our patrol consisted of three men: Captain Sadirov and two officer-cadets in their last year. Our tour of duty would last a total of 480 minutes. We would be relieved at 2400 hours. Our quota was sixty offenders, or one arrest every eight minutes. In other words, any military man we met must be guilty of something. So if, during these eight hours, we only manage to find fifty-nine soldiers, seamen, sergeants, warrant-officers and officers, then a 'bigger round' was guaranteed and, at night, where on earth are you supposed to catch another thirty men?

The success of patrol work depends to a large extent on the character of the patrol chief himself. If he is strict enough and resourceful enough then the quota can be fulfilled.

'Comrade Sergeant, you are breaking regulations on the correct form of dress.'

'No, comrade Captain.' Everything the sergeant has on is shining, and there is obviously nothing to quibble at.

'In the first place, you are arguing with the head of the patrol and, secondly, the top button of your tunic shows the symbol of Soviet power facing the wrong way. Show me your papers!'

And it was a fact that the shining button, with its hammer and sickle, within a five-pointed star, was sewn on rather unevenly, or possibly it was not sewn quite firmly enough and had got loose and, as a result, the hammer was not facing upwards as it should but slightly sideways. You could catch anyone on this pretext, even the Minister of Defence himself. How can one possibly ensure that all buttons have their hammers unfailingly straight up? The captain then scrawled on the sergeant's pass in bold letters: 'Leave cancelled at 1604 hours, owing to crude violation of the rules of dress and for arguing with a patrol.' I wrote down the sergeant's name and unit number, and the offender saluted the captain and set off for his unit. Now the sergeant was completely defenceless since his pass was no longer valid and if he was stopped by another patrol on his way back to his unit he might be clobbered with 'absence without leave'.

We caught the first one in four minutes, so during the remaining 476 minutes we had to catch another fifty-nine.

'Comrade Private, you are breaking regulations on dress.'

'No, Comrade Captain, I am not.'

'Comrade Private, you are arguing with a patrol chief!'

'No, Comrade Captain, I am not arguing, I only wanted to say that I am not breaking regulations on form of dress.'

'Guards Officer-Cadet Suvorov!'

'Here!'

'Call the duty car – this is a serious offender!'

While my fellow cadet wrote down the name of the serious offender and the captain was catching yet another, I ran to the nearest telephone box. Yes, the sergeant was more experienced, he shut his mouth before uttering the second sentence, but the little soldier was still a bit green. And that is why you, my little darling, will be taken away with honour in a car any moment now. I ran back from the telephone and saw that, beside the serious offender, there already stood a pilot officer-cadet guilty of 'sloppy saluting'. Sixteen minutes of our tour of duty gone and three offenders already in the bag, I hoped it continued that way.

'Comrade Warrant-Officer, your peak is not two fingers from your eyebrows!'

'No, Comrade Captain, it's exactly two fingers.'

'You are arguing! Your papers!'

There was no time for boredom with our captain. He was a fine fellow and no mistake. But what was that there in the bushes? Surely it was a dead-drunk defender of the Motherland? It was indeed! There were some stunted shrubs between the street and the pavement, and in their midst had fallen an inebriated warrior. Tunic unbuttoned, right shoulder-strap torn off and chest, trousers and boots all covered in vomit, there he was, completely filthy, his cap long since vanished. We turned him over on to his back. Oh, what bad luck! He was an officer-cadet of our own beloved tank school, a guardsman like myself. We never lay a finger on one of our own. There is intense socialist competition between all units of the garrison! One cannot ever let down one's own school. Air force, artillery and all the others – be on your guard – but not one of our boys! He had just drunk a bit too much. Who doesn't do the same sometimes? A car, summoned from our school, took the drunken tankman away. He was not included in the statistics, of course, he did not count, and anyway he was taken home merely to prevent him from freezing to death or catching cold. You see, the ground was cold because it wasn't summertime.

'Comrade Lieutenant, you are breaking regulations on dress.' The lieutenant obediently kept silent. He was literate, this one.

'Your gloves, Comrade Lieutenant, are black, they should be brown!'

'Yes, you are right, I am guilty, Comrade Captain.'

'Papers!'

Our own captain's gloves were also black. Where can one possibly find brown gloves? Gloves are not issued to officers, because the industry does not in any case produce brown ones. Officers are given money to buy their own gloves. Buy them yourselves, but unfortunately there is nowhere to buy them. I repeat, Soviet industry does not produce any brown gloves. Anyone who has served in Germany would have bought at least twenty pairs, a life-time's supply. And anyone who has never served in Germany is prey to the patrols. Before going on duty, all officers are issued personally by Colonel Yeremeyev with a pair of brown leather gloves for which they sign, to wear, temporarily, while on duty. But these gloves are so well worn, tattered and out of shape, that it would be indecent for an officer to wear them. This is why our captain immediately took them off and folded them tidily and put them in his pocket. God forbid that he should lose them!

'And why are you breaking the regulations, Comrade Lieutenant. Does an order of the Minister of Defence not concern you?'

'I am sorry.'

'You may go!'

'Right!'

This lieutenant's name also graced our book of statistics. When the time comes for the lieutenant to enter the academy, the top brass will look at his personal file. Oh, heavens, he has been stopped by patrols a hundred times in one year and on each occasion for the same violation! He is incorrigible! He should be locked up! And you recommend him for the academy! Use your brains, man!

'Comrade Senior Lieutenant, you are breaking regulations on dress . . . Your gloves are black. Or maybe you did not read the order of the Minister of Defence? Well then, why do you break it? Is it deliberate? Does it spring from a love of violating rules?' The captain took off one of his own black gloves and wrote down in his black book the name of the senior lieutenant.

There were two hours and seventeen minutes left before we were to be relieved. There were sixty-one offenders in the black book. In the darkness, obviously quite oblivious to us and humming something under his breath, a dead-drunk artilleryman was staggering all over the place and our captain somehow managed not to notice him.

'Request permission, Comrade Captain, to arrest this God of War.'

'Oh no, let him be, he's in the 62nd and always remember this, Suvorov, the target must be passed, but only minimally. This is the law of our life. It's time you understood that norms are scientifically based and verified many times over by life itself. In a couple of months, we will be on patrol again, and then they'd make it not 60 but 65 or even as many as 70 offenders. And you just go and try making it 70. The existing norms are the direct result of the work of the ninnies like you who tried too hard to overreach the target, and now these same ninnies are themselves being caught by patrols, that's what.'

The lucky artilleryman, quite without noticing us, staggered off. If all the patrols in his path had already slightly overshot their targets, he might quietly drift along right through town along all the main streets, drunk, unbuttoned and dirty with that fixed insolent, intoxicated expression on his face. Meanwhile, the number of drunken and half-drunk soldiers, officer-cadets and sergeants continued to grow. The vast majority had long since cottoned on to the advantages of the planned system and hid their faces until evening. The feeling was that control weakened simultaneously in all districts of the town. All patrols tried to fulfil their plans as soon as possible in order to insure themselves against the 'bigger round', and that was why everything had changed. The most experienced villains and alcoholics used this 'release of tension' for their own, far from noble, purposes. From 2400 hours onwards, all of them, even those who were paralytically drunk, put their tails between their legs precisely because they knew that the stupidest, most inept patrols, for whom a whole day was not even long enough to catch anybody, were now out on the prowl.

In spite of the growing flood of real offenders, drunks and hooligans, we had absolutely nothing to do and here we were sitting on a bench under the bare leafless willows. The captain instructed us on the tactics of the German tank forces. After all, the passing-out examinations were not very far off.

'Tactics, brothers, are the most complicated subject on earth. But just tell our generals that tactics are more complicated than chess and they laugh their heads off, they simply don't believe it. But it's really no laughing matter. Chess is the crudest form, the most superficial model of a battle between two armies and the most primitive of armies at that. In all other respects, it's exactly like war. A king is helpless and lacks mobility but his loss signifies complete defeat. A king is the exact personification of headquarters staff, cumbersome and lacking in mobility – so just destroy them and it's checkmate. The queen is the intelligence service, in the fullest sense of the word – an all-powerful and invincible intelligence service, capable of acting independently with lightning speed, and thwarting the enemy's plans. Knight, bishop and castle require no commentary. The likeness is very great, especially when it comes to the cavalry. Think of the battle of Borodino and the cavalry raid carried out by Uvarov and Platov on Bonaparte's rear. That was 'knight's gambit' for you in both meaning and form. Just you look at the map! The Russian cavalry neither fought nor charged, but simply appeared in the rear and that was that, but their appearance stopped Bonaparte from sending his guard into battle. And in many respects this one move decided both the battle and the whole destiny of Russia. And that was knight's gambit for you.

'A contemporary battle,' continued the captain 'is a thousand times more complicated than chess. If you want to model a small contemporary army on a chess-board, the number of chess-men, with all kinds of different capabilities will have to be sharply increased. Somehow, you will need to designate tanks, anti-tank rockets, anti-tank artillery and artillery, pure and simple, an air force including fighters, low-flying attack planes, strategic bombers, air transport and helicopters – you just can't list them all . . . and all demand a united plan, a united strategy and the closest possible co-ordination. Our misfortune, and the main difference between us and the Germans, consists in our habit of counting our bishops and pawns, with total disregard for their competent deployment. And, you know, the Germans started the war against us with a paltry three thousand tanks against our eighteen thousand. Now, we propound many different versions, but we refuse to accept the main conclusion, which is that German tactics were much

52

more flexible than ours. Mark my words – if something happens in the Near East, we will be smashed to smithereens; they won't give a damn for quantitative and qualitative superiority. What's the good of having three queens, if you don't know how to play chess? And our advisers simply cannot play, and that's a fact. Look at the Head of Faculty, Colonel Soloukhin, just back from Syria . . . '

'But how so?' I could not refrain from asking.

The captain looked at me and then slowly said: 'It's the system itself that's at fault.'

The answer obviously did not fully satisfy us and so he added, 'Firstly, our chiefs are appointed on the basis of their political qualifications, they don't know how the game is played or even wish to learn how to play it but they're ideologically well-groomed. Secondly, our system demands the rendering of accounts, reports, and achievements. Upon this we stand! The reports which announced the destruction of thousands of German tanks and aircraft during the first days of the war were so phoney that the political leadership of the country changed to quoting territorial indices instead, as being more convincing. This gave birth to reports of the capture of towns and mountain tops and such like. But you just try playing chess without annihilating the enemy's army, but by capturing his territory, regardless of your own losses! What will happen? The same as happened to us during the war. We won only because we showed no pity for millions of our own pawns. If our General Staff and military advisers take it into their heads to seize Israeli territory instead of first annihilating their army, it will cost us very dear indeed. Of course, the Jews won't achieve checkmate, but the annihilation of Israel by our tactics will still cost us dear. And it will be worst of all if, God forbid, we ever come up against China. In that case, our pawns won't help us at all because they have many more pawns at their own disposal.'

Here the captain spat angrily and kicked an empty tin can with the toe of his varnished boot. The can rolled along the dark pathway under the feet of a well-oiled sapper who was making advances to a young girl. The silent struggle in the darkness apparently reminded the captain that we were still on patrol. He yawned and abruptly changed the subject.

'Guards Officer-Cadet Suvorov, your conclusions please about today's patrol duty. Quickly!'

I was slightly taken aback.

'A tank commander must instantly evaluate the situation. Well? Your conclusions?'

'Uh-h, we arrested many offenders . . . Uh-h, we have improved discipline . . . thanks to you . . .' I tried, awkwardly, to interlace the flattery.

'You haven't a clue, Viktor, and you a future lieutenant, or don't you want to understand . . . or else you are just plain cunning. Listen – but it's only between the two of us. In a fully planned economy, terror also can only be a planned affair, i.e. absolutely idiotic and ineffective, this is the first point. Secondly, we have been working today according to the methods of the second five-year-plan, that is to say the methods of 1937 and 1938, the only difference being that we didn't actually arrest or shoot the offenders. Thirdly, if today the order were given to repeat the second five-year-plan, then not only the organs of State Security, but every armed man, even every ordinary Soviet citizen, would rush headlong to carry out this order: that is how we have been trained and we are ever ready. And fourthly . . . you and I too, Viktor, for that matter, are not insured against these bloody five-year-plans . . . we have absolutely no insurance . . . If the order were given tomorrow, everything would start all over again – the Berias, the Yezhovs, the NKVD, etc . . . It's just that, for the present, we have a completely spineless General Secretary in charge . . . but only for the moment! But supposing he's replaced tomorrow? . . . What then? Okay, don't get upset, let's go . . . our tour of duty is over for today.'

'Comrade Captain, maybe after all we should drive off that sapper, otherwise he'll rape her, sure as eggs is eggs!'

'Tomorrow she'll complain, that it was a soldier, and on our patrol route too,' added my other comrade, hoping to give weight to my remark.

'But this is still no concern of ours,' he smiled, and pointed to the luminous dial of his watch. We smiled too – the watch showed 0004 hours.

Kharkov 1967.

Theatre

Before the arrival in Severodvinsk of Marshal of the Soviet Union Grechko, the high command of the Northern Fleet decided to paint the shore-line cliffs grey. In all, over twenty kilometres of coastline were painted. The sailors of two whole divisions and the men of a marines regiment laboured over this titanic work for several weeks and, in the process, used up the whole allocation of anti-corrosion paint supplied to the entire fleet for a whole year. The Minister liked the colour of the rocks, and from that time forth the painting of rocks before the arrival of a high-ranking commander became one of the more remarkable traditions of our Fleet.

Before the arrival of Marshal of the Soviet Union Chuikov at the Moscow Higher Combined Arms School, the School Commander decided to level up all the pine-trees along the 'Golden Kilometre' – the woodland road leading towards the school – using caterpillar tank tractors.

Before the visit of Marshal of the Soviet Union Sokolov to the fifth Army of the Far Eastern Military District, more than 500 portraits of the Marshal were hung about the walls of the barracks of that Army's mobile rocket-technical base.

The history of our glorious army records tens of thousands of such examples, here I quote but a few of those seen with my own eyes. The system itself is to blame. That is how our army is organised. And don't think that it's only marshals who are greeted with such joy. Any major from a neighbouring division, who comes to make some check-up or other, is given the same hospitable reception. We are all trained to expect it and we cannot live otherwise. All is boiling energy, turbulent fantasy, and the rare qualities and abilities of the majority of all Soviet officers and generals are squandered on outdoing their competitors in the hospitality stakes. Rarely does one come across a general who is not keen on such displays. But our army is a huge one and exceptions do occur. I knew one such general, a free-thinker who considered the painting of grass with green paint, if not idiotic, then at least as not being his paramount task. The Head of the Tank Training School, Major-General Slukin never once appeared either at the tank training ground, the armoured troop carrier training ground, or at the artillery range. Underwater tank manoeuvres, firing practice, the battle training of tank platoons and companies he considered as being work for dumb soldiers and an unnecessary waste of time. Our general was sold on culture and considered it his duty to implant in future officers something rather higher than mere military science.

At the same time it must also be said that, as a general rule, in Soviet military schools and academies, culture is neither cultivated, taught, nor implanted in any form. And it was this very gap that our chief tried to fill. The trouble was that his notions about culture were rather peculiar. He considered, for example, that a cultured man is only one who regularly goes to the theatre and that the number of such visits defines the degree of one's culture. Literature, painting, sculpture, architecture and so on were totally beyond the general's sphere of vision. The Theatre and nothing but the Theatre! It does not matter which, as long as it is a theatre. The general's only care was a register of personal attendances.

The life of an officer-cadet at tank school is exceptionally arduous. Anyone who has experienced, if only once, what it means to load forty-three projectiles into a tank, to change a tank-track (which weighs one and a half tons), or just to sit for three hours behind the controls of a T-55, will understand to the full what it is really like to spend four years at a tank training school. But, when all is said and done, the hardest ordeal of all for us was still the theatre. And we were obliged to attend it at least once a month. The whole school had to attend, to the joy of all those theatres which were going bankrupt and were usually never patronised by anybody. And, for this very reason, the Political Directorate of our Military District loved our general very much and always quoted him as an example; and it was no joke either as our school alone provided the district with 12,000 'man-attendances' per year. This was really something to be proud of, even if there was complete failure in all other areas.

Attendance was carried out herd-fashion, in formation, with colours flying and music playing. In front of the theatre, the general assembled the whole school (a thousand officer-cadets) at attention and yelled his instructions into a megaphone so loudly that they could be heard three blocks away. 'Inside the theatre . . . No spitting on the floor! No spitting in the corners! This is a theatre! Don't blow your noses on your sleeves! Use your handkerchieves! . . . And most important . . . No swearing! I expressly forbid it! If I hear any at all, I will put you on a charge! This is a theatre!'

When we marched to the theatre for the first time, thousands of people came running out to feast their eyes upon the spectacle of these dashing defenders of the Motherland – these future officers. But after they had heard the loudly-shouted instructions, they did not know where to look for the shame of it. We meanwhile were all standing to attention, not daring to move a single muscle. The rumours about us soon spread throughout the town. Formerly, no tank officer-cadet was known in the town otherwise than as 'Guderian' after the German tank commander, but now we earned for ourselves a new honorary title – 'Snotty' – and the name stuck. No sooner did any officer-cadet appear anywhere, than there were shouts of 'Don't blow your nose on your sleeve'. Attendances at the theatre continued, accompanied by the obligatory instructions. But now, when people heard the roll of the drums and the measured tread of our boots, they fled instantly, expressly in order not to witness this disgraceful spectacle.

One night, after the usual theatre visit, I was awakened by my friend Genka Bulakov. It was probably two o'clock in the morning but the lad simply could not get to sleep, in spite of the accumulated tiredness of the previous week.

'Viktor! Please explain to me . . .'

'What do you want?'

'There is one thing I simply can't understand, I mean . . . our general . . . Of course, he is a cultured fellow, far better than other generals . . . But I cannot understand one thing . . . Why, every time, in front of the theatre, does he have to shout like that into his bloody megaphone? He could give us those instructions back at the school. What the hell does he have to shout at the top of his voice for? We know his instructions by heart and so do all the locals.'

'In the old days it would have been considered an insult.'

'Pull the other one!'

'No. In the old days, he most certainly would have been challenged to a duel . . .'

'Go on! Do you think I never read Kuprin?* I did, you know. But I still never came across any cases of cadets challenging generals to duels. Of course, it would not be a bad idea, at that, to challenge him to a duel and to shoot at him with armour-piercing shells. General he may be, and a cultured chap at that, but I bet he would fuck up shooting, on the move, with a low-energy release shell with double stabilisations. I would be the first to challenge him to a duel myself . . . But what you say is all tripe and never happened . . . and never could happen either.'

To tell the truth, I did not know for sure myself whom, and under what

---

*The descendant of a Tartar Khan, called Kuprya, Kuprin served as an infantry officer in the Tsarist army. He wrote several novels highlighting the negative sides of the private life of the officer corps. The most well-known and biased was his novel entitled *Duel*. After the Revolution, Kuprin lived as an émigré in France.

circumstances, one could challenge to a duel, and I had not come across any examples of such incidents in literature. So, then, I just expressed my own feelings.

'Of course, one could not challenge generals to duels over things of that kind, and I personally think it was because cultured generals did not exist in those days. None of the generals then was ever interested in the theatre, and that is why nobody challenged them to duels . . . The army only became cultured after the victory of Soviet power . . . It's a pity, though, that duels *were* forbidden then.'

'Yes, it's a pity,' mumbled Genka, falling asleep.

Part Two

Summer 1967. The Ukraine.

Operation 'Dnieper'

On the day after our passing-out evening celebration, all two hundred of us young lieutenants, the latest graduates of the Kharkov Guards Tank Commander School, were formed up on the parade ground and an order from the Minister of Defence concerning our re-training for our new battle techniques was read out to us. Usually, after passing-out celebrations, young officers are given a month's leave, after which time, in accordance with the Minister's order, they go to join their division or regiment and are thus scattered throughout the whole world, from Havana to South Sakhalinsk, wherever the Minister orders. And now this tradition of many years' standing had been broken, owing to the simple fact that a new tank, the T-64, had been introduced into service in the Soviet Army some few months before our graduation. Before our graduation, there had not been enough time for detailed study. As it was, our curriculum was already over-loaded with other subjects. And so it was decided to re-train all young officers, but from one tank school only, rather than from all five; and not to distribute the re-trained officers over the whole vast expanse of our territory, but to confine them to those divisions and districts which are habitually re-armed first.

It should here be mentioned that the very newest battle technology is always introduced first to the troops of the second line of defence, that is to those of the Baltic, Byelorussian and Carpathian Military Districts, and most certainly not to the Group of Soviet Forces in Germany or to any other troops stationed abroad. New technology is only introduced in such places after five to eight, and sometimes more, years after its adoption in frontier districts. Our T-64 first appeared in Germany exactly ten years after it began to be mass produced. And at the time of the first mention in the West of this tank, as a new Soviet experimental tank, its mass production had in fact long since ceased altogether—it was being replaced by the new T-72s.

This system has several aims. First, it greatly increases secrecy and, in case of war, it puts the enemy at a great disadvantage. Secondly, it facilitates the sale of obsolete technology to our allies, from Poland to the Arabs. In this way, the technology available to the Group of Soviet Troops in Germany can be made out to be of the very latest design.

Never before, at the introduction of a new tank into service, had young officers been kept back for re-training, which was formerly done at divisional level as a part of everyday service. This is understandable: all previous tanks, from the T-44 to the T-62, represent the continuation of one line of development, in that each successive model retained, in its construction, many elements possessed by the previous model, and, therefore, re-training was a comparatively uncomplicated process. Now, this line of development had been exploited to the full and the new T-64 was based on entirely new principles. Everything in it, from its general lay-out, to stabilizers, optics, signals and drive, was unusual and completely new, and, as it turned out later, also totally unreliable.

The study of the new techniques, equipment, electronics and tank's armament took four and a half months – from 1 June to 15 October, 1967. At the end of September, we had to take part in large-scale manoeuvres and to put into practice our newly-acquired skills and abilities. We had to postpone our leave until October.

The process of introducing new battle techniques into an army is always a secret. Draconian measures are taken to stop any details connected with this process from being leaked. Simultaneously, all official channels disseminate false information. For instance, at a parade, or during special show exercises, something which is absolutely contrary to actual practice may be demonstrated.

That same day, in the evening, as we stood to attention, an order was read out to us prohibiting young officers from wearing officers' uniform during re-training: only tank-crew overalls were to be worn. Tank-crew overalls in our army are standard issue and carry no badge or rank, with the result that a soldier is indistinguishable from an officer. This is an old tradition of ours, born of war. The order seemed merely to indicate a means of camouflage and there was nothing strange about that. The odd part emerged a bit later. It turned out that over a hundred re-engaged men, all instructor-drivers, were going with us. For a mere two hundred pupils, a hundred instructors were out of all proportion. Seventy would have been enough for the whole school, for all thousand officer-cadets. And yet they had assembled the school's entire complement of instructors, thus, for all practical purposes, arresting completely the whole training programme throughout the school; in addition to which, many more instructors had been sent directly from the Kharkov Malyshev Works, which officially produced railway locomotives and, unofficially, also tanks. The fact that instructors had been brought straight from the works was absolutely inexplicable. Clearly, they must be desperately needed there, if mass production of a new tank had started.

A second inexplicable factor was that our own supervisors were not going with us. The teaching process normally proceeds as follows: a lieutenant colonel, the supervisor, explains the theory, after which instructor-sergeants, under his control, give practical instruction. But there were too many instructors and not a single supervisor!

A third surprise awaited us in the train itself. After our departure, a secret order was read out in all carriages, announcing the formation of the 100th Guards Tank Training Regiment. The Deputy Commander of the School, who read us this order, introduced to us the young Colonel of the newly-formed regiment. It was also announced that the regiment would have ninety-two battle tanks and nineteen battle-training tanks.

It was dead of night as the train wended its way along the track, making a lulling knocking noise on the rails. But no one was sleeping. And there was good reason for this: as a new regiment has been formed, then, a colour must be presented to it, the more so since it was a Guards regiment, all of which made the ceremony of the presentation of the colour all the more momentous. According to regulations, a new Guards colour must be received by the whole regiment on its knees, but, in this instance, nothing of the kind was happening. And, secondly, why so many tanks for a training regiment? Thirty to forty training tanks would have been quite enough, and battle tanks were not even needed in the first place.

On the sly, every kind of hypothesis, on what all this meant, was being advanced. Some suggested that we might be sent to the Arabs, where the situation was daily worsening with lightning speed.

'It would be great, brothers, to go abroad at least once in our lifetime. To Poland or even to the Egypt place.'

'A hen is not a bird and Poland is not abroad! But to visit the GDR or Egypt, that, of course, would be interesting. Only now, with this new T-64, we will not be going abroad for five years at the very least.'

'Perhaps we really are going to help the Arabs?'

'They don't need any help! Did you read how many tanks they have? Well! . . . And which type . . . know what I mean? . . . Of course, they're not T-62s, but neither are they Shermans like those used by the Jews.'

'And they also have thousands of our advisers and all the war plans are worked out by our own General Staff.'

'Oh! They'll knock hell out of the Jews. I even feel sorry for them.'

'Better pity their poor balls! Pity, my foot!'

'How long will the war last?'

'Three to four days – no more than that. It shouldn't take long to overrun the whole of Israel with tanks. The Jews are surrounded on all sides and, if the war does drag on for a week, they'll have to surrender. As they'll be surrounded on all sides and blockaded by sea, they'll soon run out of food!'

'But I heard, lads, that the Arabs are bloody awful soldiers!'

'Do you think the Jews are any better? They'll scatter at the first shots.'

'And that's a fact!'

'In America, they're already singing requiems for the Jews.'

'Don't be in too much of a hurry to celebrate victory. Unless the UN troops are recalled from their positions and stop separating Jews from Arabs, there won't be any victory at all.'

'Never mind, our people will cook up something in that case.'

'I hope the UN troops will be removed as soon as possible, and then the comedy can really start!'

'And the golden rain of orders and medals will pour down on the heads of our advisers! There won't really be a war. We will just overrun this Israel place with our tanks and there you are, we'll be heroes overnight.'

'What is there to overrun anyway, the whole of Israel is smaller than one of our larger firing grounds!'

At this, everybody burst out laughing, although it was really no joke. In the Soviet Union, there are indeed many army firing ranges which exceed in size not only Israel but also some of her warlike neighbours into the bargain.

'And now go to sleep, lads!'

'Oh, we graduated too late. At least half those who graduated from our school last year were sent to the Arabs as advisers. Even at this minute, they're probably making holes in their tunics for the medals they're bound to receive. That's the only real preparation needed for a war like this!'

Next night, in the pouring rain, we disembarked at a small country station somewhere in the Chernigov Province. A column of lorries covered in with tarpaulins was waiting for us. After another three hours, in the haze which precedes dawn and in the midst of the warm mist, we disembarked once again close to our tents, in the forest.

What we saw before us at daybreak both surprised and puzzled us. The sight recreated visions of Batyy's* hordes at the time of his last stand before the gates of Kiev. As far as the eye could see, along the length of the forest clearings, stood the serried ranks of green tents. Here and there, small glades could be seen, and beyond them there

---

*A famous Tartar Khan.

were endless rows of marquees hidden under camouflage netting. Canvas, canvas, canvas stretching to the horizon and beyond in all directions. There were tens and maybe even hundreds of thousands of people: artillerymen, rocket men, anti-aircraft gunners, combat engineers, infantry men and commandos. Where the hell were we? What was this army all around us and what was its purpose?

Just behind us were the regular canvas rows belonging to some motorised infantry regiment – probably a show regiment, or so-called 'court regiment', where all the soldiers speak only Russian. All infantrymen invariably possess insolent faces as well as insolent tongues.

'Did you hear, brothers, about the new decree, that new coins are to be minted to celebrate the Anniversary of Soviet Power?'

'Yes, we heard!'

'We must lay in a stock of these coins – after the new revolution, these coins will be very valuable.'

Whereupon, unanimous laughter exploded from the infantry's smoking quarters.

In our life, we hear anti-Soviet remarks every day and at every turn. But, never before had we ever heard conversation of this type carried on so blatantly and in front of such a large assembly of strangers. During breakfast, we decided to send a small delegation to the infantry to explain to them, cautiously, that we were not simple soldiers but were in fact officers, only without our insignia of rank. In this way, we could suppress, at the very start, all attempts at familiarity.

I was on that delegation. The infantry greeted us with enthusiastic cries of welcome.

'The armour is strong and our tanks are fast, and our men – ah, our men, there is no need to speak of them!'*

'The infantry salute the tank men!'

'Give the tank men something to drink!' ordered a tall, slender soldier. Whereupon about thirty soldiers' flasks stretched out from all sides in our direction. But we were in a serious mood and turned down their invitation. Have you ever seen any officer drinking with soldiers and lance-corporals?

'Comrades,' Lieutenant Okhrimenko, the head of our delegation began severely, 'although we have no badges of rank, we are none the less officers!'

This remark was greeted by a friendly roar of laughter.

'And who do you think we are?'

'We also are officers!'

'Only wearing soldiers' shoulder-straps!'

*A quotation from a soldiers' song.

'May we introduce ourselves, the Kiev Higher All-Arms Commanders School. Two hundred freshly baked lieutenants!'

'On your right are graduates of the Poltava Higher Anti-Aircraft Artillery School – one hundred and eighty lieutenants in all.'

'And further down there is the Ryazan Higher Airborne Troops School.'

'So let's have a drink! After all!'

So we did.

'But, little falcons, what are you doing here?' we asked.

'It's known officially as re-training for new battle techniques but unofficially as a "big show" in honour of the glorious jubilee of our beloved Soviet Power.'

We drank some more. It doesn't go down too well in the morning but, nevertheless, we knocked it back.

So that was it! A grandiose spectacle was being organised in honour of the fiftieth anniversary, and we were taking part in it. We were to provide the crowd scenes for the film.

'It's going to be ballet like no one's seen before. And there'll be more troops than ever before.'

'Every kind of secret technology'll be on display.'

'The front-line troops will be two divisions made up entirely of young officers and instructors. The back-up divisions will be manned by officer-cadets in their last year, all men within five minutes of becoming officers.'

'There'll be specially selected soldiers, just to raise a cloud of dust on the horizon and create the illusion of vast numbers.'

'And we were told that it was a re-training exercise!'

'So were we! And we've been given a wonder-machine, the Infantry Battle Machine, the BMP-1, you may have heard about it?'

Our spirits fell abruptly, in spite of the amount of vodka we had drunk. For we knew only too well what a show turn-out is like, and what the training involves, especially for one designed to fête such a great jubilee.

That same night, the first sub-units of the 120th Guards Rogachev Motorised Infantry Division, the 'court' division of the Commander of the Byelorussian Military District, started to arrive in camp. Every district has something similar: in the Moscow district it is the 2nd Guards Taman' Motorised Infantry Division and the Kantemirov Tank Division, in the Carpathian District the 24th Iron Samaro-Ul'yanovsk Motorised Infantry Division, in Kiev the 41st Guards Tank Division. All these divisions exist solely for show. They only know parades, demonstrations, solemn visits by foreign guests, guards of honour, and they have no battle training whatsoever. All these 'court' divisions – and there are nine of them in the Soviet Army – are absolutely incapable of fighting. But they are kept always at full strength, with 12,000 men in each, which represents 108,000 of the very best soldiers and officers in all the Soviet land forces. And on this occasion, for this unparalleled peep-show, it was found necessary to reinforce even the 'court' divisions with newly-fledged officers as well.

Next day, the reforming of troops intended for the main action was carried out. Somewhere, near at hand, was located the field headquarters of the 38th Army. For Operation 'Dnieper', the composition of this army was strengthened by the addition of the 41st Guards Tank, the 79th, 120th, 128th Guards Motorised Infantry and the 24th Iron Motorised Division, the N-rocket brigade, the N-Guards artillery brigade, the N-anti-aircraft rocket brigade, the N-tank destroyer artillery regiment and the many other support sub-units including an army mobile rocket-technical base, an army mobile anti-aircraft rocket base, two liaison regiments, a pontoon-bridge regiment, as well as some sapper and CW battalions. In addition, several motorised infantry battalions representing penal battalions were included. The use of these battalions either in war or during training requires neither knowledge nor practice: the Army Commander merely hurls them into the very thick of battle, where artillery is useless, or into those areas which have not been reconnoitred. As a general rule, such battalions are deployed for one battle only. For the next battle there are other battalions, composed of other shtrafniki.* On this particular occasion, separate motorised infantry battalions were recruited not from shtrafniki but from young officers, wearing soldiers' uniform.

Alongside our 38th Army, a further three armies were being raised. Taken together, the four armies represented the 1st Ukrainian front, itself a part of the 'Eastern' forces.

On the right bank, the 'Western' forces were forming up. Troops and battle armaments continued to pour in. Every day, every night, every hour. During preparations for Operation 'Dnieper', the Soviet Army, to all intents, completely lost its combat preparedness. Judge for yourself. To build up only one show division, over 10,000 officers were required – because officers were cast in the role of ordinary soldiers. And where can such a multitude be gathered? Even every graduate from every military school and academy would not have been sufficient. And, for this reason, it was decided in addition to call upon the majority of the officers of the Baltic, Byelorussian, Kiev and Carpathian

---

*Members of penal battalions, virtually condemned to certain death by the impossible nature of the task allotted to them.

military districts. I repeat: each of these districts forms an army group. Now, just imagine four of the largest groups of armies, utterly devoid of officers. What does one do with all those soldiers? But don't panic. Four army groups represent twelve to fifteen armies. That's not really so many, after all. Five Soviet armies in Germany, that's certainly a vast number of troops, but fifteen armies spread over the entire territory of the Soviet Union is not a lot, because these armies are all 'Kadriro-vannye'* or, as we prefer to call them amongst ourselves, 'Kastriro-vannye':† many officers, lots of armament, but basically held in reserve as they have so few soldiers. As the saying goes, when the war starts, we will soon round up the peasants and throw them straight into battle. It doesn't matter that they've never even seen such weapons.They'll soon learn! Provided they're not all killed off first!

One army at full strength means 60,000 to 65,000 men. So fifteen armies mean 900,000 to 975,000 men. And, even if these armies have only ten per cent of their complement of personnel during peacetime, that represents nearly 100,000 men. What do you do with them ? Tell them to get busy digging up potatoes? The inherent danger of such a state of affairs is that the frontier districts possess the biggest adjunct of battle technology, more powerful and more up-to-date than what is available to Soviet occupation forces. In peacetime, frontier districts are very considerably under strength and are not, in essence, on a war footing. But, after mobilisation, according to Soviet practice, troops of these same districts must be superior to troops of the first echelon in both strength and in the quality of their armament.

On the eve of the great jubilee, mobilisation in these, and indeed some other, districts proved impossible owing to the absence of a basic nucleus around which the mobilisation process could be carried out. In the event of a sudden attack by the enemy, the Soviet Army would lose a colossal amount of its first-class armament and would be unable to call upon its basic striking force. Such short-sighted treatment of second-echelon troops bears witness once more to the fact that no one on the General Staff believes in the possibility of a sudden attack from NATO forces.

1967, the year of the great fiftieth anniversary, was also the year of a record harvest. Few people ever bother to ask themselves why these good harvests happen at all. But the key is quite simple. We have record harvests every year, only there is nobody to gather them in. But, if there is a chance of throwing into the business of collecting the harvest the army, students, schoolboys and girls, intellectuals,

*When only officers and technical cadres are at full strength.
†'Castrated' rather than 'skeleton'.

etc., there you are, the harvest is a record. The army plays a major role at harvest time, not because soldiers want to work more than students, but because the army brings its own machines. So, in the year of the endless peep-show, it was possible to deploy not hundreds of thousands, but millions, of soldiers in gathering the harvest. They were used also in building work and in industry in general, and, of course, to ensure our own little piece of theatre – that is to say, our famous training exercise.

Have you ever seen tanks moving under water? It is a phenomenon easily described. Through a pipe installed on the tank turret, the air passes into the battle section, and then on into the engine. Exhaust gases are expelled by the engine straight into the water. Before going into the water, the driver fixes a setting by means of a special device known as a hydro-compass on some marker on the opposite bank. Under water, the needle of this device points permanently towards the marker. In addition, a command post is mounted on the bank, which watches the movement of every pipe above water level and, in case of emergency, can give directions: '212th, keep left, still more left, fuck you . . .!' If the engine stops, divers will hook cables on to the tank and the tractors which are waiting on the bank will haul the tank out of the water. That is all there is to it, the entire science! The trouble is that a tank, regardless even of its great weight, is nevertheless a reservoir for air. And its grip on the bottom, under water, is considerably less than on dry land, and a river bed is not an evenly rolled and flat surface. That is why driving under water requires great practice. If the steering lever is pressed only a fraction too much, the tank can turn through ninety degrees, exactly as would happen on a concrete road. Indeed, this can happen to a tank even on a concrete surface. Remember, in Czechoslovakia, how many of them were lying about in the gutters. It is quite pointless trying to explain to any soldier that, under water, it is better not to touch a single lever, if the tank is not moving straight, just to spit on it, and if you must touch any levers, then turn them as little as possible. Later on, I came across one fairly sensible soldier, who could even understand Russian quite tolerably, and he drove a tank around underwater for an hour and ten minutes, while crossing a little river about thirty metres wide. At the beginning, he turned the tank to face down-stream and, when he was ordered to turn it just a little to the right, he moved it through 180 degrees to face up-river.

Having done this over and over again for some eighteen turns, eventually he emerged from the river on the same bank from which he had started his epic journey. During the 'Dnieper' exercises such epics were of course taboo and, for this reason, all sensible soldier-drivers were replaced by instructors and officers.

But the Dnieper is a great Ukrainian river, it is not the Vorskla or the Klyaz'ma, and the Dnieper had to be crossed not by mere tank battalions but by four whole armies, one of which was a tank army. (At that time, every all-arms army possessed 1,285 tanks, and a tank army 1,332 tanks, without counting any of the floating reconnaissance tanks.) The entire armada of 5,187 tanks had to cross to the other bank of the Dnieper in a strictly limited time. And the whole performance before the very eyes of the Politburo itself, to say nothing of the distinguished foreign guests!

Tanks belonging to the other advancing fronts simply crossed by bridges. Such things are permissible while there are no foreign observers actually to see what is going on. But in full view of the government observers the tanks had not only to travel under water, but they had also to tow artillery pieces in their wake. And if something were to go wrong? What if one of the tanks suddenly started dancing about under water? In that case, the simple use of instructors and officers would not be enough, even more essential precautions would be necessary. And in the end a solution was found. While the officers were undergoing training, thousands of soldiers were literally paving the bed of the Dnieper. Thousands of tons of steel armature and steel mesh were laid on the river bed at the crossing points. At the same time, concrete panels were placed along the sides of the steel mesh to form barriers, like crash barriers on a motorway. The steel mesh on the river bottom provided the tanks with a more reliable grip, and the concrete barriers prevented them from straying from the path. The tanks trundled across as if they were in a furrow. And no less than a hundred such furrows were constructed. Only God knows how much steel, concrete and human labour was wasted in the process. The structure took many months to complete and the work was first class. The furrows were completely invisible from above. First of all, the tank simply went down under water, only then manoeuvred itself into the prepared corridor, and at the other bank emerged on the surface as if nothing had happened. Such tricks are, of course, absolutely impossible in wartime as the enemy would hardly allow you to spend four months splashing about in a river paving its bed. It would also be somewhat difficult to supply so many thousands of tons of building materials while under fire! But, in Operation 'Dnieper' it must be said, all the thousands of tanks crossed the river without incident, to the great astonishment of any uniformed observer.

But this is to anticipate. While I was engaged on the construction of these 'Potemkin' crossing points, I met my friend Yura Solov'yev, who had graduated from school one year before me.

'Yurka, damn your bloody eyes, it is really you?'

'Viktor! How are you you old bastard?'

'How are you? Where the hell have you been?'

'I'm all right. And it's the devil who's brought me to Byelorussia!'

'What dizzy height did you manage to reach?'

'Battalion commander! Do you remember Sashka Starkov?'

'Of course!'

'He's with me, as chief of staff. Private Abdukhmaev!'

'Yes, comrade Lieutenant!'

'Ask the battalion's chief of staff to come here!'

'Of course!'

'And you, Viktor, what's your rank?'

'Tank-crew gunner!' I reported, loud and clear.

We both burst out laughing. It was pure Chekhov, only one of us was not fat and the other thin, we were both young and slender.

Then Sashka Starkov came running towards us, and we embraced warmly.

'Well, Commander, shall we invite the gunner to have a drink?'

'Of course!'

We drank. And we drank. We were together again.

'Where are the rest of our lads? What news of everybody?'

'They're all with the Arabs. Our lads are getting the holes in their tunics ready for their new medals. Things'll start moving there any day now. And the others like you and me are getting ready for the glorious Operation "Dnieper"! They've rounded up all the officers from our regiment, every company, platoon and battalion – some of them as gunners and the others as loaders. There are only two officers left in the whole battalion. I'm the commander and Sashka is chief of the battalion staff! That's a fact. And it's the same thing in the regiment. A captain commands the regiment, and he has a couple of old men as his deputies. Ten officers in the whole regiment! All the rest are taking part here in your comedy!'

I sympathised with my friends. We were all lieutenants and we all got the same salary. But I had no responsibility at all, while they, being one year senior to me were battalion commanders and to make matters worse, commanders with no subordinate officers.

'How do you manage, brother, to keep that mob under control? Even when all the officers are at their posts there can't be any bloody discipline at all!'

They looked at each other.

'But we don't even try to keep up discipline. The triumvirate does it for us.'

'Really?'

Yes, indeed! In all divisions of the four districts, where the officers had been seconded for the peep-show, field tribunals consisting of a commander, his political deputy and the divisional prosecutor had been created. And indeed the soldiers worked away diligently and conscientiously while their commanders were knocking back vodka in the bushes.

'You, Viktor, just pay us a call anytime. We've always got something put by for you!'

'And don't get too full of your own importance either, you may also be given command of a company after the peep-show, or even of a battalion. And then you'll know what it's like at the sharp end of being the commander! And we have nothing but this bloody peep-show the whole time!'

Nobody had a radio. Rumours were rampant, but in the main they spoke of victory.

'Our lot certainly showed them how! Thousands of Jewish tanks destroyed in a single day!'

Tales of thousands of Israeli tanks were heard at all levels – even the commander of a division gaily repeated them. It made me prick up my ears. I had been attentively reading the limited circulation magazine called *Military Matters Abroad* which was intended for officers' eyes only, and I knew perfectly well that Israel did not possess many thousands of tanks. Egypt – yes, but Israel – no! How then could our people possibly destroy a thousand, if a thousand never existed in the first place. Of course, we had destroyed all the Jewish tanks, but not thousands of them.

In the evening, a small spluttering radio receiver was unearthed at the infantry officers' quarters and we all rushed there to listen to it. As usual in infantry quarters, there was great animation. After a day spent in strenuous training, under the burning sun, they had recovered already and were slightly tipsy. A spirited song was issuing from their smoking area:

> 'This is a hammer and this is a sickle
> This is our Soviet emblem
> Reap if you like or forge if you will
> Whatever you do, you'll get fucked!'

Never before had I or any of my comrades come across such a centre of anti-Soviet feeling as in the Kiev Higher All-arms Commanders School which is named after Frunze. One does, however, encounter anti-Soviet feeling in the Soviet army at every step. Political anecdotes, songs and stories spread quickly and don't die down for a long time.

But I had never seen it so open before. Either they were not afraid of political informers, or the informers were also inclined towards free-thinking. I just do not know. The fact is that graduates from this particular school hold the record in the Soviet army for the largest number of flights to the West. Regardless of the difference between our shoulder-straps, we maintained the closest contact with them. I personally retain the pleasantest memories of them, and I am sure that if they had been in Novocherkassk at the time of those bloody events* they would not have lifted a finger against their own people. Unfortunately I cannot say the same about my own comrades, the tank men.

'Quiet, you bastards, it's working.'

After some preliminary hissing the radio started: 'Comrade Brezhnev met today in the Kremlin .. News from the fields . . .'

'You mark my words . . . there's been a cock-up there. Our advisers gave too much bloody advice!'

'Shut up, you bloody prophets.'

But the radio was in no hurry to report our victory in the Near East and the capture of Tel Aviv.

'. . . Towards the glorious jubilee . . . '

'I tell you, brothers, that it's all a lot of bullshit.'

'. . . The oilmen of the Tartar ASSR, after long hours . . .'

'Is it really true . . .?'

'. . . News from abroad . . .'

'SILENCE!'

'. . . Today Comrade Fidel Castro . . .'

Nobody could stand it any longer and a flow of the most obscene abuse was hurled in the direction of that bearded hero.

'. . . Events in the Near East . . . Fierce battles . . . Heroic resistance by Arab troops . . . Gaza . . . El Arish . . . Solidarity . . . '

The information was short and absolutely incomprehensible. Neither figures nor facts were given. The main problem was who knew where El Arish was situated, on whose territory, and how far from the frontier.

'Who's got a map?'

'Shall we take an armoured personnel carrier into the village? There's a globe in the school.'

'Go on then! Let's get it!'

'Arish is a Jewish name and El is Arab.'

'I'm telling you that if they said the word "solidarity", that's the end! The bloody end!'

---

*The 'bloody events' mentioned here refer to the ruthless suppression by tanks and machine-guns of the local population in 1962.

'What bloody end? Do you really believe that they can possibly destroy all our tanks?'

'Of course not! But the fact that our people didn't capture the capital which is close to the frontier on the very first day means that it won't be captured tomorrow either.'

'Belt up! I'll bet ten bottles of vodka that our people will capture Tel Aviv tomorrow! Don't you know how many tanks the Arabs have? How much artillery? And aircraft? And the quality of the armament? Don't you know that every Soviet internal district is totally without tanks and artillery because it was all sent to the Arabs? There's not a single officer in the frontier areas at present because they're all at the peep-show. And the internal areas haven't got officers or armament, because it's all with the Arabs as well! Can you imagine how many thousands of our officers and generals are there? There's no space left to spit without hitting an adviser!'

'You can piss off with all this talk about advisers. They're exactly like you and me, or like our battalion and division commanders. They're useless, they can't even conduct a training exercise properly. It's all show! God help us from getting entangled with China, then the shit would really hit the fan thanks to our peep-show.'

Eventually, the globe arrived and very small indeed it was. Neither El Arish nor Gaza was shown on it, and even Israel itself could only be located with great difficulty. Only the UAR and Syria were visible, threateningly covering a good slice of territory.

Our doubts and fears appeared so unfounded and unimportant that we all burst out laughing and promptly forgot the latest news and the war in the Near East. Clearly the superiority of the Arabs was undeniable, even on the globe.

Next day, however, once again there was no news about the annihilation of Israel and the capture of Tel Aviv. As usual it was confused and totally incomprehensible: 'Stubborn battles . . . heroic resistance . . .' and the names of some inhabited areas without any indication of where they were situated. In addition, there was a warning note about the Israeli air force bombing peaceful towns and villages as well as schools and hospitals. It made us all start thinking again. When peaceful people are being shot in Budapest or Novocherkassk, the radio never calls for 'solidarity', and suddenly here they were starting to mention peaceful Arabs. What did that signify?

'I told you that Tel Aviv wouldn't be captured by our advisers, even on the second day. I'm prepared to bet it won't happen. Nor tomorrow either. If our people were on the outskirts, that would have been announced immediately. But, for now, it's a very far cry indeed from Tel Aviv. Of course, in a week or so it'll be captured anyway, but our

Chief of the General Staff ought to be put on trial for such bad planning.'

'He's a fornicating old fool, Comrade Zakharov.' And it was certainly very difficult not to share such an opinion.

'Maybe our people have thought up some trick? Maybe they'll try to decoy the Jews on to our territory and then cut them down with lasers!'

'Why the hell bother to cut them down with lasers if we already possess thousands of tanks, and what tanks!'

'T-54s and T-55s. Not those prehistoric Jewish Shermans.'

'We've got overall superiority in both quality and quantity, so why not destroy them with tanks and be done with it?'

'I tell you, lasers would be better!'

'Why are you so keen on lasers? There's no such thing!'

Just take a look around you! All kinds of fireworks have been gathered together here in our camp for the big show – T-64s and BMPs and BRDM-2s and Shilkas and Luna-Ms – but there aren't any lasers to be seen. And if our General Staff can't deal with two divisions of antediluvian Shermans, what on earth will we do with the Bundeswehr? And with the British Chieftains? Shall we put all our trust in lasers? Then why the hell are we as happy as billy-goats about the T-64? And what the bloody hell are we all doing here anyway?

'I must tell you one thing, brothers, it's a pissy tank!'

'I quite agree.'

Our first introduction to the T-64 tank had taken place before we graduated from our military school, when the first machine, all wrapped in tarpaulin, was brought in at night and hidden away in a hangar. It was a very fleeting acquaintance but, from the very first look, we all liked the 125 mm gun. It was the most powerful gun in the world and no tank had ever had anything like it before. Because of its amazing initial velocity, its shells could tear away the turrets of tank-targets and hurl them a distance of about ten metres (tank turrets weigh eight or even twelve tons).

But now, upon closer acquaintance, our delight with the T-64s had begun gradually to fade. The gun was certainly all-powerful but, in their endeavour to increase the initial velocity of the shell, the designer had made it not rifled, but smooth-bored, as in the T-62, and this immediately adversely affected its accuracy. In fact, it was an all-powerful gun, which always missed the target.

The tank's tracks were also based on entirely new principles. Before, tracks had to be changed after every 2,000 kilometres and now they could stand 10,000. The only trouble was that they constantly fell off. Imagine a boxer whose trunks fall down when the moment comes for a decisive punch. And, finally, the engine itself was not only bad, it was

75

disgusting. Several teams of workers and engineers, and a gang of designers, were sent along simply to maintain our one tank regiment. But they could not hope to solve problems arising from the engine's design, try as they might.

The latest news bulletin next day put an end to all doubts. In a cheerful voice, the announcer informed us of a decisive defeat suffered by the Israeli aggressors in the area of El Kantara and the Mitla Heights.

At last everything became clear. If the Jews were being called the aggressors that meant that they had already taken a solid slice of territory from the Arabs. There could be no other interpretation. The announcer had somehow completely forgotten that, between the Israeli and Arab armies, stood the UN troops, and that Israel alone could not have jumped over them or demanded that they be removed. So how, then, had she become the aggressor?

Mention of Mitla Heights and El Kantara raised the curtain on everything that had been passed over in silence on the radio. From our course in the history of the art of war, we all knew the whereabouts of Mitla and El Kantara. It was clear to us, but not to our divisional commander. Major-General Moskalev had studied the history of the art of war a long time ago and he didn't know where the places were; he believed that our people were destroying the Jews wholesale and that, if not by tomorrow, then at least by the day after tomorrow, the final victorious communiqué would be issued.

In such situations neither officers nor generals unless they are directly involved in events receive any additional information. I do not even bother to mention common soldiers, sergeants and mere civilians. Everybody else listens to the radio and reads *Pravda* and has to make do with that. During my long service in the Soviet army I never had any connection with the war in Vietnam and, therefore, all my knowledge of events there was based on *Pravda* leaders and rumours. Officers who were not involved in events in Czechoslovakia did not have the slightest idea about the scandalous breaches of the law and the crude mistakes committed during the preparations for and execution of that disgraceful operation. I was in Czechoslovakia but my knowledge of events there and my battle experience spring only from what I myself saw. There is never any examination, let alone revelation, of mistakes, after such measures have been carried out. It is not surprising, therefore, that the same mistakes in strategy, tactics, organisation and management and guidance of troops are being repeated over and over again year after year. It is hardly astonishing either that the majority of officers have very confused notions about what we are likely to face in any future war and what we must really prepare ourselves for. It is still less astonishing that the majority of Soviet tank corps, who, of course, have never been in Sinai, are convinced that a Soviet tank is invincible, just as the majority of Soviet pilots, except those who served in Vietnam, are convinced that it was the Americans, and not ourselves, who suffered colossal casualties in the air battles there (as publicised in *Pravda*'s daily reports).

Although the news over the following days was cheerful and almost victorious in tone, it no longer held out the hope of a speedy destruction of Israel. 'The peoples of the World demand an end to aggression . . . Workmen of the Likhachev works call it a disgrace . . . Conference of the Security Council . . . Speech by the Soviet representative . . . Peoples of the World must strengthen their solidarity . . . Liberate occupied territories . . .' And so on and so forth.

Then a sealed letter from the Central Committee of the Party was sent to all communists, and read out at closed Party meetings. Its fundamental leitmotiv was: 'The Arabs are poor fighters: they were busy saying their prayers when they should have been repelling attacks.'

But there was no secret letter for officers. There was a war on, mistakes were made, but, as is well known, one learns from one's own mistakes. But what exactly was the cause of defeat, and which exactly were the mistakes made, all this remained an impenetrable secret to us. The explanation to the effect that Arabs are poor soldiers was highly popular with generals, officers, soldiers and civilians. All interest in the campaign immediately subsided. Incidentally, the overwhelming majority of Soviet military advisers, from generals down to lieutenants, also shared the same point of view: 'Poor fighters' – full stop! And somehow the thought never entered anyone's head that we had known beforehand that they were poor fighters. And that, if we did know, why the devil did we demand the removal of the UN troops, who were protecting these poor fighters? If we knew to begin with that they were not fighters, then why did we spend billions of roubles, and lose thousands of tanks and aircraft, for nothing? If we knew beforehand that Arabs are inclined to pray at certain hours of the day when they should be fighting, then why were measures not taken? There should have been much foaming at the mouth in the Central Committee, to prove that there must not be a war and that the problem must be solved peacefully and that the UN troops must not be removed. But maybe the Soviet General Staff did not know what the Arab army was really like. In that case, such a General Staff and its Chief Intelligence Administration are not worth a kopek of anyone's money. How many years had thousands of colonels been kept in Egypt and Syria and still it had not dawned on us that the Arabs were not ready for war, in spite of the billions spent on first-class equipment and on Soviet advisers? We were too busy counting the numbers of tanks and aircraft. On paper it all looked infallible.

After another whole week a top secret order came addressed to officers: 'About the lessons learned in military action in the Near East.' To this day I remember that order with mixed feelings of shame and indignation. The order of the Minister of Defence repeated, almost word for word, the text of the closed letter of the Party Central Committee. 'Disgrace to the aggressors . . . Arabs prayed, but did not fight . . .' And that was all, not another word. No reference to the casualties on both sides, to innovations in Israeli tactics and armament, not one word about our mistakes. So why this order was top secret in the first place no one knows to this very day. It could safely have been printed in *Red Star* instead of the editorial. In fact foreign broadcasts went into far greater detail. In the evening, we tank crew members, with a good few drinks under our belts, were discussing this order with the other young infantry officers.

'One should not blame the mirror if one has an ugly mug.'

'Were the Arabs not taught in our military academies?'

'In the Arab armies absolutely everything was the same as in ours: organisation, armament, tactics and even peep-shows were identical.'

'Some day it will all cost us very dear!'

'If only we had given them the T-64 and the BMP-1!'

'You're a fool, but don't be offended just because I tell you that they had overwhelming superiority in both quantity and quality!'

'Now all the advisers will probably be turfed out of the army, their shoulder-straps will be torn off, and some of them will even be put on trial . . .'

'Don't be offended, Viktor, but you're an idiot. Didn't you read the letter? The Arabs are not good fighters, didn't you understand that? Consequently, our advisers *are* good fighters! Before the week is over they'll all be getting medals and promotion. If our advisers were to be put on trial, so would the Chief of our General Staff. And the Minister of Defence must be kicked out too, as well as the Minister for Foreign Affairs, because of their policies, and perhaps somebody even higher up because of waste, stupidity and short-sightedness, and for his inability to direct the army, the country and its foreign policy.'

And, indeed, before that week was over, secret decrees from the Praesidium were signed awarding decorations to the Soviet military advisers. The decrees themselves were kept secret so as not to reveal the number of advisers or the number of posts occupied by them. But, in reality, secrecy was also maintained just to protect the new heroes from being jeered at by the West. There were thousands of names on the rolls, colonel-generals, major-generals, lieutenant-generals, majors, colonels, lieutenant-colonels. It was a wearying business listening to thousands of names in the heat of a June day.

On that same day, another order was read out in our regiment concerning the replacement of the T-64 by the T-55; by our dear old 'Fifty-fives', which we knew by heart, which we loved and which we dreamt about; the 'Fifty-fives', whose tracks never fell off and which possessed, if not that extraordinary fire-power, at least reliability and precision: those same 'Fifty-fives' which constitute the very foundation of tank troops in the Soviet Army and in the armies of its allied powers.

It is difficult to say why this decision was taken. Was it in order to hide the T-64 from the defeated Arabs, who might have complained that they had not been provided with them, or was it from fear that, during some training exercises, the engines and tracks might cause trouble. Probably both these factors played their part. In any case, the T-64s were taken away from us. They reappeared only after training, at a closed parade with no foreign guests present. They managed to cross the flat concrete without incident . . .

Meanwhile, the intensity of training increased. Each day, without rest days or leave periods, an unprecedented performance was being prepared, covering a huge territory. I do not know how many billion roubles it cost, but judge for yourself when the potential capacity of the T-55 is only 500 driving hours. After 500 hours, it must go in for a complete overhaul, and literally every part has to be changed, leaving only the hulk in which a new engine and new transmission must be installed, its whole running gear completely changed, all other apparatus, and so on . . . Then, the tank has another 250 hours of life, after which it is written off for good. A tank is not a tractor, it is too heavy and wears out very quickly. This is why the overwhelming majority of tanks spend all their life in moth-balls, waiting for war, and only the oldest of them, which have spent ten to fifteen years being preserved, are used for training. This is also why tanks are always transported in echelons or on trailers. Every hour in motion costs too much. Tanks are very rarely taken out of moth-balls and used for training. In the Soviet army there is a standard for battle tanks – 200 kilometres per year – and the General Staff, suspicious even of district commanders, watches the observance of this standard very closely. 200 kilometres per year means that if, in one year, a tank has done 400 kilometres, the whole of the previous year must have been spent in moth-balls. (If a divisional commander has used up the allocation in advance, he can be brought before the military tribunal.) And, all this does not even take into ccount the cost of technical maintenance as well as ammunition and fuel.

Now try to visualise the following picture: thousands of tanks, day

79

and night, taking part in training exercises without any notice being paid to motor resources, just as if it was a state of war. In wartime, this would have been entirely justified – that is why tanks are created, but what is the valid reason for throwing away billions of roubles in peacetime? During training, over a period of four months, our 38th Army completely ruined every one of its 1,285 tanks, and the same happened in all the other armies. One general replacement occurred before the main exercises started: all tanks, tracked armoured personnel carriers and gun-tractors were removed, and nearly new ones were distributed instead, so as to avoid breakdowns.

Twelve hours a day were dedicated to training: every movement at each stage of the coming exercises was worked out in the most minute detail. Only now did we understand how Suvorov's* principle, that 'each soldier must know his manoeuvre', is still applied in the Soviet army.

Preparations for the exercises were going on in one huge field set out with marker pegs. Every soldier (or disguised officer) studied his own task: jump down from the tracked armoured personnel carrier at this bush, move nine steps forward, give one burst of automatic gun-fire, thirteen steps forward and there's my target, another burst of fire, and there's the target of my right-hand neighbour, if he didn't hit it, I'll help him to do so, here the tank will fire armour-piercing shells – and again, and again.

These exercises seemed to have taken more than a whole year to work out, and when we arrived for our training everyone had been given a file with his role plainly indicated, not only every step but even every breath: seven steps forward, there will be a flash; hold breath: close eyes, put on gas mask, breath out; short burst of automatic gun-fire. It was the same for the infantry, for us, for the artillery corps, landing forces and everyone else: tank emerges from water, puncture the water-proofing on the gun barrel with an armour-piercing shot, throw off the pipe, remove the stopper from gun and turret, lower gun, now four hostile tanks will appear from behind that birch tree; concentrated fire by the whole company; my target is the far left tank, after having knocked it out, I shift my fire to the next target to the right and, if that one is also knocked out, I shift my fire still more to the right . . .

A week after our arrival in the camp everyone was obliged to pass an oral examination on each individual role: all the hours, minutes and

*A famous commander in the Tsarist army who, throughout his long career, never suffered a single defeat. The present writer is no relation.

seconds, when, where and what kind of target will emerge, distance towards it, its speed and angle of motion. Every one of the tens of thousands of people involved knew precisely in advance each action of the enemy, the composition of his forces and resources, and all his likely moves.

After this theoretical examination, practical training started. To begin with, each man, alone, went over the whole field, tidying up the smallest detail in his mind. At this juncture, anyone in the tank corps was on foot. After that, sections and crews started to be formed. There were four of us: the driver-instructor and three officers (the commander, gunner and loader). Once more we strode out across the field, a distance of ten to twelve kilometres.

Commander: 'Here I'll give the order Landmark – 2. 100 to the left, tank, destroy.'

Gunner: 'I'll shout armour piercing.'

Loader: 'I'll throw a shell on the rammer.'

Driver: 'I'll shout "make way", and brake slightly.'

On the left, on the right and behind us, thousands of people were walking in groups, each following its own route. Everyone was muttering the details of his own task and quietly exchanging words with his mates. For the time being, he was still permitted to do so. Behind us were the infantry, in front were reconnaissance, and sometimes aircraft 'flew past' – but even pilots were training on foot.

The following day, everything started all over again, but this time with the formation of platoons, and now only tank crews could exchange remarks inside the individual 'tanks', though one 'tank' was allowed to communicate with another. The day after, everything was repeated once again; with companies being formed. After that came the general inspection, for everybody. And, only after that, did training in battle technique actually start. One day was taken up with company exercises – every company separately and without firing. The next day, battalion exercises, the next regimental, then divisional, army, and finally the whole front. Every field was carefully covered with metal netting and armature, to prevent tanks from ploughing it all up with their tracks. Only before the final exercises was this grating removed, and within two weeks the grass had grown up.

Once every task in one region had been mastered, a new region replaced it. Thus, from the Chernigov region in the Ukraine we gradually moved over to Byelorussia, to Bobruysk, after which we returned to where we had started and repeated everything all over again, and so on ad nauseam. By this time, not only had our front rehearsed its tasks, but all the others had done the same. Then the exercises were conducted as prescribed, at full speed, with the participation of several fronts. It was still not yet Operation 'Dnieper' itself, but just the preparations for it – 'the dress rehearsal'. And only then were we returned once more to our camps, where the replacement of battle equipment took place. Meanwhile, tens of thousands of soldiers were following in our footsteps, eradicating every sign of our training and gathering up metal, filling in shell holes, removing shell cases and searching for blind shells.

. . . And then, only then . . .

A column of a motor-rifle battalion was moving forward towards the water boundary. Meanwhile the artillery and the air force were 'preparing the way' for the advance of this first of many battalions. Its task was simple: a forced crossing of the Dnieper to take possession of a bridge-head on the right side of the river and so secure a crossing place for our tank regiment with its artillery: after which the crossing of three armies would at once start, with a simultaneous tactical helicopter assault on the enemy's rear. That would be followed by the building of railway bridges and the crossing of the army's second echelon, and the landing of two airborne divisions in the enemy's deep rear. Then would come the crossing of two other fronts and engaging of the 'Westerners'. But, for the present, just one motor-rifle battalion was advancing . . .

This was an unprecedented honour for the battalion, although it had already been completely written off and would take no further active part. Two artillery brigades plus eight artillery regiments cleared the battalion's way, which meant 612 guns to support one battalion. In addition to this, a tank regiment was put forward just at the riverside cut and destroyed targets on the other bank – 600 guns and 100 tanks to support 300 men! Such a thing could only happen in honour of a great jubilee! Armoured personnel carriers plunged into the water, lifting up columns of fine spray, and swarmed towards the enemy bank which was wrapped in the smoke of exploding shells. Stumps and trunks of trees were being lifted high up into the sky. Fragments of shells rained down endlessly, sometimes reaching the middle of the river. According to plan, at the moment when the armoured personnel carriers reached their half-way mark across the river, the artillery should have switched to firing in depth, thus letting the battalion reach the bank and disembark its landing force. But the artillery showed no sign of conforming to plan. On the contrary, the rate of firing was increasing. This was either because the artillery observers had missed the right moment, or because the battalion had started its crossing two to three minutes early, but in any case it was impossible for the armoured personnel carriers to continue and they started to circle on the spot, crashing into one another as they fought against the strong current of the Dnieper.

All this happened bang in front of the government observers. The Secretary General looked in bewilderment at the Defence Minister who shouted something quite unprintable into the microphone and the gun-fire immediately stopped. About thirty guns still maintained their fire, but the main chorus had ceased. Gradually the remainder also stopped, in a somewhat bashful fashion. Armoured personnel carriers meanwhile were continuing their pirouettes on the water. Apparently the battalion commander did not dare give the order to advance, because he could not guess what the bloody artillery would get up to next. In any case, he was under instructions not to pass the middle of the river until the artillery had switched to fire in depth. But any piece of artillery needs two to three minutes to alter its gun sights, and so the battalion foundered in the water. During training it had all been so good – and now just look at that bloody mess . . .

At last the artillery, slowly and with great reluctance, started to fire in depth, and the battalion moved towards the bank . . . but not one of the armoured personnel carriers succeeded in getting out of the water. During training, the artillery had always been very well organised, but now either the gunners were nervous or something else was wrong, but the whole riverside cut, which should have been left untouched, had been ploughed up and dotted with shell-holes. So, it was time for improvisation. The battalion commander ordered his men to jump into the water and swim to the bank. The river was shallow in some places but by no means everywhere. Everything got into a tangle. Instead of an accurate deployment, there was an unruly mob.

The situation was saved by the commander of the battalion, Colonel Rubanov: 'Forget it's a manoeuvre, it's a real battle.' Later, the military correspondents praised the gallant commander to the skies. His order was especially liked by the Head of the Chief Political Directorate, General Epishev. But the battalion commander was not seeking for effect. By this command, he was simply ordering disgsed officers to forget about the big show, to forget the roles they had learned by heart, to forget all this 'ballet' and to act in the way prompted by their own common sense and by the experience obtained during their years as officer-cadets. The young officers understood their battalion commander, their lines straightened, company and platoon commanders evaluated the situation and, after a couple of minutes, the battalion commander flung his men into the attack from the very brink of the water, totally abandoning the armoured personnel carriers. After this, everything went almost according to the book, but there was just one more hitch. The armoured personnel carriers could not get out of the water and we tankmen were seriously afraid that one of them might land in one of the secret underwater channels. Then the leading tank would come up against the armoured personnel carrier, all the following tanks would stop also, and there would be an almighty scandal.

But the valiant battalion commander saved the situation once again. He had already progressed a good distance with his infantry, when suddenly he remembered the tanks and radioed for his armoured personnel carriers to go off down river, thus clearing the way for the tanks. So, every armoured personnel carrier was to be captured by the enemy, or to come under enemy fire, but at least the way was open for all the advancing troops. This decision saved the whole of our peep-show but it ruined the colonel. After the exercises, Comrade Grechko assessed the colonel's decision as 'unjustified', and ordered his dismissal from the army.

Our tanks crossed the river without incident, pulling after them, under water, the artillery of the whole division. Ammunition and crews were transported on sapper carriers. After this, the whole ballet got into its swing once again. The 'Westerners', as expected, stampeded away in panic the moment they saw us on the horizon. Targets fell all over the place, the shells did not touch them, and, most important of all, the roar was quite deafening. The high command of the 'Easterners' had 'guessed' all the perfidious plans of the 'Westerners' and delivered suitably crushing blows. In short, everything worked out disgustingly to plan.

Three days later, we were brought to Kiev. Later, of course, the parade was shown on television and in the cinema, but only after substantial work had been put in by the censor. The parade was to take place on the military aerodrome.

The very sight of the aerodrome staggered us. Countless numbers of tanks, stretching, it seemed, from one horizon to another, were standing in the field alongside the runway. Later, photographs of this field crammed with tanks were to be published in all the newspapers of the world. At the time, some Western commentators expressed the opinion that perhaps these were only dummy tanks made of rubber standing there. Certainly, there were far too many tanks, indeed it was the biggest assembly of tanks in the history of humanity, but even though they were not made of rubber, they were quite lifeless. They were tanks used for training exercises and had definitely exhausted their resources. They were not tanks any more, but former tanks, and now they represented only raw material for the steel industry. After the parade, a few went to the Kiev tank-repairing works for a total overhaul, many thousands went to the Chinese frontier to be used as immovable firing-posts, but the major part were sent to be melted down. This jubilee year turned out to be a record year for melted steel.

It is impossible to say how much this peep-show cost our peace-loving people. Even without taking into consideration ammunition, fuel, wear on artillery barrels and the thousands of tons of steel armature and concrete, and only counting worn-out tanks, the figure would approximate to billions of roubles.

On the world market, the British Chieftain, which was the contemporary of our T-62, could easily fetch 210,000 dollars a piece. During exercises, our 1st Ukrainian front completely wore out over 5,000 tanks and considerably shortened the motor resources of another 5,000 – and there were at least five fronts taking part in Operation 'Dnieper'. Out of fairness, it should be noted that, although other fronts' training exercises were similar to ours, they were still not as intensive. But, even so, we can take the amount of worn-out tanks as at least 10,000. Multiply this number by the price of one tank, and it will immediately be clear why the Soviet Union cannot overtake Spain in the production of motor cars.

The parade passed off without a ripple, as the saying goes, though there was just one jarring note. . . . The troops drawn up on the aerodrome awaited the arrival of the important guests. Those on the dais also waited. The parade, as usual, was to begin at 1000 hours, but Brezhnev, Podgornyy, Kosygin and Shelest were late, or, as we put it, they were delayed. (Bosses are never late.) The beginning of the parade was delayed, and this caused nervousness. In addition, in contrast to Moscow parades, a fly-past had been planned. The airforce was to fly from Borispol, and the flights were calculated down to the last second . . . but the big chiefs were delayed. Marshal Grechko, as he stood on the dais softly cursed our Beloved Party and Government and all the members of the Political Bureau with superbly refined abuse. Naturally he cursed them in a whisper but the microphones on the dais had been switched on at 1000 hours exactly, and his *sotto voce* was transmitted over a distance of ten kilometres – indeed over the whole of the parade. That is why the Kiev parade was eventually conducted somehow especially dashingly, I would even say gaily. Half an hour later, when the troops solemnly marched past the big chiefs' dais, there was not the usual expression of stern resolution on the officers' and soldiers' faces. Instead all the faces blossomed out into smiles. And the big chiefs smiled back and waved with their fat little hands.

1967. Moscow – The Ukraine.

Operation 'Bridge'

'Comrades,' began the Defence Minister, 'in this new year of 1967 the Soviet Army will have to undertake a number of extremely complicated and responsible tasks, and tereby celebrate the fiftieth anniversary of the Great October Socialist Revolution.

'The first and the most complicated of these tasks is to achieve a final solution to the problem in the Near East. This task lies completely upon the shoulders of the Soviet Army. The fiftieth year of the existence of the Soviet Union will thus become the last year of the existence of the Jewish State. We are ready to accomplish this honourable task, but we are held back only by the presence of the UN troops between the Jewish and the Arab forces.

'After the solution of the Near East problem, all efforts will be thrown into regulating the European problem. This task is not only for diplomats. Here again, the Soviet Army will have to solve a number of problems. In accordance with the decision of the Politburo, the Soviet Army will "bare its teeth". Under this heading, we include a number of separate measures and an unprecedented air display at Domodedovo. Immediately after victory in the Near East, grand naval manoeuvres will follow in the Black Sea, the Mediterranean, the Barents, the North and the Baltic seas. After all this, we will carry out the colossal "Dnieper" exercises and we will complete our demonstrations on 7 November with an elaborate parade in Red Square. Then, against the background of these demonstrations of force and of our victories in the Near East, we will urge the Arab countries to stop all oil supplies to Europe and America over a period of one or two weeks. I think' – and here the Minister smiled – 'Europe will then be more amenable to signing all those documents which we shall propose to them.'

'Will there be any developments in the space programme?' enquired the First Deputy of the Commander-in-Chief Land Forces.

The Defence Minister frowned.

'Unfortunately not. During the period of "voluntarism", flagrant errors were tolerated in this sphere. Now we have to pay for them. In the next ten or fifteen years we will not be able to do anything basically new in space, we shall only be repeating old successes with slight improvements.'

'What will be done concerning Vietnam?' asked the Commander of troops in the Far East Military District.

'We will be able to solve successfully all European problems only when the Americans have become tied up in Vietnam. I think we should not hurry to defeat Vietnam.'

The assembly became extremely animated, demonstrating its obvious approval.

'To finish with general matters,' continued Marshal Grechko. 'I would like everybody to give some thought to the following. Simultaneously with all our demonstrations of might, and quite apart from the number of individual troops involved and their training, it would be no bad idea to organise something which has never been seen before, something stunning and completely new. So if anybody among you, Comrade Generals, comes up with an interesting idea, do not hesitate to apply to me or to the Chief of the General Staff. I ask you in advance however, not to increase the number of tanks, guns and aircraft. You have no idea how many of them there will be – we shall gather everything we have to put on display. New technology, of course, should not be suggested. We will show everything which it is permissible to show, the BMP and the T-64, the MIG-23 and MIG-25, and possibly all the experimental machines. This, of course, is dangerous, but we must show them.'

Everyone present took the final words of the Defence Minister as a promise of high rewards for any original idea. So be it. And all the military minds started to work on the idea. Only, what could they suggest besides quantity and quality?

Nevertheless, an original idea was found. It emanated from Colonel-General Ogarkov, a former sapper officer.

Ogarkov proposed demonstrating not only the might of the army, but also that this might rested on the rock-solid base of military industry. Of course, he had no intention of revealing the whole system of supply, and there was no need to do so. To convince his guests of his wealth, the master of the house does not need to show all his treasures. One genuine painting by Rembrandt will be quite enough.

Ogarkov wanted to show just one element, but a sufficiently convincing one. What he proposed was to build a railway bridge over the Dnieper in record time, in say one hour, and then to let the railway echelons loaded with battle equipment and columns of tanks cross the river by means of this same bridge. A bridge of this kind would not only symbolize a strong back-up, but would also demonstrate to Europe that the Rhine was no protection.

Ogarkov's idea was met with delight by the Defence Ministry and by the General Staff alike. This was exactly what was required. Of course, the Soviet Army did not possess any such bridge and there was not much time left before the beginning of the exercises. This fact, however, worried nobody, the main thing was that the desired idea had been found.

Colonel-General Ogarkov was endowed with absolute power, no less than that of the general designer before the launching of the first cosmonaut. Ogarkov himself was not only a brilliant, erudite and experienced engineer bridge-builder, but also an unusually exigent and wilful commander, as only Zhukov had been before him. That, of course, made the fulfilment of the task all the easier. All the scientific research establishments and railway troops, as well as all the industrial enterprises producing the army's engineering technology, were switched to his direct leadership. The entire production of these enterprises was stopped pending the order to begin the production of something so unprecedented.

At the same time, while the designers were busy making the first sketches and outlines for the future bridge, which was to be used only once, the selection of the youngest, healthiest and strongest officers, as well as the cleverest and most experienced engineers, started. In addition, competitions were arranged in the Soviet Army railway and engineering schools, open to officer-cadets who were graduating from these schools and were therefore already officers. As a result, thousands of the best officers and officer-cadets put on soldiers' uniform and came to Kiev from every corner of the Soviet Union. And in Kiev the 1st Guards Railway Bridge-Building Division was raised.

While it was not yet clear what kind of bridge was to be built, the division was launched into a training programme of unprecedented severity, since whatever kind of bridge was to be built, it was clear that everybody engaged in assembling it would have to work like acrobats under the circus big top.

While the original idea of the ultra-high-speed erection of a railway bridge continued to be developed and deepened, it was proposed that, as soon as the erection was complete, a track-laying machine and contingents equipped with rails should go across and, just as speedily, build a section of railway on the right bank, so that troops and battle equipment could be sent over. This idea was similarly accepted and approved.

Meanwhile all the design bureaux, each engaged independently on the development of the bridge, declared unanimously that to build even a floating bridge, with a load capacity of only 1,500 tons, was impossible in such a short period of time. Ogarkov saw red. Both his reputation and future were at stake. He reacted swiftly and accurately. First, he applied to the Central Committee and obtained their positive approval that the designer who succeeded in building such a bridge would be awarded a Lenin Prize. Secondly, he invited all the designers to a conference and, having let them know the Central Committee's decision, proposed discussing all the details over again. At this conference, the plan to pass track-laying machines and echelons with rails over the bridge was rejected, as was the idea of columns of tanks crossing simultaneously with railway echelons. It was also decided that all wagons making the crossing must be empty, and that a column of empty lorries would move across alongside the train. Only one problem still remained. How to get across a locomotive weighing 300 tons? Naturally, someone suggested reducing the locomotive's weight by as much as possible. Two locomotives, a basic one and a duplicate, were urgently modernised and as many steel components as possible were replaced by aluminium ones. The steam boilers and fire-chambers were also changed. The locomotive's tenders were completely empty, they carried no coal and no water but only one very small barrel containing some kind of high-octane fuel, maybe aviation benzine or paraffin.

Time was racing past. The plan for the bridge had already been finished at the works, and the majority of the 1st Guards Railway Division's officers were sent there to acquaint themselves with its construction during the actual process of manufacture. Factories, which had not been operating for several months while the project was being planned, were now switched to a military regime. They worked twenty-four hours a day. All the workers were paid enormous wages and promised that, if they finished the work on time, they would receive unprecedented rewards from the Defence Minister personally.

The first elements of the bridge were meanwhile duly delivered to the division, and the training programme started. New elements were delivered every week, and during each training period, the bridge got longer and longer. Theoretical calculations proved that it should hold the weight of an empty echelon; but how it would work in practice no one, of course, knew. The most dangerous consideration was that, if the bridge sagged too much under the weight of the locomotive, the train's wagons could overturn into the water. Locomotive crews and drivers from motorised troops, all disguised officers, who would be moving over the bridge simultaneously with the echelon, started urgently to study the use of life-saving techniques, intended for the use of tank crews while under water. They could not, however, be given any practical training in crossing the bridge, because some sections destined to connect the two banks were still missing.

On the very day when the last two pontoons were delivered to the division, the mightiest military manoeuvres in the history of mankind began. They were code-named 'Dnieper'.

The floating railway bridge across the Dnieper was built in record time and, when the last piles were hammered in on the right bank, a locomotive smoothly glided on to the bridge from the left bank, slowly pulling behind it a long train. Simultaneously, a column of military vehicles glided on to the bridge. The leaders of Party and Government and numerous foreign guests watching the construction of this gigantic bridge never guessed that it was being built for railway communications. So, when the locomotive arrived on the bridge, all those on the Government dais applauded enthusiastically.

As the locomotive moved further and further from the bank, the sagging of the bridge beneath its weight became threateningly more noticeable. Heavy, sluggish waves fanned out from the bridge and spread towards both banks of the river, then, reflecting back, returned to hit the bridge, rolling it from side to side. Immediately, the three small figures of the frightened engine-drivers appeared on top of the locomotive. Until now, none of the foreign guests had paid any attention to the strange fact that there was no smoke issuing from the locomotive's smoke-stack, but the appearance of the engine-driver on top of the locomotive was noticed by everybody and provoked condescending smiles.

Later on, these frightened engine-drivers were skilfully removed from all photographs and films recording this famous crossing, but at that particular moment the situation was in need of saving, because the whole enterprise on which so much money and energy had been expended, could so easily have turned into a farce.

The slowly-swaying locomotive with its three engine-drivers on top lumbered nervously onwards.

'What is that there on the top?' asked Marshal Grechko slowly through clenched teeth.

All the other Soviet generals and marshals lapsed into complete silence.

Colonel-General Ogarkov stepped forward and reported smartly: 'Comrade Marshal of the Soviet Union! We have thoroughly incorporated the experiences learnt during the recent Arab–Israeli war, where aviation played such an exclusively important role. We therefore took measures to protect all rear communications against an enemy's air attack. Thus, in the event of war, we provide in addition to three engine-drivers, who are inside the locomotive, another three men with automatic grenade-launchers, Strela-2s. These grenade-launchers have not yet been delivered to the troops, but we have already started training their crews, which is what you are seeing at the present moment.'

All the foreign guests were staggered by such efficiency displayed by the General Staff and by such a lightning reaction to changes in the practice of waging war.

The Defence Minister was also staggered by this ability to lie with such speed, aplomb and aptitude, without batting an eyelid and at the psychological moment. 'Fine fellow that,' thought the Defence Minister, 'he will go far with such capabilities as those.'

After the exercises, when the bridge was taken apart and sent for melting down, and the Guards Bridge-Building Division was disbanded, as being of no further use, and after all the designers and builders had been generously rewarded, it was unanimously decided to entrust to Ogarkov the organising of all future operations of this kind. And this is how the Chief Directorate of Strategic Camouflage, the first head of which was Colonel-General Ogarkov, was born. Shortly afterwards, Ogarkov was promoted to the rank of Army General.

Ogarkov's Chief Directorate started by taking over all military and later all state censorship, and later still also the majority of all the organisations dealing with misinformation, snatching many titbits even from the very jaws of the KGB. After this, the Chief Directorate's tentacles stretched out towards the armed forces: in future training exercises undertaken by the army, air force or navy could only take place after the approval of Ogarkov. Any military building, from space centres, launching silos and nuclear submarine bases, to the barracks of the KGB's frontier troops – everything must have the approval of Ogarkov. The next step was the subordination of all industry and building in the Soviet Union to him since, in our country, all objects have a military significance. And when the post of Chief of the General Staff became vacant, no one who knew about the existence of GUSM* and its real might had the slightest doubt as to who would land it.

Having attained the rank of Marshal of the Soviet Union and the position of Chief of the General Staff, the former engineer bridge-builder did not, of course, rest on his laurels. The future belongs to him . . . unless his rivals devour him first.

*The abbreviation for Chief Directorate of Strategic Camouflage.

The 287th Novograd-Volynsk Motor Rifle Training Division.
Oster, the Ukraine, October 1967.

Training

'Puke! And that's an order!'

The young short-haired little soldier looked round pathetically for support. A platoon of equally young and equally short-haired soldiers, in front of whom he was standing, obviously did not sympathise with him a bit. In the first week of their service they had fully assimilated the iron rule of training: if one person does not obey the order, the whole section will suffer; if one section does not obey the order, the whole platoon will suffer; and if one platoon does not obey the order, then the sergeants will pick one of the platoon's soldiers and train him until he loses consciousness, or 'until he lies down' – and if he can no longer obey the orders efficiently, his section will suffer, and then the whole platoon and so on, ad infinitum. And there are too many kinds of training. For instance, you can order a section to dig trenches on an old ferro-concrete surface, and make sure that 120 centimetre-deep trenches are dug in thirty minutes, and those who do not obey the order will have to train again as a punishment.

The short-haired little soldier stood in front of the formation, but the formation was beginning to get angry – because it knew what lay in store for it if the order was not at once carried out.

I stood some way off, watching my second-in-command's actions. On the third day of my service as a platoon commander, I clearly understood one more law of the training division: do not interfere with the sergeant's work, otherwise you will have to do the work yourself.

Guards Staff Sergeant Kokhar', having waited ten seconds for effect, gave a clear order:

'Second section! Ten steps forward! Quick march! Platoon, listen to the order! Private Ravdulin was thirteen seconds late for parade, because he was in the canteen.'

Every day, every soldier in a training division has twenty minutes' free time after lunch and ten in the evening. Once he has broken away from lunch, a hungry soldier dashes off to the buffet, which is managed by only one sales-girl. There are 1,500 soldiers in a regiment of whom a good half, the hungriest ones, or the most optimistic, try to get through to the counter. The majority, having got as far as the buffet are unable either to reach the counter, or to force their way out. For being even a second late on parade they will be severely punished, but the number of those trying to break through to the buffet never decreases. One wonders where they get the money if they are paid monthly three roubles and eighty kopeks, out of which they must also buy all their toilet articles. The answer lies in the fact that every day for two or three months they try to reach the buffet and always fail – there is the economy.

At that moment, all the regiment's forty platoons were formed up in the garrison backyard ready to start cleaning their weapons. No officers were to be seen and the sergeants, each in his own way, were correcting any infringements. Some were endlessly performing 'get-up-lie-down'; one platoon was crawling *plastun*-fashion over the courtyard, which was thickly covered in a layer of pig-shit.

My deputy had decided to limit himself to forcing the buffet culprit to vomit publicly what he had eaten, or rather what he had wanted to eat. But the culprit did not carry out the order well enough, so the whole section was going to have to put this mistake right. The first and the third sections, with a mixture of hatred and hope in their eyes, were waiting for their fate to be decided. 'One for all, all for one' is, after all, the basic principle of education.

'Second section! Bend forward!'

Ten backs smartly bent forward.

'Put two fingers . . . of the left hand, IN THE MOUTH!'

The section smartly obeyed the order.

'From the right! . . . One after another! . . . PUKE!' Wriggling convulsively, the section carried out its commander's order and emptied its stomach in perfectly acceptable time.

'Section, ten steps forward! Quick march! Private Ravdulin, take your place in the formation! Stand easy!' The sergeant turned away, ostensibly to find a suitable place for the platoon to clean its weapons. At that precise moment, Ravdulin received two heavy blows in the stomach from his nearest short-haired comrades. Trying to choke back a broken, long-drawn-out moan, he crashed down on his knees, and then slowly fell into his own vomit.

During training, sergeants and officers never beat soldiers – that is an iron law in any training division.

Oster, the Ukraine. March 1968.

The Artists and the Craftsmen

The recently arrested man was brought to the regiment and locked up in the guardroom cell. He sat in the corner, looking sullenly at the floor. This sergeant had been arrested in Omsk, 4,000 kilometres from his native training regiment.

The military investigator arrived; the investigation began. How? Why? The matter is serious! and everything depends on a higher authority to look at what has happened, and interpret the present offence. If you class it as absence without leave, the sergeant will be given fifteen days under arrest, as a maximum. If you class it as desertion, it will be fifteen years at the very minimum.

If the sergeant had been caught within his own military district, the matter would have been hushed up of course, because there is good socialist competition between the districts as to which has fewer offences and violations. But since he had been caught in another district altogether, and Moscow therefore knew all about it, the commanders would do their best to show their determination to eradicate fully all such violations regardless of the consequences. But here again a contradiction creeps in – if this is indeed a desertion, then why was it not reported to Moscow six days ago, when the sergeant first disappeared?

A very unpleasant day had dawned for all the sergeant's direct superiors from platoon commander to military district chief.

The sergeant's name was Zumarov, and I was his platoon commander. That is why I was the first to see the investigator.

'Your sergeant?'

'Mine, Comrade Lieutenant-Colonel.'

'How long have you served together?'

'Fifteen months, Comrade Lieutenant-Colonel.'

He had been a cadet in the training platoon under my command, and later, after being promoted, had been left in the platoon, in command of the second section.

'What can you say about him?'

'Comrade Lieutenant-Colonel, I have never seen him before in my life!'

94

Apparently, the investigator had long since penetrated so deeply into the stern realities of the army that my statement produced no impression at all upon him.

'Was he a craftsman?' was his only question.

'Yes, a craftsman,' I confirmed.

This ended the investigation.

After me various other witnesses were called, the company commander, the political deputy of the battalion commander, and finally the battalion commander himself. Interviews with them also took no more than a minute. None of them had ever seen the sergeant in their lives before.

If all property is nationalized in a country, in other words subordinated to the state, then the natural aspiration of each person to rise, to distinguish himself and to improve his status can be achieved only within the limits of the state apparatus, which incidentally requires many (far too many) professional officials, or executives with higher education.

Any degree certifying graduation from a higher educational institution opens the way into any number of spheres: the Party, the Trade Unions, the Young Communist League, the KGB, Sport, Literature and Art, Industry, Agriculture, Transport, anywhere you like. This is why in any socialist society the following paradox can be observed: nobody seeks a profession, only a degree, and it does not matter what kind. Of course, it is better if the degree has a slight inclination towards the social sciences, rather than to the exact sciences. This is simpler, and more useful in life, because the most important thing in one's career is 'to learn to talk smoothly'.

And, owing to the fact that everyone rushes into learning Marxist–Leninist philosophy and Party history, people who can do something with their hands, and not their tongues, are few and far between. Hence, such persons are worth their weight in gold. You only have to look at how they live now – the car-mechanics, the locksmiths, the sanitary technicians and the house-painters and floor-fillers (of course, I'm speaking about those who earn additional money in their free time, and who doesn't!).

People who can make something are especially honoured in the Soviet Army, because the system of control and evaluation of sub-units, units and formations is constructed in such a way that it just cannot be managed without craftsmen.

Judge for yourself. Some kind of commission arrives in a regiment, so where will it start its check-up, what is it interested in? Before everything else comes the ideological state of the troops – are they true believers, or has the decay already set in? How are you to check whether the bourgeois, or the maoist, or the revanchist, the nationalist or the zionist or any other band of propaganda exerts any influence upon the Soviet warrior? It is very simple. First, the commission must inspect the whole camp. Are there enough portraits of the Party and Government leaders, are there enough placards and slogans, is there enough visual agitation in general. What shape is the club in? The room devoted to the glorification of battle? How is the Lenin room in each company, in what shape are each company's paper and satirical news-sheet? And what about each platoon's daily 'battle leaflet'?

After all this, one must discover what a soldier does in his free time. What is he doing? What is he thinking? And that is quite simple too: a concert and sports competition are laid on for the commission. Everything is in order! There is more evidence – cups, pennants, banners. This one is for sport, that one for amateur activities in the arts. Well, things are clearly all right there, but how do they stand with internal order, and with the observance of military regulations? Here again, there are no problems. Feast your eyes: fences are painted, paths are swept, windows are washed, beds are made and perfectly ranged in line, it would be quite impossible to arrange them any better.

Believe me, if any regimental commander succeeds in giving a better account concerning all these points than his colleagues, and in addition manages to hide all crimes and disciplinary offences, which are happening every day, his promotion is assured. The most important consideration is to be able to hide all the unattractive aspects, but exercises and manoeuvres will not be taken into consideration.

In order to win a victory in this interminable competition, every commander, from company commander upwards, must have painters, artists and sportsmen, preferably of a semi-professional level. A special term has been invented in the army for these craftsmen, they are called 'dead souls', because although they are registered as gun-layers, loaders, radio-men, etcetera, they are nevertheless occupied with quite other matters. Some are concocting newspapers day and night. Some are strumming guitars, some are defending their company's honour in sport. According to their particular qualifications, the craftsmen are divided into categories – at company, battalion, regimental or divisional level. For example, in every district there are special sports battalions, sub-divided into light athletics companies, basket-ball platoons, or even high jump platoons.

The struggle to acquire craftsmen goes on permanently between commanders at all levels. All lower-ranking officers hide their best painters and artists from the higher-ranking officers who, in their turn, haunt the various clubs and sports rooms hoping to grab the best craftsmen for themselves. It is open war, with all the rules and methods, the appropriate unwritten laws and traditions. There's enough of it to fill a novel. Direct exchanges also exist, although these take place more often between independent commanders: 'Give me a weight-lifter and a guitarist, and I'll give you a house-painter and a painter,' or, 'Comrade Colonel, don't give me a bad mark for that exercise' (this kind of bargain would be struck via a middleman from another division) 'and I'll give you a sculptor! He'll make a model of anyone you like for the officers' mess in your division. Lenin or Andropov, anyone you wish!'

All craftsmen work on the piece rate system. The principle of material self-interest is sacred. Payment alters depending on the category. Sometimes it happens this way: 'If you become an Olympic champion – we'll give you the rank of senior lieutenant!' And anyway what does it cost the Defence Minister to give away one or two additional little stars? One footballer even attained the rank of major-general without serving a single day in the army, although it must be admitted that the footballer's name in that instance was Yuriy Brezhnev.

In the Kiev military district, at the tank works, the repairing of thousands of private cars was organised. The district chiefs were filling their pockets with millions of roubles, and the craftsmen who were repairing these cars were given leave every evening, and everybody was happy, generals, craftsmen and consumers. The quality of the work was excellent and it is a pity that the shutters were eventually put up. Now there is nowhere in the whole of Kiev to have a Zhiguli car repaired.

Even if the craftsmen had not been paid at all, their work would still have been highly efficient, because to swill all day or to hit a tennis ball about is much more pleasant than digging deep trenches in the heat and the dirt; similarly, drawing a satirical paper in a warm store-room is much more pleasant than changing tank-tracks in the frost. That at least is established fact. In addition, all craftsmen receive endless periods of leave and holidays, all at the expense of others, of course. It is from this that the decay of an army springs (it is not the only cause, and certainly not the most important, but it is one of the basic ones). Let us say for the sake of argument that a drunk, dirty, scruffy soldier is walking along the street. Notice how all the patrols stand aside: it turns out that he is the personal cabinet-maker to the divisional commander. And that one over there, who is also drunk, turns out to be the personal workman of the divisional staff chief, for whom he is engaged in digging a private swimming pool. It is far better not to touch these fellows, or to have anything to do with them.

But let us return to our sergeant with whom we started this story. By profession he was a jeweller, and the son of a jeweller to boot. He joined the army complete with the tools of his trade – little saws, little vices and little tweezers. It is an everyday occurrence for young chaps to join the army with their guitars and balalaikas, with their brushes and canvas. The Soviet people have long understood our fine army customs and they exhort their sons to reveal their particular talent from their very first day in the army.

Zumarov demonstrated his talent immediately after joining our training regiment. He was promptly ordered to fashion a small silver tank which could be presented to the head of some visiting commission. He was reckoned to belong to my training platoon, and I was given six months to make a perfect sergeant out of him, a future commander of a T-62, but I never once saw him throughout his entire service. Out of a total of thirty men in my platoon I had six others like him. True, the six others – a painter, a violinist, a pianist, and three sportsmen – were non-residents; so that sometimes, perhaps once or twice a week, they did turn up in the platoon, and I managed to teach them something.

Officer-cadet Zumarov was not even present at the passing-out inspection. How could he be? He had seen nothing except miniature tanks which he was carving from bronze and glass. The regimental commander took the test for him and whispered to the inspecting commission. As a result, Zumarov became an excellent soldier, was awarded the rank of sergeant and then left behind in our regiment as a section commander in order to train a new generation of tank commanders. He was posted as a section commander to my platoon and, from that day to this, I never clapped eyes on him.

Do not imagine that I was the only one who had problems with the 'dead souls' – every other platoon commander had six or seven corpses on his register. Here at least distribution is just and no one is offended. This is how we train cadres for our beloved army. When such a tank commander/ignoramus arrives from training to join his battle regiment, he honestly reports at the very outset, 'I am not a tank commander, I am a singer.' Of course, they are pleased in the regiment. 'You are just the thing we've been waiting for!' As a result, the tank is commanded by the gunner, and the baritone just sings his way through operatic arias, and everybody is pleased. The best craftsmen, such as our jeweller, would never under any circumstances be surrendered by a training regiment to a battle regiment, but would be held on to, under any pretext, most frequently as nominal instructors.

But Sergeant Zumarov had come to the notice of the divisional commander, and then of the army commander, and had consequently moved first to divisional, then to army, level. He could have risen even higher, but unfortunately he was arrested by a patrol and, what is even worse, in another district.

After the first interview with the military investigator, I promptly decided that there would not be a second one, as I knew absolutely nothing about the sergeant – at what level he was now, who his real commander was, or how many times a week he was given leave. But the second interview nevertheless did take place.

'Where is his oath of allegiance?'

'I do not know.'

I really could not know that.

The fact is that every Soviet soldier after a month of primary training eventually takes the oath of allegiance. This can be done only after the soldier has fired his weapon for the first time. The oath of allegiance is printed for each soldier on a separate piece of paper and is signed by him personally. This is done so that this separate sheet can be put on his criminal file, if the need arises.

But, at that moment when the whole training platoon was on the shooting-range prior to signing the oath, Zumarov was making his first tank.

'Never mind,' the regimental commander had said. 'You can go with the next platoon.'

But then the regimental commander apparently forgot to see to it – poor chap, he had so many problems! I, too, as his immediate commander, was unable to see to it. I was told not to interfere in matters which did not concern me. So I didn't. I simply had no means of doing so.

Now it became clear that Zumarov was neither a sergeant nor even a soldier. Nor was he under military jurisdiction as he had never signed the oath of allegiance – so he could not even be judged under military law, and under civilian law he had not committed any offence as he had just gone from one town to another. And of course he lost the whole year and a half which he had spent in the army. This period could not be counted because time in military service is calculated from the day of signing the oath. Now, Zumarov could have started a commotion. 'I don't know anything about it. I joined the army and served conscientiously. It is not my fault but yours! Why didn't you put me under oath?'

And indeed a scandal flared up and had to be nipped in the bud, because not only pawns like regimental commanders might have suffered in the process but some people much higher up. The scandal was hushed up at the level of the Kiev Military District. A compromise was found. According to the law, Zumarov had another six months to serve but he was offered immediate demobilisation on grounds of health. Zumarov accepted the compromise. It was reported to Moscow that Sergeant Zumarov of the Kiev district had indeed been arrested in Omsk but that he was no longer on active service, but had been prematurely demobilised. The sergeant was said to be suffering from mental derangement, as a result of which he did not produce the relevant documents when requested to do so by the patrol.

The Zumarovs of this world are the lucky ones, but there are a lot of them in our indestructible army – more's the pity.

Misha

'The little key?'

'Comrade Private, first button up your tunic, you are addressing a Lieutenant-Colonel, the duty officer of the military district staff.'

The private simply did not react at all to the lieutenant-colonel's words.

'The little key!' quietly repeated the young soldier with the broad peasant face which showed such superiority and contempt that the duty officer simply did not dare exercise the power of his nearly limitless authority.

The duty officer of the district staff is a very superior being altogether. So much so, that having caught sight of him from afar, any officer absentmindedly assumes a dignified air and straightens his belt and the peak of his cap. Whereas now, a young soldier, who should tremble in front of any lance-corporal, stood in front of him and simply did not react at all to his reprimand.

'The little key' repeated the soldier, evidently savouring the situation to the full. Deliberately, he did not say which key he wanted, and the key itself, in defiance of regulations, he called 'little key', which theoretically is quite inadmissible between a soldier and an officer.

At this moment, a major with a red stripe on his left arm – the duty officer's deputy – entered the room. Having appraised the situation in a trice, the major suddenly gave a radiant smile, and jumping up he went to a huge safe and jerked open its massive doors. He snatched one of the hundreds of keys hanging there and, with an obsequious smile, stretched it out towards the arrogant soldier. The latter took the key between two fingers, measured the staff duty officer with a contemptuous gaze, unhurriedly turned his back and, after deliberately spitting on the floor beside a spittoon in the corner, he left the room, slamming the door behind him.

The duty officer was white with rage. Turning towards the major, and enunciating every syllable, he asked deliberately: 'Comrade Major, to whom did you dare give that key without my express permission?'

'But that's Misha, Comrade Lieutenant-Colonel,' said the major obsequiously.

'Which key did you give him?'

'The key to the study of the district commander's first deputy.'

'But you . . . but you . . . do you understand? Did you read the instructions? . . . There are state secrets in that study . . . Only a senior aide-de-camp or an officer on a special mission is entitled . . .'

'But that is Misha!'

'I don't want to hear anything about any Misha, you will be put under arrest together with your Misha! Only the senior aide-de-camp or an officer on a special mission can be given that key and then only after the deputy commander's order and only after the said officer has signed in duplicate for this key, in case anything should disappear. Surrender your pistol and cartridges . . .' Whereupon the lieutenant-colonel turned to me, the guards commander, and said, 'Arrest this Misha and the major!'

'Misha', declared the major suddenly, 'is the relief driver of the Commander of Leningrad Military District's First Deputy, Lieutenant-General Parshikov.'

'Ah!' The lieutenant-colonel stopped short. 'So, why did you not say so before?'

'And that's not all,' the major cruelly continued, 'that's only officially, but unofficially . . . he . . . he drives Maria Michaylovna, his wife . . . that's what!'

The duty officer slowly left the room.

'Now there you are, Lieutenant, you learn from that! They keep sending all kinds of idiots here . . . They've got accustomed in the regiments to shouting at anyone, without knowing the particulars . . . But here you've got military district staff! Here, one must have a head on one's shoulders! Staff work is subtle, not everyone can . . . It's a good thing that Misha is not touchy . . . or we'd now be in a fine old mess!'

The whole night through I thought about Misha. The lieutenant-colonel was old enough to be his father, but because of his status he was not simply a lieutenant-colonel, battalion commander or some kind of a regimental commander's deputy, no, this was a lieutenant-colonel of a special kind, not a duty officer on the staff of a division, corps or army, no, a duty officer on the staff of a military district! One could clamber all one's life up the slippery career ladder and still not reach such a dizzy height. And suddenly Misha breezes in, just like Misha – no more and no less – a chap who has served no more than six months in the army, while the lieutenant-colonel has been through the whole war . . . If fate had sent this same Misha to our training division he would now be grovelling even in front of the lance-corporals . . .

Where did he get his swaggering conceit from? Where did he acquire that look on his face? It goes without saying that a relief driver for

Lieutenant-General Parshikov's spare car is not the lowest figure on the militay district staff. But, still, where did all that contempt come from?

Maybe our leaders have some kind of special system for selecting people who are marked with a stamp of churlishness? The lad could only have driven the manure lorry on a farm, nothing more, so where did he manage to acquire all this veneer? Or maybe we are all like him and, when we reach the foot of the pyramid of power, we forget everything except ourselves and, blinded by our own authority, we show nothing but contempt for all those lower than ourselves?

In that case what liberties must the cook and chamber-maid permit themselves, they who are so much closer to Parshikov's own person than Misha, and who have been in the job for years? And supposing Comrade Parshikov suddenly becomes a colonel-general and not only a deputy but the commander of the whole military district? What liberties will Misha permit himself then? The very thought made me feel giddy.

In my uneasy sleep, that swine-faced Misha pursued me along the endless nightmarish corridors of absolute power with no one to control him and nothing to stop him.

Part Three

The Way towards Commander-in-Chief

Every commander of a platoon or a battalion or a regiment must seek a way of distinguishing himself and showing himself off to his immediate superior, otherwise younger, more pushing officers will trample him underfoot.

The commander of our division was very clever at all kinds of tricks and probably owes to this his promotion to the rank of major-general. He looks like going higher still. In military matters, he rated an absolute zero, but this of course plays no role in the Soviet Army nor does it have the least effect upon one's military career. What one must possess is a talent for organisation and some 'savvy'! So it was that the divisional commander worked out that his career prospects would depend not on spotless parade grounds or neat rows of beds in the barracks, but on something more original.

His particular plan was as simple as it was original: to invite the Chief of the Kiev Military District, Army General Yakubovskiy, to a meeting with the officers of the division to say, 'Look, dear Comrade Chief, in our division, while all the others are busy with battle training and other assorted shit, if you will forgive the expression, our division is not. Our division can't sleep or eat, we only long to see our beloved Chief and to hear how he defended our beloved Motherland from her enemies and why he was awarded his many orders and medals. And, in general, please take good note of our love for you. Indeed, we love you so much that we recognise no other authority. This is the kind of division we are, and we have a remarkable divisional commander.'

A top-secret conference of the district's military commanders was in progress. Questions concerning mobilisation preparedness were under discussion. The walls of the big hall were covered with maps, graphs and diagrams. The discussion was serious and businesslike. Worthwhile ideas about how to raise our battle readiness and the improved training of troops were being put forward.

There were strict time limits: three minutes for divisional commanders and their chiefs of staff, five minutes for army commanders and their deputies and chiefs of staff, ten minutes for the district comman-

107

der, his deputies and for the chief of the district's staff. Everybody, without exception, must take part, but only with specific criticism and specific suggestions, there must be no waffle.

When our divisional commander's turn came, he rose and, without even glancing at his notes, began:

'We lack battle experience, Comrades, we have lived so many years without war that we have forgotten everything. Many regimental commanders, let alone battalion and company commanders, have never even smelt gunpowder. And just look what a chance we are missing! We are serving under the command of such a glorious general as Comrade Ivan Ignat'evich Yakubovskiy, who fought throughout the whole of the last war. This is where we must accumulate our experience! In my division, I held a meeting, and my young officers advised me . . . They said, Comrade General, invite Comrade Yakubovskiy to visit our division, let him tell us about war! Comrade Commander, I take this opportunity of passing on to you the request of our division's young officers!'

All the other generals present were disgusted by this blatant flattery. The main thing was that our general had avoided making any specific criticism or any specific suggestions. And yet his speech was accepted as making a specific suggestion and the most valuable one to boot.

'Well, all right, I'll come then,' mumbled dear old Ivan Ignat'evich. 'Why not, after all?'

When the military chief had left the hall, the army commander's deputy, Lieutenant-General Gelenkov, turned towards our cunning divisional commander and, in a sugary voice, loud enough to be heard by all the others, he asked whether it was not perhaps his post that our efficient divisional commander was aiming at. Everybody laughed appreciatively. But the divisional commander was not offended: the deputy army commander was still his direct superior for the time being, and the divisional commander never took offence at his superiors. This was one of his basic principles which had never let him down.

After returning from the conference, the divisional commander got busy. All battle training was immediately stopped – tanks, armoured personnel carriers, guns, all were put into mothballs. Every soldier was thrown into 'sprucing up' work, cleaning and repainting cars and redecorating the barracks. More than half the division went off to do 'illegal' jobs: some to collective farms, others to unload railway wagons or to work in factories.

The director of any factory and the chairman of any collective farm are always asking military commanders to help them out with men. Nowhere are there enough people, in collective farms or in industry or transport. Such 'illegal' operations are mutually profitable. The military commander illegally receives cement, asphalt, bricks, steel, timber, nails and, what is even more important, paint, while the directors and chairmen are able to report increased productivity and an over-achieved budget. At present labour productivity is very much the fashionable criterion. Even Vladimir Ilich Lenin taught us, long ago, that in the end productivity is the most important single factor in the victory of new economic structure. Plan fulfilment is of paramount importance.

So, industry, agriculture and transport all welcome activity of this nature by the army. They are ready to accept any number of soldiers at any given moment and to pay for their labour generously in kind. The only problem the directors ever have is how to coax military commanders to let them have more soldiers on a more regular basis. The army is equally pleased with the practice. Indeed, the only person opposed to it is the Defence Minister. He carries on a merciless campaign against the system, but how can one person resist the will of the collective?

Suppose the Defence Minister gives a resounding order: only he personally, and then only in exceptional circumstances, may order the troops to tear themselves away from battle training. The district commanders listen attentively, nodding their heads. Who could possibly impinge upon the monopoly of the Defence Minister? The Minister orders one of the divisions to work for three days in the fields or at the factory, and to pay all the proceeds into the Defence Ministry's fund. Very well, it shall be done!

For three days, the division works for the Defence Ministry, but on the fourth day it works for the military district commander. If a Moscow commission should arrive unexpectedly, it is always possible to justify oneself: 'We are working for you on your own orders.'

Every district commander issues a similar directive: only on his explicit orders may troops engage in collateral work instead of battle training, in all other instances their work will be considered illegal. The army commanders, of course, agree, but promptly issue similar orders in their own name to stop all unofficial work. In my own experience, our regiment nevertheless used to spend exactly half its time moonlighting. This state of affairs is quite common in the Soviet Army and exists everywhere, except among troops stationed abroad. Indeed, it seems that the Soviet Army could be halved without any damage to its fighting efficiency. This was exactly what Khrushchev attempted, but he failed to provide the army either with sufficient rations or with the necessary supplies. Khrushchev's reforms were not a success, and the army, though cut by nearly half, still continued its moonlighting operations just as intensively as before.

But let us return to our brave divisional commander, who so resolutely directed 4,000 soldiers to carry out unofficial work.

He was a bold man, but he took a calculated risk. Neither the district staff nor the army staff could reproach him for anything, because Army General Yakubovskiy had consented to make his unofficial visit, thus allowing the divisional commander to prepare an appropriate welcome for him.

Having allotted jobs to every soldier in his division, he ordered the chief of staff to take charge of building materials, and his deputy to organise the complete renovation of the whole barracks. He, together with the chief of the Political Department, busied himself with the most important task of all – the planning of the reception itself.

There was not much time left, only two months at the most, during which it was necessary to learn by heart the life history of our beloved general, to select from it the most striking and memorable details, and to prepare suitable questions; seemingly innocent questions, but ones which would stimulate the general to go into detail about his most heroic and amazing feats. It was also necessary to organise a competition among the young officers, to choose those who would ask questions from the floor, as well as supplementary questions, and then to carry out lengthy training for both these groups. Another competition was arranged to discover the best painters and craftsmen, who were then ordered to draw a gigantic map pinpointing events in the commander's war career and to prepare souvenirs to be presented by the personnel of our division. And, of course, there would be a big concert and banquet, to be laid on by the Political Department and the chief of the divisional rear services.

In the competition among young officers, I happened to be one of those selected and, at the distribution of roles, became the third relief for the officer who had to ask: 'Comrade Commander, please tell us how you shoed Churchill.'

All my friends and I too had heard this story a thousand times, and now we had to stimulate Yakubovskiy into telling it yet again. During the war, Great Britain provided the Soviet Union with Churchill tanks. But they were not ideally suited to the conditions of a Russian winter, and their tracks skidded on the snow. Then, one of the soldiers in Lieutenant-Colonel Yakubovskiy's tank brigade proposed putting spikes on the caterpillar tracks, as a result of which the practicability of using the tanks in the snow increased greatly. That very day, it was reported to the front commander that Yakubovskiy's brigade had 'shoed' Churchill. At a suitable moment, the front commander reported to Stalin that Lieutenant-Colonel Yakubovskiy had shoed Churchill. The joke pleased Stalin and the Lieutenant-Colonel after many months at the rear in the front line reserve, became a Hero of the Soviet Union and a personal favourite of Stalin. Gradually, with the rise of Yakubovskiy, this story began to change in detail and became encrusted with new heroic overtones.

These two months preparation for our important guest in a small Ukrainian town called Oster were for me the very best time n the whole of my service in the training division. My soldiers were working away somewhere, I did not know exactly where. Every morning after breakfast, all those who had been selected to put questions to our guest gathered in the officers' mess and the rehearsal started: first question, first question understudy, second question, second understudy, etcetera. After a week of intensive training, a theatre director was invited down from Kiev and the whole thing started to go with a swing.

There is no doubt that our commander was a genius, but even if he had been an absolute idiot we could have turned him, in the space of two months, into a veritable Napoleon Bonaparte. That, at least, was the considered opinion of all the division's officers, of everyone who took part in the preparations for the reception of our beloved general.

After marinading for a month in this extraordinary ragout I fully understood the whole process of the cult of the personality for the rest of my life. It became quite obvious to me why we loved Lenin and Brezhnev so much, and why we loved Khrushchev and Stalin so much. All of us who were preparing for the reception of Yakubovskiy were mere amateurs, we were about to glorify one of the sixteen district commanders, not even the Commander-in-Chief, Land Forces; we had a mere two months at our disposal. Give me a couple of years, a staff of professional speakers and all the State's resources at my disposal, with the right to annihilate if necessary millions of dissatisfied people, and I will create for you from a bald, stuttering, impotent, mad Herod, a genius for all times and for all peoples!

The great general mounted the platform, took a sip of water, put his papers in front of him, cleaned his spectacles with his handkerchief, checked them against the light, cleaned them again, coughed slightly, put his spectacles on his nose, drank some more water and started to read.

'Comrades! The whole Soviet people in-spi-red by the his-tor-ical de-ci-sions of the Party Congress . . . etc . . . with seven-league boots . . . astronauts ploughing the furrows of space . . . milking and wool-shearing . . . millions of tons and billions of cubic metres . . .'

Then smoothly, as if through habit, he switched to the Imperialists, the Maoists and the Zionists, the enemy intelligence services and other disruptive elements; and then, equally smoothly, to the glorious Soviet Army, vigilantly watching over . . .

After two and a half hours, he neared his conclusion: 'And the gallant soldiers of our Red Banner District, and the gallant soldiers of the whole of our army, will spare no pain . . . or effort . . .'

Two and a half hours without once deviating from his prepared text, two and a half hours reading at dictation speed about things which we are all obliged to read every day in the editorials of Red Star. And that was all! Nothing else. No questions, no answers, not a personal word. Not a single word.

He collected up his papers, finished off the bottle of water, took off his spectacles, and departed to the accompaniment of thunderous applause.

Hundreds of officers, ready for anything, but not for this lunacy, were wildly clapping while trying not to catch one another's eyes, for the shame of it. Everybody was struck by the dullness, callousness, colourlessness, absolutely inhuman heartlessness of a stupid, corrupt, overfed official who was as fat as a bull.

'Where did such an idiot spring from?' I asked rhetorically after the first glass. Of course, I didn't expect an answer, knowing Yakubovskiy's background maybe better than he himself knew it. However, I was deeply mistaken, as we clearly knew only the visible part of the story.

'He distinguished himself at the battle for Moscow.'

This answer, totally unexpected, revolted me.

'At the battle for Moscow there was certainly no trace there of Yakubovskiy.'

'I'm not talking of 1941 – I mean 1953.'

'Get on with it then. Your audience is waiting for you!'

'Being one of Stalin's favourites, our old friend Yabukovskiy* had become commander of the Kantemirov court tank division. When the trouble started the commander of the Taman' Division was reluctant to raise his hand against the State Security people, and he was eventually put up against the same wall alongside them. But Yakubovskiy did not hesitate. He's always ready to carry out any order from Party or Government, but it all depends whose order comes first: if Beriya had given the order first, Yakubovskiy would happily have hanged the whole Politburo, but Beriya didn't give the first order . . . After that, his star rose even further as all the leaders were so grateful to him.'

'He may become a marshal, or Chief of the General Staff.'

'No, never. Men like him are given more delicate posts, governing peoples' democracies for instance.'

These prophetic words came true exactly three months later, when

---

*By means of this simple juggling with the letters, his surname becomes a thing of ridicule and approximates in meaning to 'Fuckerskiy'.

Army General Yakubovskiy was promoted to the rank of Marshal of the Soviet Union and given the post of Commander-in-Chief of the Combined Armed Forces of the Warsaw Treaty Powers. On the other hand, maybe the lieutenant who predicted this was not a prophet at all, but just had a contact somewhere at the base of the power pyramid, where everything is known already – the past and the future of all 250 million souls.

About two days after these changes in the upper echelons of the Soviet Army, our battalion was ordered to go urgently to Kiev 'to carry out the work of transferring equipment from the command points'.

We were taken to Yakubovskiy's country house (not the one where his wife lived, but his own personal house). A young aide-de-camp and about ten soldier-gardeners were directing the work there. There is, believe it or not, a famous horticultural training school in Moldavia, whose graduates are drafted into the army and appointed not as machine-gunners or snipers, but as gardeners at numerous military 'establishments'. That is actually how it is put on their military cards. Gardeners serve two years in the army, three years in the navy, and they acquire extremely high standards in their art.

Our work at Yakubovskiy's villa was somewhat unusual. We dug up the best trees according to the gardeners' instructions, wrapped their roots in sacking and then carried them to the airfield, where heavy aircraft of Military Transport Aviation, especially allotted for this operation, awaited us.

It is difficult to say what the point of all this was. Maybe Yakubovskiy or his wife did not want to be separated from familiar trees or perhaps, by removing them, he wanted to demonstrate his contempt for his successor, Lieutenant-General Kulikov, who was then a complete nonentity, and only later received the rank of colonel-general.

My deputy, Sergeant Kokhar', was more puzzled than the others by this air transportation of trees.

'Why the hell by air? Look what a long way it is from here to the airfield – the roots will get damaged. It would have been much simpler to give us a railway detachment since the branch line runs just beside the house, and it would have taken them only one night to reach Moscow. What a crazy idea – aircraft! A train would have been much more economical!'

New Ideas

The rumour that the Head of the Chief Political Directorate of the Soviet Army, Army General Epishev, suffers from the severest form of sclerosis has been persistently repeated. Sharp tongues maintain that, when he turns over a page, he promptly forgets completely what he has just read.

I don't usually believe rumours, simply because I know only too well where so many of them originate. But, subsequently, I had an opportunity to prove that, in this instance, the rumours were very accurate indeed.

Epishev mounted the platform, cleared his throat, drank some water and, in a dreary monotone, started to read about the historic decisions of the Party Congress (decisions which, incidentally, for some funny reason, never seem to bear fruit), concerning the care of our beloved peasant workers and the further development of agriculture, and the strengthening of our defences.

At the speaker's first words, the many thousand-strong audience lowered their heads over their notebooks and started compulsively to summarise the words of this man who occupied such a high position in the Party, the Army and the State. I too lowered my head and pretended to write. Personally, I have a deep antipathy to writing summaries and, in the present case, it was anyway completely absurd – first, because his speech would be published in all the military newspapers, and secondly because Epishev would certainly not tell us any more than is printed every day in *Red Star*.

Everything was going just as usual when suddenly the audience flinched. Epishev's vivid and memorable harangue had suddenly stopped in the middle of a word. Then he began to read it all over again from the very beginning. 'In the name of and at the request of . . .' he welcomed all those present, who answered him with a storm of applause. And everyone started to write down precisely what they had already noted down only a moment before.

After about five minutes, Epishev again stopped and began to read a new sentence, absolutely unconnected with the previous one. The

114

audience sensed, rather than understood, that the speaker was repeating himself, that he was giving the same examples which he had already given, and that he was shouting out the same slogans which he had shouted just a short while ago.

Suddenly, everybody guessed, everybody understood, what the matter was. Owing to the negligence of the researchers (why must they consume so much caviar?), Epishev had been given a speech written by somebody else, but *in duplicate*: beginning with the two first pages, followed by the second ones, and so on. In our army, no one reads his speech before he delivers it in public, and Epishev was simply following this unwritten regulation. The audience was somewhat perplexed. But the speaker, who was obviously not accustomed to noticing public reaction of any sort, continued his monotonous reading. In this way, he read forty pages instead of twenty.

After finishing his historic speech, the Head of the Chief Political Directorate returned in triumph to his place on the platform where the Minister of Defence, Marshal of the Soviet Union Comrade Grechko, was sitting with the other sclerotics and decrepit senile old bodies. None of them even so much as noticed what had just happened.

A cynical critic may not believe this story, but I have more than 2,000 witnesses; indeed, more than that, since many of them summarised this speech in their notebooks with two introductions, two conclusions and twenty repetitions, starting and ending in the middle of a word.

The most astonishing thing is that all this happened in 1969 at the time of the USSR young army officers' congress. A good ten years have passed since then and the young officers have become mature ones, but Comrade Epishev is still at his post. Untiringly he fights on. Boldly he instils the most advanced and effective methods throughout the broad masses of the army. He resolutely reflects, through the prism of the class struggle, the newest development of world history and brings to the army the unfading light of Leninist ideas.

The Group of Soviet Troops in Germany. Spring 1970. As one of a group of observers, I took part in 3rd Shock Army manoeuvres.

Determination

The Commander-in-Chief of the Group of Soviet Forces in Germany, Army General Kulikov, liked to control everything himself. Sometimes, he flew over the roads in a helicopter, watching Soviet military vehicles exceeding the speed limit. Sometimes, he lay in the bushes, eavesdropping on what his officers were talking about in their smoking room. But most of all he enjoyed putting on sports clothes and bicycling through Vünsdorf, especially in the evenings.

It was a Saturday evening and officers' pay day. All the beer houses were packed with staff officers, as everyone was taking the opportunity to drink as much of that lovely beer as he could, because when you returned to the Soviet Union where would you find such good beer?

The Commander-in-Chief flitted like a ghost past the brilliantly-lit windows of restaurants and beer houses, and anger welled up inside him. He could not understand the passion of Soviet officers for German beer. The sated can never comprehend those who are hungry, and he was always supplied with the best wines and had eight cooks, who are always in the Commander-in-Chief's baggage train ready to prepare the most recherché dishes for him. Like any true communist, Kulikov roundly condemned drunkenness and crusaded against it with great determination.

'Drinking, eh? Well, I'll soon show you, with your drinking!'

A sudden idea flashed across his mind, he smiled to himself, turned his bicycle round and rode back towards the Group of Soviet Troops Headquarters.

Without changing his clothes, he entered his study, thought for a moment and picked up a red telephone which had no selector dial. It was answered at once. The Commander-in-Chief blew into the receiver as was his wont and then imperiously ordered: 'The 215th independent sapper battalion – battle stations! Version 7, cypher 2323777.'

'Right, Comrade,' came the answer.

Half an hour later, the Commander-in-Chief was at the forest clearing where the sapper battalion was waiting for him. After a short consultation with the officers, the Commander-in-Chief finished with the

116

words, 'Give no warning before destruction, just destroy and be done with it. Forty-five minutes to reach Vünsdorf, twenty-five minutes to perform the operation!'

Bellowing wildly and much the worse for drink, officers were jumping out of the windows, and wild shadows rushing about in the darkness. Tank engines were roaring into life. The noise of crashing was horrible. Everything was falling about. 'It must be war!' was the only thought which coursed simultaneously through a thousand heads.

'I always said that everything would happen exactly as it did in 1941,' shouted a lieutenant-colonel whose left shoulder-strap had been torn off.

Heavy army bulldozers quickly destroyed the fragile glass pavilions, and within a moment the clean little town was filled with dust and the spicy smell of good German beer. By morning, the soft green lawns were all that was left of the former restaurants and beer-houses. The warm summer rain settled the dust, and there was nothing to remind anybody of the night raid by a sapper battalion.

That is how drunkenness in Vünsdorf was eradicated for good. The Head of the Political Directorate delightedly reported to the Chief Political Directorate and to the Central Committee about the remarkable determination of the new Commander-in-Chief in his fight against drunkenness.

Exactly one month later, on the next pay-day, the Chief of the Finance Directorate for that group of troops timidly entered the general's study and reported that there was no money in the till to issue the officers with their salaries.

'Well,' said the Commander-in-Chief, 'write a report and we shall bring the guilty ones to trial before the military tribunal! But what, by the way, is the real reason? Is it because the cashiers have been embezzling?'

'No,' the man from Finance explained shyly, 'we normally receive only a very insignificant part of the necessary money from Moscow. The bulk came from the military trade system – from the beer-houses, is what I mean. The deutschmarks were circulating, we gave them to the officers, they brought them to the beer-houses, we took them back and gave them back to the officers. But now there are no Soviet beer-houses in Vünsdorf, so all the officers are using the German ones, which are fifteen kilometres away. All the marks go there now instead. We have asked Moscow, but Moscow doesn't give us any money.'

The Commander-in-Chief ground his teeth. Then he grabbed the red telephone, the one without the selector dial.

This time the Commander-in-Chief did not himself go to the spot where the sapper battalion was assembling, but sent one of his aides-de-camp instead, with the order: 'Restore all the restaurants and beer-houses in Vünsdorf. You've got a maximum of a fortnight!'

Durov's Way

He pushed the remains of a herring backbone complete with tail up his arse and shouted in tones of mock pathos: 'Comrade officers, don't come near me. I'm a mermaid and I'm shy!'

It happened at a New Year party, during a competition for the most original fancy dress. Senior Lieutenant Durov possessed neither sharp reflexes nor a sense of humour, but when the competition was announced, Durov responded in a flash, if you'll forgive the pun. Apparently he had prepared his act beforehand. The Senior Lieutenant stripped off his guards uniform, and simply donned the aforementioned herring.

Everyone was deeply shocked, regardless of their state of intoxication and an age-old habit in the Soviet Army of never being astonished by anything. The chief of the regimental staff stood up and left the room, banging the door behind him. The other senior officers followed close on his heels.

At the first officers' meeting in the New Year, the commander of the 3rd Battalion tabled a motion that Senior Lieutenant Durov be brought before an officers' court of honour for insulting the regimental staff. This proposal was supported by the chief of staff, the technical deputy regimental commander, the head of artillery and all the battalion commanders, except the 1st, and all the company and battery commanders, except the commander of 3rd Company. There is no prize for guessing that the senior lieutenant served in the 3rd Company, which is part of the 1st Battalion. If a platoon commander is found guilty, it puts a stain on the company's reputation, as well as on the battalion and, of course, on the regiment itself, or, more precisely, on the regimental commander and his political deputy, since it indicates a weak programme of education. This was exactly why the flushed political deputy jumped up and shouted:

'To condemn people, comrades, is the easiest thing in the world but to educate them is far more difficult. Too hasty a decision by us and we could spoil the career of an officer with a bright future before him.'

'His future belongs in a madhouse,' remarked the reconnaissance company commander.

Durov sat in the first row, unconcernedly staring at the dark window. It was all the same to him. The only thing he wanted in the whole world was to have another drink. January had only begun and there was still a long time to wait until pay-day, cherished date the 13th. And they had long since stopped giving him vodka on tick in the small garrison restaurant. Everybody could get vodka on tick but not him: it was a kind of discrimination. He did not care a damn about anything being said at this officers' meeting, only deep down it was all somehow distasteful.

It was not, however, a matter of indifference to the regimental commander. The decision to bring a young officer before an officers' court of honour was a matter for him alone. If he said yes, it would mean that the officers of the regiment would band together and remove one of the stars from the senior lieutenant's shoulder-straps, and they might even remove the shoulder-straps altogether – then you can go anywhere you like, former senior lieutenant, there'll be no pension for you because you are too young, and no future either as you are already too old to begin life anew. The divisional commander, the army commander and the district commander will automatically ratify the decision of the officers' court because, otherwise, the one who approves the decision takes upon himself all future responsibility for faux pas committed by dipsomaniac senior lieutenants. If the regimental commander says no, then the senior lieutenant will go on being educated until the next incident, after which the question of the commander's decision again arises.

A decision in the affirmative is always a painful one to make for every Soviet commander because, basically, his own personal career depends on the extent to which he manages to reduce the number of offences and breaches of discipline, as well as on how well the soldiers make their beds and on how well the fences of the cantonment are kept painted. The actual registration of offences is not governed by the quantity of offences but by the quantity of penalties meted out. Discipline in the Soviet Army is exceptionally low. In many areas, the army amounts almost to an undisciplined herd, precisely because every commander is busy struggling for his own survival. The victor in this endless struggle will be the one who, in general, never punishes his soldiers and officers, irrespective of the kind of offences they have committed. The only department which enforces some form of discipline is the Military Commandant's Office and that is only because its allotted task is to catch any soldiers and officers who might fall within its grasp. The Commandatura offices have another way of operating and a completely different system. Everything there is the other way round. They are anxious to detect as many infringements and breaches

119

as possible. But, generally, the offices of the Commandatura operate outside military cantonments: in towns, at railway stations and at airports. It is their activities which create the illusion of discipline and order, but when all is said and done it is only an illusion.

The regimental commander had long been awaiting an opportunity to exercise his power, but this particular case was too risky. Discipline in the regiment had anyway already fallen to the lowest possible ebb and to start the new year with such a decision would have been ill-advised. Just suppose something really serious happened tomorrow which it would be impossible to whitewash or hush up. Then what? Then somebody would have to be punished and there would already be two infringements on the statistics. Meanwhile, in other regiments everything would be peace and light.

The commander stood up. To go against the almost unanimous decision of the other officers was not a good idea either, so he said grimly, 'Let's not be hasty: we must think it over.'

And they had to think it over for a very long time indeed.

A week later, the chief of staff telephoned the regimental commander and asked him immediately to forward the papers of his best platoon commander with a view to appointing the latter as a company commander in the neighbouring regiment. In ten minutes flat, the political deputy commander of the 1st Battalion and that of the 3rd Company were in the regimental commander's study.

'Comrade Officers, I have been commanded to send the best of our platoon commanders to the neighbouring regiment to be promoted. I think that Senior Lieutenant Durov will fill the bill. Of course, he does make slips from time to time, but who does not? I think he has fully realised his guilt and that this new responsibility will only help him. Is that not so? Trust does great things for people. With responsibility for a whole company, he will not have time to get drunk. One thing is clear, we must give the man a chance, otherwise he will be pecked to death. Just try telling a man every single day that he is a swine and he will soon start to grunt like a pig!'

The company commander wrote a brilliant character reference for Durov. The battalion commander added: 'I completely endorse these conclusions. Signed Commander of the First Tank Battalion, Guards Lieutenant-Colonel Nesnosnyy.' The regimental commander also agreed: 'Deserves to be nominated for the post of commander of a tank company. Signed Commander of the 210th Guards Tank Regiment, awarded the orders of Bogdan Khmel'nitskiy and Aleksandr Nevskiy, the Port-Arturskiy Regiment, Guards Colonel Zavalishin!'

The political deputy wrote a separate reference relating to Durov's

120

moral and political qualities: 'Party activist, sportsman, social worker,' and everything else appropriate in such circumstances.

The papers went on their way to divisional staff where they were approved by the commander of the division.

'I've found a real winner to be the commander of the fifth company of the 299th regiment. He's not just an officer but pure gold. A falcon. He's an experienced activist, a sportsman and a social worker. You'll be grateful to me for the rest of your days.'

'And may I ask, Comrade General, who this man is?'

'Senior Lieutenant, what was his name . . . Yes . . . Durov . . .'

The Colonel turned pale.

'Are you joking, Comrade General?'

'Why? What's the matter?'

'But I know this Durov like the back of my hand, we live in the same mess. And not only me, but the whole division knows him though they don't live in the same mess with him.'

'Wait, just a moment, it isn't the same Durov who got so drunk that he vomited his insides out at the 7th of November parade?'

'That's the one, Comrade General, and remember also how he once ruined a tank engine, this very same Durov?'

'Well! That's Zavalishin for you, the scoundrel. He must have decided to pull a fast one. But just you wait, I'll make you dance for your pains.'

'Well, Zavalishin, we've confirmed your little falcon as company commander.'

'Thank you, Comrade General.'

'Do you think he'll be able to cope?'

'He's proved his worth, he'll be okay.'

'But Zavalishin, all is not well with discipline at your place, is it? Eh? What?'

'We are doing our best, Comrade General. We didn't start this year too badly and we hope to continue in the same vein.'

'Do you know what occurred to us at Staff HQ? In order not to deprive you of one of your best officers, we decided in the circumstances to leave this excellent fellow, Durov, with your regiment, as commander of the 3rd Company. The neighbouring regiment is in need of a company commander, so we shall give them the present commander of your 3rd Company, and replace him by this same Durov. Let him remain in your regiment. Let him command a company and help to strengthen discipline there.'

And then, suddenly changing his good-humoured banter to those steely tones employed sometimes by all commanders, the divisional commander announced bluntly: 'The order relating to the switch-over of the said officers was signed today.'

And that is how Guards Senior Lieutenant Durov became commander of the 1st Battalion's 3rd Company of the 210th Guards Tank Regiment. There were practically no changes at all in his lifestyle. The only thing was that his income increased and so consequently did his drinking. Nothing could now be said about the court of honour – since his promotion in itself indicated confidence in him on the part of his superiors and forgiveness of all past sins. Neither the regimental commander, nor his political deputy, nor the battalion commander could possibly complain about Durov or take any steps towards his demotion, because each of them in turn had written such a brilliant character reference. Unquestionably, they must have expected their ruse to be discovered eventually, but they could never have thought that it would happen so soon. If the truth had come to light in, say, a week's time, after Durov's transfer, the commanders of the 210th could have put their hands on their hearts and sworn that to the best of their knowledge he was a good man and that surely something had suddenly gone wrong with him. Generally speaking, of course, subterfuges of this kind produce no complications when an officer is transferred to another town or even to another army or division. There is a cast-iron law: once the order is signed, it's done with! Of course Colonel Zavalishin was well acquainted with all these subtleties, he just did not have the time to wait for another opportunity to transfer Durov to another division. He had to move quickly and take a risk. As things turned out, he risked and lost.

With the appearance of its new commander, discipline in the 3rd Company broke down altogether. Battle-training and battle-preparedness also fell off sharply. The divisional commander, in no mind to forgive and forget what had happened, always hurried to inspect the 3rd Company whenever he visited the 210th Regiment, after which he invariably summoned the regimental and battalion commanders and had long talks with them. He had decided to teach them a lesson. In the end, of course, he would have to remove Durov from the company but for the time being he was in no hurry to do so, and any suggestions about Durov's replacement were invariably dismissed by the divisional commander.

The divisional commander was away on leave and his duties were being performed by his deputy, who had recently arrived from Egypt. The deputy commander had not yet had time to get to know the ropes.

Zavalishin and the battalion commander were both on the prowl, like caged tigers. The absence of the divisional commander must be quickly and resolutely exploited. Durov must be urgently disposed of. Where to was immaterial – Syria or Hungary, or the Transbaikal region or the far north; promotion or demotion – no matter.

After he had been presented with a dozen bottles of brandy, the chief of the divisional cadres department came up with a piece of advice: Send him to the Academy.

Brilliant character references were again concocted for this best of all company commanders in the 210th Guards Tank Regiment. They were approved by the divisional commander's deputy and urgently despatched to Moscow.

There were only six character references in Durov's personal file: two written at the time of his graduation from military school, two stating that he was the best platoon commander in the regiment, and two stating that he was now the best company commander in the same regiment. The references written at the military school were pale and inconsequential, neither fish, nor fowl nor good red meat (at school he simply had no opportunity to reveal himself as an alcoholic because an officer-cadet's pay is too low), but all the rest of the references were simply brilliant. Within a week, Durov was summoned to Moscow to sit an extrance examination for the Armoured Troops Academy.

'If he fails to get in,' said the regimental commander, biting his nails nervously, 'the divisional commander will have us for breakfast.'

'No, he won't get in, not that bloody alcoholic. How could he?'

'But why not? Maybe he will, idiots are invariably lucky. In any academy, idiots are given preference.'

'We've blundered . . . and how!'

'What do you mean?'

'It's time he was made a captain, and of course we did nothing about it. How can you make a captain out of a man like him? But in the Academy they're bound to harp on about it. Why, they will ask, when you have a company commander with such a distinguished service record, did you not promote him to captain long ago?'

The very next day, a recommendation to confer the rank of captain upon that excellent commander of a tank company, Senior Lieutenant Durov, was urgently despatched to Moscow.

Durov joined the Academy and a month later was promoted to Guards Captain. His unexpected rise could not leave even Durov unimpressed. The psychological shock produced by his elevation suddenly woke in him a superiority complex. He did not stop his drinking, but he did considerably reduce his activity in that direction.

Now, he only drank alone, not so much out of any consideration for safety as out of contempt for his comrades.

His scant intellect never gave birth to a single original idea but he compensated for that by cramming and by learning the academic text books off by heart, thus staggering his professors by the exactness with which he reiterated the thoughts once expressed by these same professors, who had written the books in the first place.

He was held up as an example of a conscientious, competent and contemporary officer. After three years' study he graduated from the Academy with honours (it must here be stated that, to achieve this in the command faculty of the Armoured Troops Academy, one does not need to be very clever; a degree of application is called for and nothing more).

After graduation, Durov duly received the next military rank of major, by order of the Defence Minister himself. Having graduated with honours, he had the right to choose his posting and Durov chose his own regiment.

By order of the Minister of Defence, Guards Major Durov was appointed deputy commander of the 210th Guards Tank Regiment, that same regiment, in which only three and a half years previously, he had merely been the commander of the worst tank platoon. As well as all regimental majors, all nine lieutenant-colonels of the regiment were also subordinate to him, including the chief of staff, the chief of anti-aircraft defence, the chief of the rear column, the technical deputy commander, the commander's deputy and four battalion commanders.

The system of conferring ranks in the Soviet Army differs in many respects from that adopted in other armies. When a vacancy arises, it is not filled by an officer who is senior in rank, with prolonged good service, experience or official position, but by someone who, in the high command's opinion, is most suitable. One consequence of this policy is that high-ranking officers often find themselves directly subordinate to lower-ranking officers.

To quote one example, after the death of Marshal Grechko, Colonel-General Ustinov was appointed to the post of Minister of Defence. Simultaneously with his appointment, Ustinov received the next military rank, that of army general, and all other army generals, marshals and chief marshals of the other arms of the service, even Marshals of the Soviet Union Kulikov, Ogarkov, Sokolov, Batitskiy, Moskalenko and Admiral of the Soviet Fleet Gorshkov, all found themselves directly subordinate to Ustinov.

This system has one unquestionable advantage, which is that it allows 'our people' to be pushed forward without consideration for any laws or regulations. 'In our opinion, this captain is the most capable and he should be put in charge of all the majors.'

Position has an overwhelming advantage over rank. For instance, Major-General Salmanov, Commander of the Kiev Military District, enjoys incomparably greater authority than any colonel-general of a second-rate district like the Ural or Odessa Districts. And a major, who is also the regimental commander's deputy, has many more privileges than a lieutenant-colonel who is the commander of a battalion.

The conferring of ranks depends on the post occupied, on long service and on relations with the higher authority. Army General Ogarkov received the rank of Marshal of the Soviet Union on the same day that he became Chief of the General Staff, while his predecessor, Army General Kulikov, only managed to become a Marshal when he left this same post!

To revert to Durov, when the latter returned to his old regiment, the regimental commander, Colonel Zavalishin, had already retired and been replaced by a young lieutenant-colonel from the Chinese frontier. The majority of the officers, however, including the first battalion's commander, Lieutenant-Colonel Nesnosnyy, still remained in their posts.

Yet another entirely objective factor had influenced Durov's rise. During the second half of the 1960s, frontline officers who, after the war, could not make a way for themselves at the Academy reached the peak of their service career at battalion level. They could not be promoted any higher as they had not graduated from the Academy, and to send them to the Academy now would be inexpedient as they were too old. There was also no reason to lower their ranks as all of them were experienced, worthy and disciplined campaigners, while to retire them was also impossible because, after Khrushchev's reforms, the army was terribly short of officers.

The front-line officers had a tight hold at battalion level on the posts of battalion commander and battalion deputy chief of staff, and they thus created a blockage on the promotion ladder. On the one hand, it was absolutely impossible to promote young officers above company level, and on the other hand, there were no replacements for officers retiring at regimental level. That is why many young officers, who managed to join the Academy from company level, returned at regimental level, thus jumping two rungs on the promotion ladder, often those of deputy battalion commander and battalion commander. This was a general phenomenon.

Durov himself was extremely vindictive. He remembered all those who had suggested censuring him before an officers' court of honour, though the one man who spoke out on his behalf also felt the sharp edge of his tongue. He found fault with the smallest, most insignificant detail and berated the guilty party with intolerable abuse. Durov entered without mercy any error committed by any officer in the officer's personal file, thus destroying that officer's career and deciding his fate for good.

Every officer changed his style, trying not to give Durov any cause to find fault. And it was in this way that the fame of Durov came to spread among higher-ranking officers as an exacting commander of principle. It was not surprising, therefore, that in a couple of years, while he was still only a major, he was given command of a regiment and that, only one year later, as the best of the regimental commanders of our division, he was sent to Syria in the capacity of military adviser to the commander of a Syrian tank division.

I knew Durov for many years and had to serve under his command. I met many officers who knew him at all stages of his career. Those small unwinking snake's eyes and that low threatening whisper still haunt me to this day in my worst dreams.

He had not the slightest idea about army problems or the possibilities of the army's development. However, those dogmas which he had learnt by heart were completely unshakable. The expression of any opinions differing from those expressed in text books written ten years before Durov entered the Academy of Armoured Troops was not only useless but even dangerous.

The way he behaved towards his subordinates could not be called uncultured, it was simply ill-mannered boorishness. We were astonished that he never read any books. We, his subordinates, saw in him only a combination of cruelty, intolerance and bestiality. I have never met anyone who served under his command who had a different opinion of him. But, to the powers-that-be, he was a model of how one's duty should be performed.

He was lucky: throughout the years of his stay in Syria he was never called upon to demonstrate his qualities as a commander in any battle with the enemy. After Syria, Durov's fortunes rocketed. I would not be surprised if, one fine day, I read in the newspaper that Colonel-General Durov has been appointed Commander of the Moscow Military District. That's just the place for the likes of him. They like his sort there, and then again perhaps I underestimate him? Maybe men of his ilk should be promoted higher still?

126

As a result of the unfortunate experience of the Middle Eastern adventure, the Soviet Army was hurled into the task of building aircraft shelters in the winter of 1967–68. These are my impressions of the Soviet combat airforce.

The Brick Bomber

Good luck fell from the sky.

An American B-29 strategic bomber made a forced landing on Soviet soil. The bomber had been taking part in an air raid against our common enemy, Japan, and after getting shot up in battle somehow managed with great difficulty to reach the nearest airfield – Baranovskiy near Ussuriysk. The damage was superficial – its wings had been pierced in several places by machine-gun fire from a Japanese fighter, as a result of which the bomber had lost a lot of fuel. The commander had the choice of either bringing the bomber down in the ocean, thus dooming the crew to certain death, or trying to reach a faithful ally, repairing the holes, refuelling the bomber and, in a couple of days, resuming bombing Japan. The captain chose the second alternative. The bomber is worth a fortune, he reasoned, the damage is very slight. The crew is safe, and very experienced, and in war this is probably the most important thing. Why should I let such a crew be eaten by sharks while there is an ally right at hand? That is how the best strategic bomber in the world landed upon Soviet territory.

The news covered the distance from Ussuriysk to the Kremlin, which is all of 10,000 kilometres, clearing all bureaucratic barriers in its path, in a matter of minutes. The event was reported to Josif Vissarionovich Stalin himself while he was in a meeting. Stalin thought for a moment then, having asked only the Politburo members to remain, he passed the news on to them and, with a cunning smile on his face, asked them to give their opinions.

The opinion was unanimous: to detain the bomber for a week under any pretext so as to enable specialists to acquaint themselves with the structure.

'And what if we do not return the bomber at all to our allies?' asked the Great Leader and Teacher, drawing on his pipe.

'The allies will be offended, Comrade Stalin,' Molotov objected cautiously.

'They may stop sending us supplies,' added Kaganovich. 'Then what shall we do without their Studebaker lorries?'

That splendid American army lorry was universally acknowledged as the best military vehicle by everybody from common soldier to marshal. The famous Russian Katyusha BM 13s were mounted exclusively on these American vehicles. The Soviet artillery was the mightiest in the world but its prime mover and ammunition transporter was that same American Studebaker. And, in addition to lorries, the allies supplied much else besides which was very important for the Soviet Army, including means of communication and jeeps, Aircobra fighters, armoured personnel carriers and tanks.

The supply could be stopped at any moment and, with that fact very much in mind, all the Politburo members fell to thinking. Very cautiously, everybody declared themselves against the proposition not to return the bomber. Only Beriya sat silent, trying to guess which way the Great Teacher's mind was inclining.

But the Teacher scoffed at the apprehensions of the Bureau and declared: 'As it is, we shall soon strangle Germany and what will be our next objective? How can we turn against England and America without a strategic bomber? The allies will put up with it,' he added, sucking his pipe. 'They will be a bit agitated for a while and then forget all about it. The bomber must be copied exactly, alike as two peas, and it must fly within the year.'

Beriya energetically supported Stalin while the other members of the Political Bureau readily agreed. They all knew only too well that the basic principle of their Leader and Teacher was that friends and allies should be treated like a woman – the more you beat her, the more she loves you. But every one of them doubted strongly in his heart that the allies would put up with it.

But the allies did put up with it. The American crew was returned, but not the best bomber in the world. The Soviet side did not even bother to invent any kind of explanation. We are not going to return it – full stop. Lease-lend supplies continued as usual because American diplomats were accustomed to discussing problems which arose without regard for questions of military supplies.

A. N. Tupolev, the best Soviet aircraft designer, was put in charge of the copying team and the new Soviet strategic bomber was named, after him, the later TU-4. A further sixty-four design bureaux and scientific research institutes joined in, copying the engines, the fuel and other materials used in the B-29's construction, as well as all its systems of navigation, sighting, internal and external communication network and much else besides. Co-ordination of all the work was entrusted to a member of the Political Bureau, Comrade Lavrenity Pavlovich Beriya, and the aircraft designer, Yakovlev, was appointed technical consultant. The latter understood Stalin better than anyone else and he knew how to please him.

A huge new workshop was hurriedly built at the restored aircraft factory in Vorohekh where, incidentally, twenty-two years later, the unsuccessful attempt to copy the Concorde was made.

The B-29 was dismantled into thousands of the smallest possible parts, which were distributed among the various ministries, departments, design bureaux and scientific research institutes with the explicit command to copy each detail, aggregate or device and then to embark upon its mass-production within ten months.

The bomber probably received the unfortunate nickname, 'The Brick Bomber', owing to all these small parts and mechanisms being sent all over the Soviet Union. Many years later, in his book *The Aim of Life*, Yakovlev said that in 1945-46 we somehow missed out on the development of jet-propulsion. And, no doubt owing to his inborn modesty, Yakovlev completely forgot to explain why this happened. This was precisely the time when dear Comrades Yakovlev, Beriya and Tupolev were up to their necks creating the 'Brick'. Well might he have missed anything else. 'It must be ready to fly in a year's time' – this was all that Comrade Yakovlev remembered even while he slept.

Indeed, after the TU-4, all unsuccessful aircraft, especially those copied from foreign models, were unofficially nicknamed 'Bricks'. The most famous is, of course, the TU-144 Koncordskiy. But, on that occasion, there was no actual model to hand, only a few documents. Maybe also its failure was due to the absence of Lavrentiy Pavlovich's iron fist, without which all technical progress withered.

Difficulties arose from the very beginning of the copying process. To begin with, the use of the metric system of measuring was quite out of the question. If the weight of each rivet is only ten milligrammes less than it should be, it could lead to the whole structure's durability being diminished whereas, if the weight is just a bit greater, it could adversely influence the weight of the whole aircraft. Tupolev knew full well that if the aircraft was to be copied it must be copied in every detail, down to the last rivet, screw, nut and bolt.

Soviet trade representatives in Canada, England and the USA started to buy up measuring equipment in small quantities in order not to create any suspicion. And the retraining of thousands of engineers, technicians and workers, to switch over to calculating in inches, feet and pounds, began urgently.*

*This system of measurement is still used in the Soviet Army.

The training of thousands of crews and tens of thousands of ground staff, engineering and technical personnel for the hundreds of future new bombers began with the same urgency.

How many gallons of fuel would be needed at the normal rate of fuel consumption with no wind for a thousand-mile flight at a height of 30,000 feet? Elementary problems of this kind nonplussed not only the experienced aces, who had been through the whole war, but also the professors of the Aviation Academy.

Pressure in the piping is twelve pounds per square inch – is that a lot or a little?

It may not be so difficult for American and English specialists, accustomed as they are to operating with two different systems of measurement, but for the Soviet specialists it was problem number one. Thousands of mistakes were made and every one of them was mercilessly punished.

While the new system of measurement was becoming accepted in the Soviet aviation industry as a whole, another no less complicated problem emerged, that of keeping the secret, because in the eyes of the KGB anyone who displayed any knowledge of English measuring systems might easily be a potential carrier of State secrets to the enemy.

Everybody who saw Tupolev at that time remarked upon his gaiety and rather childlike, carefree attitude. Apparently, the old man was tormented by jealousy. He loved and yet he detested the B-29 and he tried to hide it from the others. The mechanical work of copying was sickening him and he concealed the fact under a mask of indifference. Tupolev had no problems then, solving with ease even the most complicated.

A little hole was found on the left wing of the aircraft. No aerodynamics or durability expert had the slightest idea what the hell it was for. There was no tube or wire attached to it and there was no equivalent hole in the right wing. The opinion of a commission of experts was that the little hole had been bored by a factory drill at the same time as the other holes for the rivets. So, what to do? Most probably, the hole had been drilled by mistake, and later no one had bothered to fill it in as it was much too small. The chief designer was asked his opinion.

'Do the Americans have it?'

'Yes.'

'So why the hell are you asking me? Weren't we ordered to make them absolutely identical! Alike as two peas?'

So, for that reason, a very small hole indeed, made with the thinnest possible drill, appeared on the left wing of all the TU-4 strategic bombers.

130

Here's a narrow pipe, through which one can crawl on all fours the whole length of the aircraft, and it has been painted light green (some design bureau or other struggled for a very long time in an attempt to copy it exactly) but, at its very end, several metres have been painted white. Maybe some soldier simply did not have enough paint. But the order was to copy it exactly, which is why all the Soviet bombers are the same colour as the American one. It was calculated exactly how much green paint there was and how much white paint. Later, this ratio was included in all instruction books on how to paint the interior of the bomber.

Meanwhile, another two B-29s made forced landings on Soviet territory. It was discovered that there was no hole in their wings, while the paint on one of them was light green and that on the other white. The chief designer was again asked what to do. But, once again, Tupolev had no problem. He had been ordered to copy the bomber which had landed first, and there were no orders concerning the others. So just go on copying!

It was later discovered, from the factory number, that the aircraft which had landed first had been built earlier than those which landed subsequently. It was therefore decided to follow the first model without a single deviation. Gradually, the number of problems started to decrease. Everybody got accustomed to the chief designer's standard answer, to do everything as it was on the first American aircraft. No one asked questions anymore. A little anecdote grew up. The question was, what kind of stars should be put on the mass-produced aircraft – white American stars or red Soviet ones? It was this question that completely foxed Tupolev. If you put white American stars, you risk being shot as an enemy of the people. And, if you put red Soviet ones, first it will not be a copy, and second maybe the Supreme Commander-in-Chief wishes to use the bombers against America, England or China and therefore keep the American markings. The question about the stars was the only one which Tupolev ever addressed to Beriya throughout the whole period of copying, pointing out to him that this was not a designer's business. Beriya was equally nonplussed. He was not accustomed to asking Stalin questions. He had risen to the very top precisely because, like any dog, he could anticipate the wishes of his master.

People say that Beriya told Stalin about the stars as if it was a funny story and that by the way in which Stalin laughed at the joke Beriya knew unerringly which stars should be used. This last problem was solved and mass-production started.

A 'golden rain' fell upon all those who had taken part in the creation of the 'Brick Bomber'. Ninety-seven prizes were distributed over a short period of time 'for the development of new battle technology'. In addition to which Beriya, Tupolev and Yakovlev all received the Order of Lenin.

Part Four

Tension was building up in Czechoslovakia. Because of this, our training division held an extra pre-term graduation of students. They were replaced by other cadets in a pre-call up age group. The word 'training' disappeared from the division's title and henceforth it was designated only as the Novograd-Volynsk Motor-Rifle Division. The Ukraine. Beginning of summer 1968.

Preparation

The devil only knew what was going on with the armoured troop carriers. The standard allocations for every motor-rifle regiment should be 31 tanks, 6 howitzers, 18 mortars and 103 armoured personnel carriers. Tanks, howitzers and mortars were all in order, but there was only a total of 40 armoured personnel carriers. Trouble was obviously in the air. Something similar had happened in brotherly Hungary in 1956 and was obviously about to happen in brotherly Czechoslovakia. It was obvious that we would have to help. But how could we with such a shortage of basic armament such as armoured personnel carriers in our motor-rifle regiment?

After our third glass together, I put this question to a captain whom I had known at military school and who now occupied the post of Assistant Chief of Staff for Mobilisation. The captain regarded me attentively and, it seemed to me at the time, a trifle foxily, and then said vaguely, 'Hm . . . m,' filled up our glasses, ate a piece of cucumber and suddenly asked:

'But do you know why we've got any at all in our regiment?'

'What an odd question. We've got them because they're prescribed under our allocation, the only thing is that there aren't enough of them to go round.'

'We've got them in our regiment because once a year they take part in a parade at Kiev. Thirty-six of them are needed in the parade and that's why our regiment has them. The other four are just in reserve.'

Apparently the captain rightly felt that he had not satisfactorily dealt with my question, so he asked me another leading question.

'Do you know how many motor-rifle regiments there are in our district?'

'Of course not!'

'But approximately. Just try to guess without being too exact.'

'Well, if only approximately . . . First there's a tank army and two all-arms armies. That makes . . . ah . . . ah . . . six tank divisions and eight to ten motor-rifle divisions.'

'Right!'

'That makes twenty-six to twenty-eight tank regiments and thirty to thirty-six motor-rifle regiments.'

'Right again. So then, of all the district's motor-rifle regiments, out of all thirty to thirty-six, only our regiment has forty armoured personnel carriers, and all the others haven't got a single one.'

'Go on, that's a lie,' I blurted out.

'I'm not lying.'

I was certain that the captain knew his job, and I knew he wasn't lying. I also knew for certain that two other regiments in our division had no armoured personnel carriers. But I did not want to believe that our regiment was the only one in the whole district which had any at all.

'Then where are they?' I finally asked. 'In Egypt? Or, to be more exact, in Israel?'

'Yes, there are some there but not very many. Israel captured a lot of tanks and artillery but no armoured personnel carriers.'

'But where are they then? Were they given to the Warsaw Treaty Powers?'

'Yes, but very few. Czechoslovakia, which receives nearly all its armament from us, still produces her own armoured personnel carriers, to her own standard specifications, and supplies them to the Germans and the Poles, while the Rumanians, because they're so poverty-stricken, usually transport their motor-infantry in ordinary lorries.'

'But when all's said and done, where are ours then?'

'Nowhere!' He looked at me searchingly and repeated 'Nowhere. They don't exist!'

'But how so?'

'Just like that. How many of them did we produce before or during the war? Not one – not a single one. Isn't that so? All the armoured personnel carriers were American.'

'That's right,' I agreed. 'M-3s they were called, half-tracked, and there were some others with wheels and they were American too.'

'And now let me ask you another question. How many types of armoured personnel carriers have we produced throughout the whole of our history?'

'Lots! Let me see. There were the BTR-40 and BRDM.'

'No, we can't count those, they were only reconnaissance machines and not infantry ones.'

'Of course,' I agreed. 'We won't count them.'

'We don't count the BTR-50 either.'

No, that armoured personnel carrier could not be included in our calculation. It is a splendid machine, but apparently much too good for us.

There is only one of them in each regiment and then only for the use of the regimental commander himself. The chief of the regimental staff and the commander of the artillery and regimental reconnaissance are considered as part of the hierarchy, but even in battle they have to travel on ordinary lorries. The BTR-50 is solely for the regimental commander, so it cannot be considered as an infantry armoured personnel carrier. In fact, one regiment of the Taman division was fully supplied with the BTR-50P, but they were only for parades. The whole army knows that this regiment has never taken part in any real manoeuvres but only in peep-shows, like all other 'court' divisions.

'We can't count the BMP either,' continued the captain. 'For a start, it has only recently appeared and second the BMP is not the BTR and its existence does not solve the problems of transporting infantry during battle. The BMPs were supplied only to some selected, privileged infantry units. What about the others, the majority of the ones who'll actually decide the outcome of any war? What will we transport them on during the war? . . . So then, how many types of armoured personnel carriers have we actually created throughout our whole history?' he repeated his question.

'Two,' I answered, and blushed, 'The BTR-152 and BTR-60P.'

'You do know, of course, what kind of armoured personnel carriers they are?'

Unfortunately, I did know that the BTR-152 was the very first Soviet armoured personnel carrier. It was a simple lorry, a ZIS-152 with armoured plating fixed on top. The BTR-152 was a copy of that splendid American lorry, the Studebaker. The copy, as distinct from the original, was not a success and, after another five tons of armour had been added, it looked like anything on earth but a battle machine. It was impracticable, it lacked manoeuvreability and speed, and had no armoured protection. In addition it was produced by the same factory which produced the ZIS-151. And this factory has many problems. Either brotherly China needs machines, or brotherly Indonesia, or brotherly Korea, or brotherly Albania, and we need machines ourselves either for the undeveloped areas or for the Bratsk Hydro Electric Station.

The second Soviet armoured personnel carrier, the BTR-60P, was developed to replace the first one, though there was really nothing to replace as the overwhelming majority of the Soviet divisions only possessed them in theory anyway. This new armoured personnel carrier had the shape of a coffin and it was never known by any other name except the 'coffin on wheels'.

Owing to the shortage of diesel fuel in the country the BTR-60P, like its predecessor, was powered by petrol and as a result burned in battle with an especially bright flame. But diesel fuel was not the only problem – when it was built the country did not possess a single really strong and reliable petrol engine, so two weak engines from the normal collective farm lorry, the GAZ-51, were installed in the BTR-60P. So, it began life with two engines, two clutches, two transmissions, two distributors, four transmission boxes, two starters and two distributor and contact-breaker units. Of course, all these mechanisms were neither reliable nor synchronised, and when the synchronisation of the two engines broke down, which happened every day, one of the engines started to throttle the other. So, one of the engines had to be urgently disconnected, and then the 'coffin on wheels', weighing twelve tons, was hardly able to move on the one 90 horsepower engine.

The letter P in the BTR-60P stands for amphibious. And, although the coffin's shape gives it some buoyancy, even so it floats only in theory. The armoured personnel carrier goes bravely into the water and doesn't swim too badly, but it can hardly ever get out of the water under its own steam since its weak engines can only turn either the wheels or the screw propeller, but not both simultaneously. As it leaves the water, the propeller screw is no longer effective in the shallows, and the wheels don't have sufficient grip on the ground. If the engines did operate simultaneously, it might somehow be able to clamber out but, as it is, when faced with even a small river the whole of the infantry remains without means of transport and reserve supplies.

The BTR-60P is produced by the Gorkiy car factory, which, as well as its own army, must also supply the whole of the national economy and all the Soviet bureaucrats with personal cars. In addition, all Soviet taxi-cabs without exception are produced exclusively by the same works, plus supplies for brotherly Egypt, brotherly Chile, brotherly Sudan, brotherly Somalia and many more besides. And there is still only one Gorkiy works!

'So we should build more car works!'

At this remark he smiled, but not without a certain malice.

'We would if we could but, as it is, we are compelled to buy from Italy! Up to now, we have not built one single automobile factory ourselves.'

I was forced to agree with him. True, I had only visited a Soviet car works once in my life but it had produced a very bad impression on me. Its equipment had been built in America in 1927 and sold to Germany, where throughout the whole pre-war period as well as during the war it had been used mercilessly, to the point of exhaustion. In 1945, this completely worn out and damaged equipment was transported to the Soviet Union where construction of Moskvich cars started. This Moskvich factory does not anticipate replacing its equipment before the year

2000. And what will really happen then remains to be seen! But it is highly probable that yet one more record will be established in the Soviet Union.

'But how, Captain, shall we be able to save Czechoslovakia?'

'By pure cheek, as usual! Of course we've got armoured personnel carriers in the front-line troops, in the GDR, in Poland and in the frontier districts. But here, in the rear, in the second and third echelons, we must just make a lot of noise and generally demonstrate our readiness.'

'But what if the war does really start? What if the Americans really do intervene?'

'Don't worry! Nobody will ever intervene. They'll put up with anything. The more impudent we get, the more patient they will be. Of course they'll hurl stones at our embassies but later they'll repair everything at their own expense, down to the very last penny, and then the usual improvement in international relations will start and in a week's time everything will be forgotten. It is in their government's interest to allow things to be forgotten as soon as possible. Well, let's have one last drink and that's that. Mobilisation will start soon.'

The 1968 mobilisation went on openly without any attempt at camouflage. First, the press announced large-scale exercises, then the call-up of the reservists followed and, when the exercises were over, the reservists remained in the army.

Large-scale exercises involving the strategic rocket troops were carried out over some months, then there were naval exercises, and exercises for anti-aircraft defence and of the military air force, as well as countless exercises for the armies and divisions of the land forces. Then followed training of liaison forces, during which all elements connected with the direction of a gigantic army were checked; and there was training of rear forces, during which thousands of tons of ammunition and tens of thousands of tons of fuel were moved to the western frontiers; and finally command-staff training took place on Czech territory, and all commanders down to battalion and, in some cases, company level studied their tasks actually in situ, in the event of an invasion. All this looked very impressive from the outside. But from the inside it looked rather different.

The process of complete mobilisation of any army consists firstly in bringing the existing units, sub-units and formations up to strength, secondly in forming new ones, and thirdly in their training and knitting together into overall battle preparedness.

The process of bringing our division up to strength proceeded generally without any special difficulties. In peacetime, most Soviet divisions have a reduced personnel, for instance each artillery crew, instead of seven men, has only two – the commander and the gun-layer – and on mobilisation the vacancies are filled by reservists. Even in those cases where they have not even served in the army for ten years and have forgotten absolutely everything – after a short training period, they are fully prepared for war. The same thing happens with the infantry, tank-men, sappers, etc. In a far worse position, at times of mobilisation, are the units of liaison, air defence missiles, anti-tank rockets, reconnaissance and chemical warfare. After a full four months of training, all these units were still not ready for battle.

In official terminology, as we have seen, divisions with reduced personnel are called *Kadrirovannye*. And this really is a fact, especially for units where the percentage of reservists is very high. For instance, in our tank battalion there were three men to every tank instead of four – the loader was missing. When he was added to the crew, the tank promptly became ready for battle. In all remaining tank battalions – and there are seven of them in every motor-rifle division – there was only one man in each tank – the driver. There were only twelve men in a company: the commander of the company, a captain and ten drivers. At mobilisation all the missing members, gunners, loaders, tank commanders, even the company sergeant-major and the platoon commanders, came from the reservists. All except the platoon commanders had served in tank units five or ten years previously, sometimes in other types of tanks. But the platoon commanders had never served anywhere before and knew nothing, not only about tanks and contemporary techniques and tactics, but about the army in general. The platoon commanders are all former students, who once upon a time in some civilian institution attended a course of lectures on military questions and on graduating received the rank of reserve junior lieutenant.

After four months of intensive training, only one tank battalion in seven, the one which had reservists only as loaders, was accepted as being ready for battle. If war had started then, the division would not, of course, have had four months for training, but only one to two weeks maximum. It would have been thrown into battle and would have been destroyed. And no wonder, since only one out of every seven battalions would be fighting fit. Now just imagine a division without reconnaissance, without liaison, without a communications network and without anti-aircraft and anti-tank rockets!

But the biggest problems lay with the infantry – not only because in peacetime its cadres are reduced by an even greater extent, nor because the infantry is recruited from among the worst soldiers, who very often do not understand either their commanders or one another. The worst fact of all is that the infantry has no support technology. A motor-rifle division should have 410 armoured personnel carriers and we had only forty – and that was in our special parade regiment. In the other regiments of the division, in other divisions of the army and in the other armies of the district, there were none whatsoever. Many regiments had three to four armoured personnel carriers for battle training but even these immediately became the personal machines of the battalion commanders, thus leaving nothing at all for the battalion.

Of course, in case of necessity, the infantry can be transported by lorries. But there were no lorries either. The lorries which were in moth-balls in our division were only sufficient for two battalions. The third battalion was issued with armoured personnel carriers, and the remaining six battalions had to make do with vehicles received only on mobilisation.

All Soviet civilian cars are military-registered. If you buy a Volga car, you are warned that at any moment it may be requisitioned for military purposes. This includes dump-trucks, taxis and petrol-tankers. Each and every one of them is specially registered and, at mobilisation, goes straight into the army. At mobilisation, the whole country's national economy comes to a standstill because all the cars, tractors, bulldozers, cranes and excavators – all go into the army. It is difficult to say who created such folly. The system has existed for a long time but it could pass muster in the 1930s and 40s when the country was still able to feed itself, when even at times of general famine some food reserves still existed, when the basic means of transportation in a village was the horse. But now, when the country is unable to feed itself, when it has no food reserves (as was demonstrated to the whole world in October 1964), and when the national economy has no more horses, it is complete madness to take away all the men, all the tractors and all the cars simultaneously. Those who plan any future war must, in these conditions, count on a sudden, short, lightning war, using nuclear force within the first few minutes, or anticipate defeat if the war lasts longer than one month.

Meanwhile, the division began to receive these mobilised machines. What we actually got was a sheer mockery. These were machines which had entered the army long ago directly from the works. The majority of machines absorbed by the army are put into long-term moth-balling. Ten years later, they become normal working army machines whereupon new machines replace them in the moth-balls. After three, four and sometimes five years of vicious use, in adverse conditions and on appalling surfaces, the machines are deemed to be totally useless for further exploitation. Only then do they go to agriculture, though every one of them remains on the military register and has to be returned to the army in case of mobilisation.

In 1968, before Czechoslovakia, we were issued with machines built in 1950 and 1951. During their lifetime, Malenkov had replaced Stalin, Khrushchev had replaced Malenkov, and Brezhnev had replaced Khrushchev. During their lifetime, the Soviet Union had performed a titanic leap into space with the Sputnik and Gagarin (but then, having used all the advantages of surprise as well as of captured German technology, had refused to participate further in the space race). But these superannuated vehicles remained, like old spinsters still waiting for their day to dawn. And now indeed their hour had at last come!

After receiving its 'battle technology', the infantry was forbidden to leave the cover of the forests. On the roads and fields, only tank crews, the artillery and one parade battalion of armoured personnel carriers were training. All the remainder were standing along forest cuttings and in forest clearings. Viewed from outer space, it must have looked menacing, but not from the ground. The military hierarchy was afraid of frightening the locals by the look of our army: fat, untrained and undisciplined soldiers, who had forgotten all they ever knew, in old worn-out vehicles of all possible types and painted all the colours of the rainbow.

The Soviet military leaders must be given their due. None of these 'wild divisions' ever appeared in Europe, or even moved in daytime over Soviet territory. But their very existence gave the Soviet Union a considerable advantage. From outer space, the Americans saw new divisions increasing like fungi. Their reconnaissance noted mighty tank columns on the roads and calculated that innumerable infantrymen lay hidden in the forests. And so it was, in fact, but this infantry was neither organised nor controlled and, what is most important of all, was incapable of fighting.

After the first stage of mobilisation – the bringing up to strength of the existing units – the second stage started: the development of the new units, sub-units and formations.

The reservists continued to arrive, and 'battle vehicles' as well. The units were becoming swollen and, one beautiful night, the order was received to divide into two. The deputy divisional commander became the commander of the new division, while the deputy chief of staff became the chief of staff. Battalion commanders became commanders of regiments, and company commanders became commanders of battalions. The only pity was that platoon commanders, former students, who had never seen a real army, also became company commanders. And reservists were pushed up to become platoon commanders.

After this splitting into two, every division and every regiment started

142

once more the process of bringing itself up to strength, though this time with even older reservists and vehicles. The number of reservists became a real threat, and the army totally lost its professional face. Of course all this did not happen within the divisions intended for the seizure of Czechoslovakia, or if it did happen, it did so to a much smaller degree. But it did not make our position any easier. Those divisions, too, had to be brought up to strength somehow, and suddenly we saw with horror that, from what had already become our two divisions, they were starting to take away, little by little, both men and machines; and of course they were the best men and the best machines which were taken. From the tank crews created with such difficulty, they started to take away combat soldiers, replacing them with simple reservists.

In a couple of days, this wave reached us. We were ordered to get ready to send twenty of our forty armoured personnel carriers to the Carpathian Military District. The next day, twelve of our regular young officers received orders transferring them to the same district. And after that the process really snowballed. There was more news every day: all the tank drivers were taken away, the regular liaison men and the regimental chief of staff went too. It was our second month in the forest. Reservists were still joining us; discipline was lapsing. In early June, an order was received for the creation of field tribunals in each division. It was about this time that the number of 'wild divisions' had so increased and each of them was so drained by the constant departure of regular officers, sergeants and soldiers, that it had become impossible to govern this horde other than through field tribunals.

In a short while, the tribunals restored order, but not troop training. Every day, training sessions were going on. New difficulties arose in our regiment. After sending away half our armoured personnel carriers, we only had twenty left. The commanders of the 2nd and 3rd Battalions were given two each, so that left only sixteen in the 1st Battalion: and they were divided, as between brothers, one to the battalion commander and five to each company. A company consists of seventy-six men. Each armoured personnel carrier accommodates fifteen men apart from the driver, so everybody had his place, in theory at least. In practice the first armoured personnel carrier goes to the company commander, and with him travel his political deputy, the medical instructor, the company's machine-gun section with a very large provision of cartridges, and the sergeant-major with all the company's belongings. The commander's armoured personnel carrier is not only absolutely full on the inside, outside it is hung about with all manner of cases, casks and canisters.

For the three remaining platoons, consisting of twenty-two men each, there were four carriers: one for each platoon, and one to be shared between them. The fact that, in battle, the platoons and sections would all be torn to pieces, perturbed no one at all because, for the moment, one must not think about the battle, but how to accommodate men in armoured personnel carriers. Nobody would give us any additional machines, even if they were broken down and worn out. Where were they to come from? And, even so, our regiment was the luckiest in the three armies of the district. This had to be appreciated. No one else had such privileges.

So, in each armoured personnel carrier accommodating fifteen men, we had to put sixteen – that wasn't really too bad. During training, we used to transport far more than that. We managed about thirty men and even that wasn't too bad! But training and pre-battle conditions are two different things. In pre-battle conditions, every armoured personnel carrier, in addition to all infantry armament, also has one grenade-launcher RPG-7 with ten grenades, and ten grenades constitute two big cases. In addition there are twenty hand grenades, F-1s, which means another case, and one machine-gun, the SGMB, with 2,000 cartridges, which means another two cases. An armoured personnel carrier must also have two additional fuel tanks, which are suspended on top of the spare wheel, and can only be accommodated on the armoured roof, after which one of the hatches will not open. Then, in addition, every soldier carries on his person an automatic rifle or machine-gun or a grenade-launcher, 300 cartridges for every automatic rifle and 1,000 cartridges for every hand machine-gun. Every soldier also has two grenades, a bayonet, a gas-mask, protective rubber overalls, anti-nuclear rubber boots and gloves, greatcoat, rain cape and ground sheet, a change of underwear, rations for five days, a water bottle, a spade, and individual medicine and anti-nuclear pack. When all this is put into an armoured personnel carrier, there is no room left for one person, let alone sixteen. It was much better before, when armoured personnel carriers had no armoured roof and one could put everybody one on top of the other like peasant wenches on a hay-cart. After Hungary, the production of such armoured personnel carriers was stopped. Now we have to push all sixteen in through the hatches under the carrier's roof.

This is not an easy task, especially if you take into consideration the reservists' corpulence. The sergeants just have to hammer them in under the roof. Sometimes, this operation takes about forty minutes. If something happens, if the machine overturns or catches fire, no one, except the driver and the commander whose positions are separated from the others, will get out alive. We are not even talking about the battle itself. How do they breathe there, squashed together worse than sardines in a tin? The soldier's good sense, however, soon finds a way out of that situation. Everyone puts on his gas-mask after disconnecting the filter container from the pipe; then the pipes are fed out through the open hatches and embrasures. During the summer it is not very pleasant in a rubber mask, pressed from all sides by backs, bottoms, boots, barrels and butts, but at least there is air to breathe.

During training exercises, especially when overseas attachés are present, things happen quite differently. Exercises are one thing, especially peep-shows, while harsh army reality is another matter altogether.

Late one evening, after the usual training practice of loading soldiers into armoured personnel carriers, which left no time for any other type of training, I received an order to go immediately to the staff of the Carpathian Military District. My post was to be taken by the 1st platoon commander, a junior lieutenant-reservist. When he heard about his appointment as a company commander, he looked sadly at our armoured personnel carriers, at the reservists, whom the sergeants were extricating with great difficulty from the hatches, then he gave a long-drawn-out whistle and swore loud and long.

The hurricane of transfer, re-groupings, re-formations and
bringing up to strength caught me too up in its wake and hurled
me into the 2nd Battalion of the 274th Regiment of the 24th
Samaro-Ulyanovsk, Berdychev, Iron, three times holder of the
Red Banner and holder of the Order of Suvorov and Bogdan
Khmelnitskiy, Motor-Rifle Division of the 38th Army, which
forms part of the Carpathian Military District.

Liberators

What a thrilling sight the changing of the guard at the Mausoleum is! I've been to Red Square hundreds of times and I'm still lost in admiration at their accuracy and military bearing. I am simply drawn there and could stand for hours feasting my eyes.

And how could it be otherwise? The very cream of the cream, trained to the point of artistry, trained better than Soviet gymnasts for the Olympic games. Handsome fellows.

Their regiment is stationed within the Kremlin Walls, a whole regiment of the KGB! Just go round from the side of the Alexsandrov-skiy garden and count the storeys in their barracks. It looks like two, but if you look more closely there are really four. The windows are too vast and there are two storeys to each window. Look carefully and you will see that there are indeed four. They extend above the Kremlin wall. And how many storeys are covered by this wall? Now go inside the Kremlin itself and look at the barracks from the side of the Tzar Bell and you will see that it is not just an ordinary house but a huge rectangular construction with an inner courtyard. Now go out again through the Troitskie gates into the Alexsandrovskiy garden and try to calculate the length of this building by pacing it out. So, there you are – not just a regiment but something far bigger can be accommodated in there, without tanks and artillery, of course.

And now, any Sunday, go towards the Kremlin and see how many of these lads are just strolling around aimlessly. But the regimental commander can only give leave to five per cent at any one time: that goes for the commander of an ordinary regiment, but the one in the Kremlin is no ordinary regiment. And, even if the commander allows only five per cent of his eagles to go in to town to enjoy themselves, there must still be plenty left in the Kremlin. And if it's not five, but only two to three per cent we're seeing, then how many of them have been left inside?

The lads strut up and down importantly and they look very proud. And why shouldn't they be proud? Their uniform is most imposing: greatcoats, caps, boots – all officers' issue. They have blue shoulder-straps with the letters 'GB' shining like gold. But why not 'KGB', why only 'GB'? It needs to be explained. 'K' stands for Committee. That's certainly not solid enough. 'MGB' would be better ('M' could mean Ministry), but 'GB' is best. It stands for State Security – plain and simple! How weighty it sounds, how imposing! It takes precedence over all ministries and committees, including even the Central Committee of the Party. 'GB' is a crystal-clear dream. But not only a dream of course.

So they are the cream of the cream. A whole regiment, lacking only tanks and artillery. But the tanks would not really be necessary – the Kremlin's walls are still strong.

But suppose something happens, some kind of revolution breaks out, especially one by the army with tanks against the Leninist Central Committee? What then?

Don't worry on that score, brother: there is a whole Dzerzhinskiy Division created for just such an eventuality, with tanks and artillery and everything else which may be required. Of course it is true that the division is called a Division of Internal Troops, which means that it is part of the Ministry of Internal Affairs. But don't you believe in such a masquerade. The KGB has used plenty of disguises in its time! So, don't give a glance at the Dzerzhinskiy Division's uniform. It's indeed a masquerade! Since when did the protection of our beloved leaders fall into the hands of the MVD? It has always been the KGB's prerogative: that's why this division was created. This is what is written in all the reference books raised on Lenin's personal instructions and for Lenin's personal protection. But then you have Comrade Roy Medvedev writing about the protection of our beloved Lenin, and the existence of the Dzerzhinskiy Division is somehow forgotten. In contrast, the division itself is very proud indeed of its role: 18,000 men guarding one man, Lenin. The Latvian riflemen pride themselves on their role just as much as the Moscow Military School named after the Supreme Soviet, and the Kremlin machine-gun detachments – just see how many of them there are.

In addition to the Dzerzhinskiy, the KGB possesses other regiments and divisions. All are made up of the very best soldiers, and there are a great many of them. Some liaise with all ministries and departments, with all republics, territories and regions, with all test-firing grounds, space centres, prisons and camps, with works, factories, mines and pits, with all military districts, armies, corps and divisions and, of course, with the brotherly socialist parties. And there is liaison within liaison: cables, switchboards, cypher machines, eavesdropping posts. And all such things have to be built, maintained and guarded; and all this needs troops, troops and more troops. The very best ones, of course. Because every day one is forced to hear secrets and tell no one. And, even though the secrets are far from comforting, one is not allowed either to hang oneself, or to run away to America. And so many soldiers are needed for this job! But it is still not the Soviet Army nor is it the Defence Ministry. These same troops eavesdrop and report even on what is said within the Defence Ministry. And that is not the end of it, that is not even the main arm of strength of the KGB. The frontier troops – there lies their strength, and they control nine districts! All the rest of the Soviet Army has only sixteen military districts. There are nine frontier districts controlled by KGB troops, with tanks, helicopters, artillery and warships.

Each one is, of course, made up of the best crack troops, since a frontier guard was invented specifically to prevent anyone from running away from this splendid society of ours. But he is not guarded by anyone. He stands on the very frontier itself: one step sideways and he is over the border. So, to prevent that, the very best soldiers are chosen for all nine KGB districts.

All those who have not eventually landed up in this gigantic organisation go into the Internal Troops. This too does not come under the Defence Ministry but under the Ministry of Internal Affairs. It is still not the army although it has regiments, divisions, tanks and guns.

'What are you doing, brothers?'

'Guarding a camp!'

'Well, it's a necessary job, responsible too. How many people are there there?'

'Oh, there are a lot of people. Under just one law, the one about the intensification of the struggle against hooliganism, over the last ten years, eight million people have been imprisoned. But there are many other decrees and laws leading to imprisonment. We have to guard all those people.'

'And I suppose they take on only the very best for this job.'

'Of course. They need people who have never themselves been convicted, nor anyone in their families. And also those, who, after being in contact with the prisoners, don't pick up any wrong ideas, and if they do happen to pick up any ideas they should not absorb them, and if they do happen to absorb them, they must not disseminate what they've picked up from the prisoners, or in any case not disseminate it too widely.'

'But where can you find such people?'

'Well, we do our best.'

148

So then, those who have landed up neither in the GB nor the Internal Troops – they are the ones who join the invincible and legendary Soviet Army.

Every self-respecting army consists of three types of armed forces, each of which is split into different kinds of troops. The Soviet Army has more respect for itself than all the others and, therefore, does not consist of three but of five arms. In addition to the land forces, the air force and the navy, there are two other branches of equal importance, the anti-aircraft defence troops and the strategic rocket troops. And, in addition to all these, there are also the VDV or airborne forces, which are not separate but are answerable solely to the Defence Minister and commanded by an army general. And the VDV consists of eight divisions, no less, whereas the whole of the British Army, for instance, consists of four divisions: three divisions in Germany, and one actually in the United Kingdom. When one compares these simple statistics, one's ideas about the aggressiveness of NATO tend somewhat to fade.

So the VDV are selected also from the best soldiers, the most courageous, the most convinced, developed and physically strong. They would have to be: jumping in all weathers, often at night, operating in the enemy's rear against its most important targets; completely isolated from their own troops, without any supplies of ammunition, fuel, food, and without their wounded being evacuated. Paratroopers must kill their own wounded, so they are never taken prisoner and give away the operation's plans and intentions. The air descent must always be a surprise attack.

Those who have not been taken into the VDV join the strategic rocket troops or RVSN. Again, they need the very best. The real question is: how many of these crack soldiers are really required for the RVSN? The RVSN has three armies altogether: every army consists of a number of corps, and every corps of several divisions. So, it would be futile to make any comparison with the British Army.

After the RVSN, it is the turn of the country's anti-aircraft defence. That requires enormous numbers of soldiers and, again, all of them must be the best. They are intended to deal with sputniks, intercontinental ballistic and other missiles, and strategic bombers. The country's anti-aircraft defence consists of three types of troops: air force, air-rocket and radio-technical troops. The anti-aircraft air force possesses the fastest aircraft-interceptors. The radio-technical troops operate thousands of locators which guard the sky day and night. Finally, there are the air-rocket troops. All three arms are concentrated in two districts, Moscow and Baku, and each district forms a group of armies for anti-aircraft defence. But, apart from these two districts,

149

there are also several separate anti-aircraft defence armies, which are directly subordinate to the Anti-Aircraft Defence Commander-in-Chief.

Next comes the air force, which is not to be confused with the anti-aircraft defence air force. In general the air force, or to be more exact the VVS, or military air force, has nothing in common with the anti-aircraft defence air force. The VVS has many air armies, ranging from a front-line force through the strategic air corps known in Soviet terminology as the long-range air force, to the divisions of military transport aviation. Each front-line army consists of six divisions, and the corps of long-range aviation have two to three divisions each. Without doubt, the air force must have the best soldiers.

The navy comes next. It, too, is huge. It has a colossal· number of strategic rockets, and the demands made on the sailors operating them are extremely high, because the launching of a rocket from a submarine underwater is so complicated. The navy also has its own anti-aircraft defence and a mighty air force separate from the VVS and the country's anti-aircraft defence. And, of course, the cleverest, the most literate, the boldest and most resolute, the strongest and the sturdiest, are essential. And everything that's left goes into the land forces!

The best are sent abroad: let the liberated admire their liberators! The best are needed there so that our reputation in Europe is not spoiled. That is perfectly understandable. But how many soldiers are needed to be sent into liberated Europe? Let us take, for instance, West Germany and its fierce Bundeswehr, with which, in the Soviet Union, they frighten everybody from pioneers to pensioners. Well, that Bundeswehr has twelve divisions. Against these twelve divisions, we maintain five armies in the field and one air army from the VVS. These six armies are called the GSVG – The Group of Soviet Troops in Germany. But, apart from the GSVG, there is the Northern Group of Troops, which are the Soviet forces in Poland, the Central Group in Czechoslovakia, and the Southern Group in Hungary. And these four groups must be made up of the very best soldiers. It was not for nothing that the poet Yevtushenko composed a song:

> It's not only for their Country
> The soldiers perished in that war
> But to provide quiet sleep
> At night over the whole World.

So, Europe can rest in peace – our armies and their crack soldiers will never leave it. We like Europe!

Those young soldiers, who for some reason have not joined the hundreds of thousands of picked troops in liberated Europe, go into the land forces at home actually on Soviet territory. It must be said that the remaining soldiers are very good, though perhaps not as perfect as for instance those in State Security, the Frontier Troops of the KGB, the Internal Troops of the MVD, the Airborne Forces, the Strategic Rocket Troops, the Anti-Aircraft Defence, the Navy, the Group of Soviet Troops in Germany, the Central Group of Troops, the Northern Group of Troops or the Southern Group of Troops. They are, of course, first class, but not of quite the same calibre.

The Soviet Army Land Forces, representing sixteen districts, is a gigantic organism. Neither China, nor America, nor anyone else, not even all of them put together, can match it in size. But how can this army be brought up to strength? The biggest one in the world? And what happens if there is no one left to harvest the crops?

I inspected my guards company, bit my lip and said nothing. I did not call the officers in for a talk. I did not speak to the sergeants. Nor did I go and meet the commanders of the neighbouring companies. I just looked at my company and that was enough.

After he has met his men, the done thing is for the commander to examine the battle vehicles and armament of the company and later its equipment and ammunition. But I didn't do that. No . . . I went straight to the officers' bar which rejoices in the lyrical name 'Little Star' – which particular star is not specified, the one in the sky, the one on the shoulder-straps, or the red one on the chest.

I placed an extra crumpled rouble in the hands of a big-bosomed barmaid, and bribed her to bring me a bottle, because an officer officially should not drink. I put this small bottle under the table and gradually emptied it, in proud solitude. But it did not make me feel any happier, in fact it only increased my depression. Why the hell I wondered, did they invent this bloody system? Who invented it? However you interpret things, it is the tanks and the infantry who will fight on the battlefield, not the rocket men or the KGB people. You have to fight your enemy not with numbers alone but by your skill. And my guardsmen didn't even understand the Russian language! The language of their commander! Nor did they understand one another because all the nationalities had been mixed up. Those who did understand at least something had all been sent to the artillery or liaison a long time ago. What was the good of having this pack? Why hadn't they all been sent off to building units, that would have been much more useful! Have a smaller army if you must, but at least let them all understand one another a little better! If war were to break out, it would be a hundred times worse than the Arab troops, who could at least understand one another. What on earth was I to do with them?

Well, I thought, leaving war aside, it is peacetime and they all have to be drilled into some sort of shape. Tactics, for instance. If the pupil doesn't understand his teacher, you can't even teach him to play chess. And at least, in a game of chess, the whole situation is like the palm of your hand, any threat is clearly visible. The situation in battle is far from clear, and a threat can appear suddenly from anywhere. The enemy does not wait for you to work out your counter move, he acts and goes on acting. And payment for losses on the field of battle is not a chess title, not even a couple of million dollars, but the lives of millions of people. And everyone wants to win. The enemy is not an idiot! Each one of his moves on the battlefield he has previously worked out a hundred times over on his electronic calculator. So how shall we manage to fight? In 1941, there were no rocket troops but at least our best infantry divisions were made up of first-class soldiers. Maybe, that is why we were able to hold out. And there were also national divisions in those days – Latvian, Georgian where the divisional commanders understood Russian and that was enough. But what now?

I ordered another little bottle and, having drunk half of it, I felt so sorry for myself and my unfortunate Motherland that it was quite unbearable.

Just before the bar was due to close, two infantry captains sat down at my table. Perhaps they wanted to get to know me or perhaps they were just looking for a third drinker. I didn't answer their greeting very politely.

'New officer, eh? . . .'

'Crying, of course . . .'

'All the new ones cry in this corner . . .'

'Never mind, he'll recover . . . he'll get acclimatised. All of us start this way.'

Those were the last words I heard. Probably these two captains, having understood perfectly the state I was in, somehow dragged me off at the dead of night to the officers' mess.

The same night, dead drunk, I was dragged again from the officers' mess to my own company. I was put into the commander's car, and the column moved off.

That very night, our regiment was put on alert. Our brothers in Czechoslovakia had asked for our help and protection.

The Carpathian District is transformed into the Carpathian Front. The Western Ukraine. August 1968.

On the Border Line

'The grain will soon start to fall from the wheat as it stands in the fields.'

'What are the people at the top thinking of?'

'Do you think things are easy for them? The Czechs are not giving us real grounds for going to protect them. Communists still haven't been killed there and no "Chekists" have been hanged from the lamp-posts. There is no one to protect them from. So, how can we move our troops in?'

'They must consider themselves and their own country first, and not bother about some Czechs or about public opinion. It's the right time to go in and that's all there is to it.'

'Those people up there understand whether it's the right time or not.'

'They bloody well don't understand anything. If our troops are not in Czechoslovakia within a week, it'll be the end for all of us.'

'Why?'

'Because the wheat will start to fall, because there's no one to harvest it, because all the peasants and all the machines have been taken away from the *Kolkhozes*. And if we don't harvest our wheat everything will start all over again just like 1964.'

'The Americans will help us!' said the assistant chief of staff confidently.

'And if they don't?'

'They will, what else could they do?'

'In any case, they wouldn't be able to feed all of us. Did you see how many people were being mobilised! In 1964 at least some of the harvest was gathered in, but now there'll be nothing. The Americans wouldn't be able to feed all of us.'

'Don't you worry about the Americans. They're rich. They've got plenty of food. There's enough for everybody.'

Doubts about what would happen if the Americans failed to support us did not evaporate, however, and conversation to the effect that it was about time we finished these long drawn-out proceedings and let the peasants get on with the harvest kept on cropping up.

'What about letting the peasants and the whole army get on with the harvest now without delay and then liberating Czechoslovakia afterwards, in October or November?'

'That would be disastrous. It would be the end of us and the end of all Soviet power and all Socialist achievements. We have to go in now, otherwise everything will collapse, and there will be nothing left to protect.'

'They say they are building a different socialism, with a human face.'

'That's enemy propaganda,' interrupted the political deputy, 'all socialism has the same face. The bourgeoisie, Comrades, have invented this theory of compromise. This theory contradicts Marxist teaching and does not contain a single drop of common sense. You cannot sit on two chairs with one bottom, it's just not comfortable. Judge for yourselves: what compromise can there possibly be if not a single advantage can be torn from socialist achievement. You surely remember how one anti-Soviet, during the era of Voluntarism, penned an infamous slander against our regime. It was called *One Day in the Life of Ivan Ivanovich* or *Ivan Trofimovich* or something like that. What came of that? All the politically immature elements got on the move and started disseminating the slander. There was even some distrust of Party policies, and so on. It was nipped in the bud at the right time otherwise who knows how it might all have ended?'

One could disagree with that. I myself had never read about this Ivan, the book just did not come my way, but I distinctly remember that the effect it had was deafening.

'So, what did they think up, these Czech communists?' continued the political deputy. 'They completely abolished censorship. They opened the sluices to the full force of bourgeois propaganda! Let everyone print whatever they like! And where will that lead? To compromise? Not at all! To capitalism! It's enough for the bourgeois influence to make a small hole in the dam and then the flood will destroy the whole system! We've already had one small hole like that but, thanks to the Party, it was closed in time. But in Czechoslovakia it's not just a little hole, it's already a full flood of water! It must be urgently quelled. What kind of compromise is it if everyone is allowed to say just what he likes? It's not a compromise, it's sheer bourgeois anarchy!'

One could not disagree with this either. If, owing to one little story, the whole system had nearly collapsed before, what would happen if censorship were completely abolished? There is no third way – either you have censorship or you don't, either you have the necessary organisation or you don't, either with a Central Committee or without it. Really, what talk can there be of any compromise? If there is a Central Committee, that implies that there is a Party policy. The necessary organisations protect the Central Committee and censorship protects the Party's political line. This is what socialism is all about. And, if you take away any one of these elements, the whole orderly system will collapse and anarchy will ensue with all its inherent vices, like unemployment, crises, slumps, inflation and all the rest. This is what this obscenity Capitalism is all about. Indeed, however you look at it, there is no room for any compromise or for any so-called human face . . .

'Please continue, Comrade Lieutenant-Colonel,' they shouted from the rear ranks. 'We fully support you.' The new political deputy was different from the previous one, the new one spoke persuasive good sense.

'Yes, I will continue, Comrades. There was somebody here who suggested sending the army in to do the harvesting and waiting to liberate our brothers until October. I consider this proposal disastrous for the whole socialist system. Let's say for the sake of argument that we don't liberate Czechoslovakia in the immediate future: by October there'll be nothing left there, neither socialism nor any human face. Socialism is an orderly system like a diamond and as strong as a diamond, but if the diamond-cutter makes one false move all the stability of the crystal may be shattered. In Czechoslovakia, it has already happened. The diamond is falling to pieces. But it represents one organic component of the whole socialistic camp. The diamond formed by World Socialism can also fall to pieces and very rapidly too. Bad examples are highly infectious! If the bourgeoisie triumphs in Czechoslovakia, do you really believe that Hungary will not follow her example? We've already had one example of this kind. There, too, everything started from this business of a human face. Of course Rumania is already moving further and further from Marxism. If there is the smallest change in Czechoslovakia, then the same will happen in Poland and in the GDR. We've already had this experience once. You know yourselves what kind of situation already exists in Poland! And in the GDR – I won't even speak about that! The bourgeoisie is already calling for compromise. That means removing the Berlin Wall. Isn't that so? If that's done, the immature elements of the population will all rush off into West Germany! Comrades, our revolutionary vigilance must not be slackened. The frontiers must be kept under lock and key. We must neither remove the wall, nor abolish censorship. Otherwise, you know yourselves what will happen.'

The political deputy took a sip of water from somebody's flask and then continued:

'Let's say for the sake of argument that some socialist countries break away from the socialist partnership – the infection could quickly reach our own Baltic Republics like Estonia, Latvia and Lithuania, where bourgeois nationalism is still strong, as well as the Ukraine and Byelorussia, especially their western parts, which are precisely those adjoining Poland and Czechoslovakia. I won't elaborate further. You yourselves understand perfectly well what might happen there.'

We answered him with cries of indignation. The chief of staff of the 3rd Battalion smiled foxily and then calmly asked, 'But when will it happen, Comrade Lieutenant-Colonel? For a long time now we've been ready to carry out our international duty.'

The political deputy was not confused by this new question, although he himself, of course, had not the slightest idea of the answer.

'We must be ready for the moment!'

We all applauded the gallant political deputy for organising such a successful improvised meeting.

Events were coming to a head. Everybody could plainly see that we should be going in soon, but no one knew exactly when. Two days previously there had been a secret order, for officers' eyes only, concerning the formation of the Carpathian Front on the basis of one tank, one air and two all-arms armies. Colonel-General Bisyarin was appointed commander-in-chief.

The same day we learned of the movement of the 8th Guards Tank Army from our front on to Polish territory. Our 38th Army, with which I had taken part at the Dnieper exercises, was still in the Ukraine and would probably enter Czechoslovakia from Soviet territory.

That day, we learned of the formation of the Central Front under the command of Colonel-General Mayorov. The Central Front was developing in the GDR and Poland to the west of Krakow. It consisted of two armies taken from the Baltic District and the 20th Guards Army of the Group of Soviet Troops in Germany, in addition to which it had some Polish and German divisions. Some of the Polish divisions were included in our Carpathian Front. Apparently one further front had been developed in Hungary, which was to consist of Soviet armies and Hungarian corps, plus some Bulgarian units. But, at that time, we had no definite information, we just guessed. Later I learned that a Southern Front had indeed been developed on Hungarian territory, plus an operative group called 'Balaton'. The Southern Front did not go into Czechoslovakia. It only covered and protected the active group of troops. Only the 'Balaton' group, which was more than an army and less than a front, actually entered Czechoslovakia. As part of the Soviet forces, there were also Bulgarian and Hungarian units in this group, as we used to say, in order 'to make up the furniture'.

And now the grains of wheat were really falling on to the ground.

We had already been standing in the forests for several months.

There had been training, check-ups, command-staff training and general training followed yet again by further checking of equipment. After more time had elapsed, an order was issued concerning the creation of the Danube High Command, to consist of the Central and Carpathian Fronts, the 'Balaton' group and, as a fourth separate element, two airborne divisions. For the first day of the operation, in order to ensure the success of an airborne landing, five divisions of military transport aircraft were put at the disposal of the Danube High Command.

Army General Pavlovskiy was appointed commander-in-chief, and his command post was established somewhere in Poland.

Everything was ready, but the liberation still didn't start: somebody at the top still had doubts about something, though there was really nothing to have doubts about. If we invaded Czechoslovakia it might lead to catastrophe for everybody including our own system, or on the other hand maybe not ... If we did not invade Czechoslovakia, it would lead to catastrophe for our system. There was no choice for the Soviet leadership. The first alternative was obviously the better. To drag out the liberation process was also impossible. The harvest could not wait.

Our regiment was ordered to stand to at 2300 hours. The order 'Now is our time' was passed by secret channels to all fronts, armies, divisions, brigades, regiments and battalions. Commanders were instructed to open one of the five packets in their possession and, in the presence of their chiefs of staff, to burn the other four without opening them. The operation had been worked out on the basis of five different alternatives. Now that one of them had been approved, the others lost all significance.

The directive signed by the Defence Minister ordered Operation Danube to be put into effect. Military action would be necessary, continued in accordance with the two plans 'Danube-Channel' and 'Danube-Channel-World'.

The liberation had begun.

The final stop before the state frontier. Outskirts of Uzhgorod.

White Stripes

The battalion chief of staff looked at me with leaden eyes and imperiously commanded: 'Repeat!'

I straightened myself and, clicking my heels, repeated parrot-fashion the words known to us all for so long – 'Instructions for mutual support during Operation Danube'. 'A white stripe is the distinguishing mark of our own and allied forces. All battle equipment of Soviet and allied origin without white stripes is to be neutralised, if possible without a shot being fired. Tanks and other battle equipment without stripes are to be destroyed immediately in case of resistance without prior notice of orders from above. In the event of contact with NATO troops, immediately stop and do not shoot without first being ordered to do so.'

The chief of staff moved away down the line, ordering first one then another officer to repeat aloud these instructions which had been dinned into us all. At last he finished his round, came to the middle of the formation and ended his briefing with the words:

'Comrade officers! Not shooting at NATO troops does not necessarily mean any hesitation in showing firmness and resolution! Where our first tank meets their first tank, a platoon or a company must immediately deploy into formation. If possible without firing, try to push them back from the territory they have occupied. Our task is to seize as much territory as possible. Let the diplomats decide later where the frontier between Eastern and Western Czechoslovakia is to be drawn. It is a matter of honour that we should make Eastern Socialist Czechoslovakia larger than Western Czechoslovakia. If shooting does start, do not lose your heads. It is better to retreat one or two kilometres. Do not spoil for a fight, as they too have no wish to start it. But, if the affair does come to a fight, be prepared for the worst.'

The chief of staff struck his dusty boot with a willow branch and added in a low but distinct voice:

'Any scoundrel who takes it into his head to desert to the stripeless or Western side will be immediately shot. Any attempt to eradicate our white stripes and desert to the camp of the stripeless can be dealt with with the utmost severity. This right is given to every one of you.

158

Unfortunately, one must remember that the elimination of white stripes is possible, not only among Hungarian and Polish units, but among our own units too. Let's hope for the best.' And, changing his tone, he roared, 'STAND TO!'

We all rushed to our vehicles, where sergeants and soldiers were bustling about carrying out a last inspection before departure. Suddenly, from the other side of the column, a sizeable group of soldiers and sergeants who had just received their instructions from the officer of the special department of the KGB, came running towards us. *Stukachi*, as KGB informers are nicknamed, are always given their instructions secretly. But here, at the very frontier, the special department had apparently received new instructions, which had to be passed urgently to its executives. All around them was nothing but open fields, and no time to spare. How could they hide? The only way was to give them their instructions in sight of the whole battalion. What they were talking about was not difficult to guess: they were being given the power to kill us, the officers, if we started to wipe the white stripes off our vehicles or tanks.

I started to run as fast as I could, and saw that all my brother officers were also running. Each one of us wanted to reach the column before the *Stukachi* and to see them all together in a group before they dissolved into the grey-green mass of the other soldiers.

Here we come! A single tight group of like-minded individuals. We were starting to divide into smaller groups, each running towards its own company. Familiar faces – oh hell, that dark fellow! I would never have thought he was an informer. As far as I remembered, he couldn't even speak Russian. How had the KGB found a common language? And now they had melted completely into the dense mass of soldiers. Their comrades did not seem to have the least idea of the reason for their absence: they were still young soldiers and even spoke different languages. They did not understand too much of what was going on. But the KGB was not quite as silly as all that. As they were out in the open, the KGB had not gathered together the whole lot of them, only some. I would have staked my head on it that my own signals operator was a KGB informer. But he had not been called out for instructions. Maybe he had been given his instructions earlier, or maybe one of those who had attended the meeting would inform him secretly later what had been said.

Meanwhile, another dense group of soldiers and sergeants had detached itself from the armoured troop carrier belonging to the battalion commander's political deputy and run towards their machines. These, too, were *Stukachi* – but of a slightly different kind. They were the legal *Stukachi*, with their own line of responsibility.

They were Party servants. In every platoon consisting of thirty soldiers and sergeants there is a Komsomol secretary and his two assistants, plus a platoon agitator, plus an editor of the *Boevoi Listok*. Indeed each detachment of seven soldiers has its own *Boevoi Listok* correspondent.

In the same platoon, some of the soldiers must belong to the company bureau, to the company board and company agitators' group. Provided they can say at least ten words in broken Russian, then one of these positions is open to them and they become the creatures of the political deputy, or indeed of the Party. They listen to what the Party says and the Party, through the ears of the political deputy, very attentively listens to what they say about me, my comrades, my commanders and my junior officers. Looking at the insolent faces of the legal and political *Stukachi*, it was only too easy to guess that, only a moment before, the Party had given them the right to shoot without warning any officer who dared to obliterate any white stripes.

Now, there was one last man running from the vehicle of the regimental propagandist. He ran fast, but not so fast as to disturb his special decorum. He was nineteen years old; he had a well-shaped face, a well-shaped nose, a well-built figure, well-shaped thoughts and a careful haircut. Such men's names generally figure on the board of honour and they are elected to the Praesidium at solemn gatherings. He was a Candidate Member of Our Great Party. There was only one like him in my company. He was quite another matter. He represented a particular thread of information with direct access to our regimental political God. He was yet another man authorised to shoot me in the back, if the KGB *Stukachi* just happened to hesitate. And he would shoot at both the obvious and the hidden KGB *Stukachi*, if they faltered, and if, of course, I happened to be a second late in killing them.

The Candidate Member of our Great Party climbed into my vehicle and took his seat at my left side. On my right was a signals operator (a hidden KGB *Stukachi*), behind me sat the machine-gunner (an obvious KGB *Stukachi*), in front was the company's agitator, the Party right-hand man. The huge fuel supply vehicles pulled away with a roar from the armoured column, and we started smoothly on our way.

160

Invasion

Throughout the entire night, in an endless stream, the troops were marching past our armoured personnel carriers and tanks. Towards morning, in spite of the dew, our machines were covered with such a thick layer of dust that neither identification signs nor numbers could be seen; and the troops were still marching on and on.

The only command was to close up, and this was broadcast repeatedly over the air. We all knew our battle standards only too well. On the march, the distance between battle vehicles should be 100 metres and, between auxiliaries, 50 metres. So the length of one division on the march is 150 kilometres. But now, through the narrow roads of the Soviet-Czechoslovak frontier, two armies were on the move, consisting of twelve divisions in all, plus replacement and supporting units and the reserves of the Carpathian Front.

All established standards went by the board and were forgotten, for, if it had been decided to observe them, troops would not have entered Czechoslovakia in less than a week. 'Close up!' This categorical demand was accompanied by highly select abuse and threats by all commanders to their subordinates. At 0820 hours came the order from the Carpathian Front commander to push off the road any broken-down vehicles, regardless of type or responsibility. Hundreds of tanks, artillery tractors and vehicles containing top-secret cypher equipment rolled down the slope. In the 79th Motor-Rifle Division, a rocket-launcher whose engine had failed was also pushed off the road.

At 0930 hours the 38th Army commander ordered all repair vehicles to be moved out of the column so that they could be left behind on Soviet territory. Ten minutes later a similar order, covering all three armies, was issued by the Front commander.

Meanwhile, we were still standing at the roadside allowing the first echelon to pass. The call to 'Close up' still echoed. The commanders' helicopters hung in the air over the dense clouds of dust. Divisional and army commanders, generals and officers of the front line staff urged on their hapless regimental and battalion commanders from immediately above their heads.

At noon, we were joined by the helicopters carrying the generals from the commander-in-chief of the Danube Staff. Orders to remove regimental and divisional commanders who could not sustain the speed of marching and did not 'Close up' were issued on the spot. Battle vehicles were scattered in the gutters. Units of sappers, chemical and medical troops had already been removed from the composition of the column. But, still, thousands of tanks awaited their turn on Soviet territory to enter the narrow mountain passage and to fulfil their noble mission. A mechanised Genghis Khan was rushing headlong into Europe.

At 1500 hours our division finally received the order to start moving in column formation. By then the roads were in such a bad state that to adhere to the prescribed speed of advance was absolutely impossible. The dust was so dense that all vehicles were moving forward with their lights switched on.

Towards evening our regiment reached the state frontier, but was then commanded to position their machines along the roadside to allow the Front commander's reserve to pass.

This enforced stop allowed us to have dinner. Some weeks earlier, during the training period, provision points had been established along all directions of troop movement. And it was here that the miracles started to happen. The provision points were equipped with a monstrous capacity, to serve thousands of people in only a few minutes.

The first surprise was an unprecedentedly luxurious table containing all kinds of foreign delicacies. It was announced that from now until the end of the operation all troops would be supplied only with foreign products, which were being provided by the governments of the USA, France, Canada, Australia and their other allies.

Towards daybreak on the liberation's second day our column finally left Soviet earth-roads and reached the extremely well-surfaced Slovak roads. The dusty haze which had pestered us for nearly two days was left behind on the Soviet side, but instead there came the frenzied crowds of people. Stones and rotten eggs, tomatoes and apples, were thrown at us. Insults and curses were hurled in our wake, but the thicker the crowd became, the more abundant became our food. This was a very precise psychological calculation and Bonaparte's words that the way to a soldier's heart was through his stomach were not forgotten. The food was of the very best quality. We had never seen such multicoloured labels printed in every language under the sun. The only Russian product among our rations was, of course, Vodka.

All officers were constantly reminded that they must keep their troops' battle spirits up to the mark. But there was no need for that, first because sergeants and soldiers alike hardly understood where they

162

were and what was going on, and secondly, owing to the abundant supplies of food, they were all ready for battle anyway.

Most of my company's sergeants could understand a little Russian. They were generally recruited from the distant-wooded districts and had encountered electricity for the first time in the army. There was no need to worry about them. Only, after five or six hours of moving through the infuriated crowds, one of them suddenly noticed the fact that the numbers of the machines were not quite standard ones, and he asked me a question about it. I answered his question with another question of my own. I asked him to name all the republics he knew. The sergeant was one of the cleverest and quickly named Byelorussia, the Ukraine, Lithuania, Poland, France and Uzbekistan. Then I told him that, in some republics, the numbers of vehicles are not standard; and that was that. The other sergeants did not even notice the cars' number plates.

It was even simpler with the soldiers. All of them came from beyond the clouds, from mountainous kishlaks and distant reindeer-breeding farms. They did not understand not only me but also one another: all the nationalities had been mixed up with the alleged purpose of developing friendship between the peoples. They knew only ten commands: Get up, Lie down, Right, Left, Forward, Back, Run, Turn round, Fire, Hurrah.

At our next halt in the forest, during supper, I decided to fulfil the order of the political deputy and to raise morale still higher. It was not difficult.

I climbed onto a box marked 'Made in the USA', lifted high above my head a tin containing stewed beef, smacked my lips in a sign of appreciation and shouted out 'Hurrah'. In response, a mighty and joyous 'Hurrah' rushed from hundreds of throats.

The tinned stewed beef was really excellent.

The Reconnaissance Battalion of the 6th Guards Rovno, Order of Lenin and of the Red Banner, Order of Suvorov, Motor-Rifle Division of the 20th Guards Army, in the centre of Prague. August 1968.

The Banker

Of course Lenin was truly a genius, thought the battalion commander, Major Zhuravlev. Take possession of the banks, the post office and telegraph, the railway stations and bridges. That's all very well, but there's one thing that's still not quite clear. Is it possible that no one thought of such a simple thing before he did? The Major spat on a heap of cases packed full of money and angrily kicked one of them.

The day before yesterday, in the morning, the 508th Separate Reconnaissance Battalion of the 6th Guards Motor-Rifle Division of the 20th Army of the Central Front had been the first to set foot in the streets of a still sleepy Prague. The Reconnaissance Battalion was moving fast, having left behind its radio-reconnaissance company, and as a result had considerably outstripped the advanced detachment and the main forces of the division. The battalion's task was clear and categorical: take possession of all bridges and retain them until the arrival of the main force.

The commander of the Reconnaissance Battalion, Major Zhuravlev, knew all the town's roads off by heart. For four whole months, the battalion had worked at its task with maps and models. The battalion chief of staff had a complete set of photographs of all the crossroads along the route. Before Operation Danube, staff commander exercises had been held during which all twenty officers of the battalion had visited Prague and travelled by bus along all their future routes.

Zhuravlev was in the turret of the leading tank and gazed with renewed interest at the unusually colourful town. Suddenly on the façade of an old building he noticed the huge letters: BANK.

Zhuravlev knew perfectly well the distribution of responsibilities between the division's units, and he was absolutely sure that, at the time of the 'distribution of roles', the central bank had been completely missed. This entire area was to have been occupied by the 6th Guards Division and no other troops were supposed to be stationed here.

164

Zhuravlev swore blind at the commanders' muddle-headedness and kicked the dozing radio operator, who had not slept for three nights.

'Closed channel to the divisional chief of staff!'

The radio operator answered after a few seconds.

'Closed channel to the divisional chief of staff, Bullfinch four, go ahead.'

Zhuravlev pressed the button on the speech control panel and, filling his lungs with air, he began:

'Bullfinch four, this is Kursk, Square 21341 – bank. I have decided to take the bank myself with a reconnaissance company and the first tank reconnaissance platoon. My deputy will carry out allotted task together with armoured reconnaissance vehicle and the second reconnaissance platoon. This is Kursk. Over.'

'Kursk, this is Bullfinch four. Okay. This is Bullfinch four. Over and out,' came the short answer, and the transmitter fell silent.

When reporting his decision concerning the modification of the approved plan, Zhuravlev had secretly hoped that the chief of staff would not agree to his decision or that he would order somebody else, his deputy for instance, to deal with the bank and not him. Therefore, upon receiving the answer, he again cursed the stupid bungling of the leadership, meaning all those higher than himself.

'Kursk two, this is Kursk,' he addressed to his deputy over the open channel. 'Proceed with task, Kursk five and Kursk forty-two, Kursk three and Kursk forty-one to the left, into battle!'

Three amphibious tanks at once turned to the left without reducing speed, while the long-range reconnaissance company left their machines and followed. The remaining column, filling the street with the roar of its engines and the clank of its tracks, quickly disappeared round the corner.

Major Zhuravlev pressed down the safety lock to point at 'automatic fire', and called out, 'Assistant to chief of staff.'

'Yes.'

'Blockade the entrances with tanks. Put one in the yard and two along the street!'

'Right!'

'Company commander!'

'Here.'

'Hand over the 5th Reconnaissance Group to the tankmen and, with the remainder, take possession of the objective. Don't touch any papers! I'll have you shot if you do! Go ahead!'

The long-range reconnaissance company rushed forward to the main entrance and knocked repeatedly at the metal grille covering the glass doors with the butts of their rifles. An old watchman in a grey uniform appeared behind the doors. He looked in terror at the fierce faces of the men knocking at the doors. Then he glanced uncertainly behind him. He looked again at the soldiers hammering at the doors and hurried forward and opened them. The company rushed into the echoing central hall and spread out along the staircase and corridors.

For some reason, it reminded the battalion commander of that famous painting *The assault on the Winter Palace*.

Ten minutes later, all the bank's personnel – mostly night-watchmen—were gathered together in the big hall. Zhuravlev collected all the keys, ordered all the personnel to be searched and then locked up in the guard-room. The battalion commander went round all the rooms and sealed them with a notice reading 'Military Unit 66723'. The massive safes he secured with a secret seal: '508th Reconnaissance Battalion'. Then he personally checked the positions of the inner and outer guard, after which he returned to his command tank to report the completion of his task.

The closed channel was working normally. The divisional staff answered within a minute.

'Bullfinch four, this is Kursk. Bank taken. This is Kursk. Over.'

'Well done,' replied the divisional chief of staff, ignoring the call-signs. 'Remain there until they relieve you. A tank regiment will arrive in a couple of hours.'

'Armoured reconnaissance vehicles alone, without our help, won't be able to hold the bridges,' implored Zhuravlev, breaking regulations. He did not want to sit there in the bank – if some kind of papers were lost, it would be his fault and he would be shot. So he tried every means to get somebody to replace him – for instance the battalion's chief of staff – so that he could go off to the bridges. He could not have pretended not to notice the bank as he moved along the street, things then might have turned out badly for him: the guilty party is always found out, and who else in this situation would have been guilty if not the reconnaissance battalion commander? And so there was only one possible decision: remain himself at the bank. The manual on reconnaissance treats such a situation very clearly. Simple and easy tasks must be given to the deputy; complicated and risky ones, do yourself. Furthermore the divisional chief of staff had just confirmed it: 'Kursk. To hell with the bridges. Hold the bank. Over and out.'

The battalion commander switched off the transmitter and swore loudly. Somewhere close by, there was a short burst of automatic fire followed by three long machine-gun bursts. The sound was rather muffled but the machine-guns the battalion commander could not fail to recognize unmistakably: SGMs. Somewhere on the bridges the

Czechs had obviously fired their automatics, and then our people had replied with machine-guns. Then everything became quiet again.

At the sound of shooting, astonished, sleepy faces began to peer out here and there from their windows. Apparently the entry of several reconnaissance battalions into the town had remained virtually unnoticed, but the sound of shooting woke them up. An elderly woman stopped in front of the commander's tank, surveyed it and quietly went away. A yard-cleaner with a brush, instead of the usual home-made broom, stopped by another tank. The Czech army is equipped with the same tanks, and reconnaissance units wear camouflage overalls instead of field uniforms.

The camouflage overall had no insignia or badges and it was probably owing to this fact that it had not occurred to the inhabitants of the neighbouring houses that this was not the Czech army but something quite different. It is in any case only the 'court' divisions who wear badges, white piping and other adornments; tanks and armoured personnel carriers have no identification marks except the three-figure numbers on the armour, plus, in some cases, the identification marks of their division: a little rhombus, a deer, or oak leaves. On this particular occasion, in addition to these marks, the famous white stripes had been painted along and across the tanks. And it was precisely those stripes which had interested the elderly cleaner. He had a scar on his left cheek. For a long time he gazed, examining the tank, and then put a question to the reconnaissance troops sitting on top of the tank. The latter obviously did not understand the question, but, to be on the safe side, without answering they went down inside the tank and slammed the hatch shut. After standing beside the tank for a further few minutes, the elderly man moved away, shrugging his shoulders in puzzlement.

Zhuravlev, who had observed the scene from the bank window, ordered all the officers to gather in the central hall.

'Now the questions will begin . . . what is what, and why are we here . . . I tell you now to send them all to hell or even further. I've great experience in these matters after what happened in 1956 – is that clear?'

'It is!' answered the officers cheerfully in unison, but Zhuravlev noticed that something was not clear to one of the youngest officers, the commander of the fourth long-range reconnaissance group.

'What's the matter with you?'

'Comrade Major, what about the political department's order: 'Every Soviet Soldier is a diplomat and agitator?'

'Let the political deputy do his agitating on the bridge, that is what he is paid for,' the battalion commander interrupted, 'and as long as he's not here, everybody can go to hell!'

And then, realising that his words might reach undesirable ears, he added in a more conciliatory tone, 'We are guarding an objective of special importance and, until we get reinforcements, there is no point in getting involved in discussions. The tank regiment will soon be here, then we shall start the agitation work.'

At this point, Sergeant Prokhorov, the deputy platoon commander, rushed into the hall.

'Comrade Major! Tanks. Without any identifying marks.'

'What type of tank?'

'Fifty-fives!'

'Battalion, prepare for battle!'

Broad white stripes had been painted on all the fighting machines taking part in Operation Danube, in order to distinguish them from the same types of machines in the Czechoslovak army. Any fighting machine – tank, assault gun, armoured personnel carrier or artillery tractor – without white stripes should be immediately destroyed.

There was at least an hour before the tank regiment was due to arrive and no help could be expected from any other source. Zhuravlev looked with anguish at the approaching leading tank, whose front armour plate bore not even a trace of white paint.

The long-range reconnaissance company took cover inside the bank and the three PT-76s* prepared to meet the Czechs with armour-piercing shells.

We are done for, the battalion commander thought sadly. Why the hell did I allow myself to get such a long distance from the main force?

The PT-76 barrel was smoothly lowered a little, and the turret slightly turned. It was ready to fire.

Convulsively, Zhuravlev pressed the button of the tone generator: Don't shoot!

Perhaps, he thought, the incident will pass peacefully. When the time comes to engage the Czechs perhaps our people will arrive, maybe the Czechs will not open fire first? And it did look as if the leading tank had no such intention because its gun was still pointing at the sky, and the tank commander himself was clearly visible on the turret. The tanks were approaching quite fast, knocking sparks out of the old blocks of the roadway with their tracks. The column seemed endless, as more and more tanks appeared from round the corner and engulfed the narrow street with the suffocating stench of their exhaust gases.

'Comrade Major, they look like ours.'

'Of course they're ours, look at their dirty overalls.'

'What the hell! They've arrived much too early.'

*The PT-76 is an amphibious reconnaissance tank. For that reason, it possesses neither heavy armour nor an impressive armament. In comparison with the T-55, it is utterly defenceless.

168

'Hello, lads!'

'Salute the liberators!' The head tank turned sideways and then stopped, leaving the way open for the column.

Zhuravlev and his escort hurried towards it.

A broad, impudent and utterly filthy face appeared from the turret. His overalls were soaked in oil – he was Russian. He was about forty, which meant he was not an ordinary soldier, but who knew what kind of shoulder-straps he had under his overalls? Perhaps he was an over-ripe junior lieutenant. On the other hand he might be a young colonel; one could only guess. If he was in the leading tank he might be the battalion or even the regimental commander. In overalls everybody looks the same.

'Why the hell are you roaming about over this brotherly country without any white stripes, like some counter-revolutionary?'

'We were in the reserve, they didn't want to bring us in but later they decided to do so, and by then there was no white paint left,' said the dirty-faced fellow, with a conciliatory grin.

'You bugger, I nearly hit you with our armour-piercing shells. Thank God your face is Russian and your overalls are dirty. You might at least have had a white stripe on the leading tank.'

The dirty-faced man looked contemptuously at the reconnaissance tanks: 'You and your advice can go and get stuffed.'

The passers-by listened with astonishment to all this foreign conversation, and the most intelligent among them clearly sensed that something was wrong. Meanwhile the head of the tank column had stopped and those behind were catching up and taking up positions straight across the tram-lines.

'Did you come to reinforce me?' Zhuravlev asked.

The dirty-faced tank commander raised his eyebrows in astonishment. Like most Soviet commanders he was pretty ill-bred and boorish, and he didn't bother to answer. Zhuravlev spat.

'Who are they?' the divisional chief of staff shouted into the receiver. 'Our first tanks are expected to enter Prague in about thirty minutes!'

The battalion commander switched off the transmitter, summoned his escort and went to find out who those tankmen were.

'Look here, lads, aren't you from the 6th Guards Division?'

'No, we're from the 35th.'

'Where's your commander? There's something wrong!'

'He's there,' said a young soldier, pointing at the dirty-faced fellow with whom Zhuravlev had just had such a nice chat.

'What's his rank and post?'

'He's Major Rogovoy, the regimental commander's deputy.'

Zhuravlev approached him again.

'Comrade Major' – this time Zhuravlev addressed him officially – 'I am the commander of the 6th Guards Division's Reconnaissance Battalion. I have just been informed from HQ that your regiment is not in its proper position.'

The dirty-faced officer whistled. A commander can commit no worse error than to take his unit to the wrong place, and Zhuravlev's words produced the appropriate effect. Quickly, he produced his map and opened it out. Right in the centre of the map, there was a big red oval with an inscription in black: '35th Motor-Rifle Division.' Slightly higher up, in sprawling handwriting, there were the words: 'Confirmed by the Chief of Staff of the 20th Guards Army, Major-General Khomyakov.' There was no doubt about it, the tankmen were exactly where they should be.

'Right then, take over the bank,' said Zhuravlev. 'It's on your territory. It looks as if I am the one who made a mistake.'

'I don't know anything about a bank, there was nothing about capturing a bank in my assignment. Telegraph, yes – telephone also – but not a word about a bank!'

'Since it's on your territory, you've got it. I don't bloody well want it. My guardsmen will be off in a moment. I've been ordered to take possession of the bridges.'

'Seizing the bridges is the task of our division's reconnaissance battalion,' the tank man said confidently, 'and we came to reinforce them.' Once again, the tank man pointed at the map. The circle covered the bridges as well, there could be no doubt about it.

'Look here, does your reconnaissance battalion not have any white stripes on its armour as well?'

'I believe so, why?'

'I think that just now our two reconnaissance battalions were shooting at each other!'

'Oh, come off it!'

'I tell you!' Zhuravlev was hurriedly opening his map, trying to find his mistake. But on his map there was just the same red circle covering the town's central points together with the bridges. Exactly the same inscription was at the top: 'Confirmed by the Chief of Staff of the 20th Guards Army, Major-General Khomyakov.' The only difference was that on Zhuravlev's map was written the 6th Guards Motor-Rifle Division and not the 35th.

The commanders swore simultaneously. The army staff had given the same task to two divisions, and one of these divisions had no markings.

'Show me your photographs,' said the dirty tank man, laying out his own photographs on a board. The two sets of photographs were absolutely identical. They showed the same crossroads and in the very same order.

'But why didn't we see your reconnaissance battalion?' said Zhuravlev in surprise. 'It must have followed the same route.'

'Who the hell knows! Maybe there was something wrong with its route too!'

Both commanders ran to their machines to inform headquarters about the misunderstanding which had just come to light. But headquarters had already realised for itself that a great many serious mistakes had been worked out a whole eight months in advance. The columns of different divisions, armies and even fronts had been mixed up together, and control of the troops had in many cases been lost. All the call signs had got mixed up as well, there were hundreds of 'Cornflowers' and 'Cupids' and 'Nightingales' and 'Simfoeropols' all using the same frequency, obstructing one another and trying in vain to shout one another down. Central Front Headquarters had issued a directive not to shoot vehicles which did not carry white stripes. Apparently, headquarters had guessed that there had not been enough white paint to go round, or perhaps they had already received information about Soviet tanks shooting at one another.

It was half an hour later when Zhuravlev managed somehow to get in contact with divisional headquarters. He was ordered to remain where he was. He was also informed that he would not receive reinforcements that day, as the division's tank regiment had got lost and probably overshot Prague.

Zhuravlev again visited the dirty tankman from the 35th Division. The latter told Zhuravlev that he could not contact his headquarters. The lines were blocked. Zhuravlev described the general picture to him and invited him to the bank for a glass of 'tea'.

'To hell with your bloody bank! You'd better come and see me this evening. I've something to really entertain you with.'

Whereupon they parted.

Friendship between Soviet officers usually blossoms in such situations.

Meanwhile crowds were filling the streets. Young and old, men and women, they all rushed towards the Soviet tanks.

'Why did you come?'

'We didn't call for you!'

'We can solve our own problems without tanks!'

The soldiers really had no way of answering these questions, and they did not try to, except occasionally.

'We came to protect you.'

'The Americans and the Germans want to take you over. Have you really forgotten the war already?'

'Well, you come when they do start to take us over!'

Th(officers, especially the political activists, plunged into the crowds, but without any noticeable success.

'We were invited in by your own government.'

'You just name one member of the government who invited you to interfere in our affairs.'

'Comrades!'

'We're not your comrades!' And the political deputy was struck in the face. He reached for his pistol, but the soldiers pulled him back out of the crowd.

'Bloody fascists!'

'It's you who are the bloody fascists!'

'You brought your own country to a state of starvation and now you want all those around you to sit and starve!'

'Those are only temporary difficulties, later things will be much better in our country.'

'And without you it would have been better than ever!'

'Get the hell out of here, wherever you came from! And take your Marx and Lenin with you!'

'Citizens, keep calm!'

'Go to hell!'

'Citizens, by your unreasonable behaviour, you are putting all the victories of socialism on the verge of . . .'

'Your socialism should have been tested on dogs first, just as all normal scientists do. Your Lenin was stupid and no good at science.'

'Don't you dare speak in such a way about Lenin!' A rotten egg landed smack in the middle of the political deputy's red face.

'But if Pavlov had been given the task of introducing communism, he'd have quickly proved, by experimenting on dogs, that this way of life isn't suitable for a living soul!'

At the very back of the column, the discussion had taken on an even more agitated form. Youths were hurling stones at the last three tanks, forcing the crews to hide inside, and then with crowbars had broken open the spare fuel tanks which are fixed to the outsides of tanks during long advances. A minute later, the last but one tank began to smoke, and then another. Disorganised shooting could be heard. The crowd reeled back from the last tank, but only for a moment.

Two crews tried vainly to put out the flames while the third tank swivelled its turret sharply round, trying to throw off the youths who had climbed on to it. Two platoons of tankmen from the centre of the column fought their way through the crowd to help their comrades.

172

'Keep clear! The shells in the tanks will start exploding at any moment!'

'You bloody fascists!'

Zhuravlev, who had watched all this from the bank window, secretly rejoiced at the others' misfortune. Why the hell start a discussion? You've come here to liberate them, so get on with it. Don't start any political discussions!

The reconnaissance tanks of Zhuravlev's battalion were standing there too. But the crowd somehow didn't notice them. The soldiers were obediently carrying out their orders and swearing at everybody right, left and centre. The Czechs either understood the tones only too well, or else preferred not to carry on any discussions in such tones, or they were simply convinced that they would be unable to out-swear the Russians. In any case the people just did not linger near the reconnaissance tanks. All the swearing and scuffles took place in the tank column itself at those places where the political deputies were especially active, trying to convince the people of things that they did not even know for sure themselves.

'Stalinism and the personality cult in general were accidents in our history! Like hell, they were! For thirty years out of fifty, it was Stalinism. And how long during the last twenty years did you live without a cult? Without the cult of Lenin, Khrushchev and the others?'

'And why is there no personality cult in America? And never has been?'

'There is imperialism in America, Comrades, and that is much worse!'

'How do you know it's much worse? Have you ever been there?'

'Why is there a personality cult in every single socialist country from Cuba to Albania, from Korea to Rumania? All these countries are different: their communism is also different, but the personality cult is always the same. It all began with the cult of Lenin . . .'

'Don't you dare insult Lenin! Lenin was a genius for all mankind!'

'Lenin was a pederast.'

'Silence!'

An old man with a little wedge-shaped beard twisted one of the buttons on the regimental political deputy's tunic.

'Now don't go and get too excited. Have you read Lenin?'

'Of course I have!'

'And Stalin?'

'Ah . . . Ah . . . well . . .'

'Well, my old lad, you read them both and count how many times each of them uses the word 'shoot'. There are some very interesting

173

statistics. Did you know that, in comparison with Lenin, Stalin was a pitiful amateur and ignoramus. Lenin was an out and out sadist, one of those degenerates who happens only once in a thousand years!'

'But Lenin didn't annihilate as many innocents as Stalin did!'

'History stopped him in time. It removed him from the scene at the right time. But remember that Stalin didn't let himself go completely from the very outset, but only after ten to fifteen years of unlimited power. Lenin's start had much more impetus. And, if he had lived longer, he would have done things which would have made Stalin's thirty million dead look like child's play in comparison. Stalin never, I repeat never, signed orders authorising the killing of children without trial. And Lenin did so in his very first year of power, isn't that so?'

'But, under Stalin, children were shot in their thousands.'

'That's right, Comrade Colonel, quite right, but you just try and name me at least one child who was shot without trial on Stalin's orders! There you are, you can't say anything! I repeat, Lenin was one of the most bloodthirsty degenerates who ever lived. Stalin at least tried to conceal his crimes, not so Lenin. Stalin never gave official orders for the murder of hostages. But Lenin killed children as well as hostages and never felt the least compunction about it. Lenin, Comrade Colonel, should be read attentively!'

'But now you're criticising not only Lenin and Stalin but Marx too!'

'What's the difference? Marx or Mao? Of course, neither of them called for the deaths of millions of innocents. But both Lenin, and even more so Stalin, didn't call for them either in their pre-revolutionary writing. In Lenin's works, the word 'shootings' appears only after the October revolution, and in Stalin's works it never appears at all. But you, my fine fellow, must agree that, where any form of communism appears, with a human face or without it, it always engenders a personality cult. Always! It is a rule with no exceptions. Of course, if it appears in France or Italy, the shooting of millions of people will not start at once, the conditions are different. For the time being! But if, as Marx taught us, communism eventually wins in the majority of all developed countries, such atrocities cannot be avoided, and there will be nobody left to be ashamed. There will always be a personality cult. There will always be a Mao or a Fidel or a Stalin or a Lenin. And the cult will always have to be defended by strength and by terror, a great wave of terror. The freer the country previously, the greater will be the terror. Your ideas are beautiful but only in theory: in practice, they can only be thrust upon people with tanks and brute force like yours, Comrade Colonel!'

'You . . . you . . . you're an Anti-Soviet! That's what you are!'

'And you . . . You are a Marxist–Leninist which, translated into human language, means a child murderer!'

174

A rotten tomato flashed through the air and landed on his peaked cap and splashed itself all over the colonel's face.

The crowd pressed close again. Somewhere, in one of the neighbouring streets, came the sound of renewed firing. And a light breeze from the river brought with it the smell of burning rubber.

At first glance, and before taking into consideration the huge responsibility involved, work in a bank may not seem too bad. There is a washroom with hot and cold running water, and it is a big house with railings. You are not taunted with stones or with rotten eggs: but, what is even more important, you can have a good kip after so many sleepless months. From his very first day in the army, Zhuravlev had understood that no one is ever compensated for lost sleep – if you do manage to snatch a couple of hours, it's yours; if not, no one will ever give it to you. Besides, this first night in Prague promised to be a very disturbed one. He checked the guard once more, looked through the window at the seething town, and then lay down on the sofa in the director's office.

But they did not let him sleep. About ten minutes later, in ran his personal driver, Junior Sergeant Malekhin, to report that two armed Czechs wanted to speak to him. Zhuravlev seized his automatic and carefully looked out into the street. At the entrance to the bank between two reconnaissance tanks stood a van with grilled windows, and two Czechs with pistols in their holsters were quarrelling with the sentries.

'But they've come to deliver money.'

The junior sergeant just shrugged his shoulders. He didn't understand.

Zhuravlev had an irresistible desire to yawn, but those two Czechs with pistols were trying hard to explain something to him. Then a third man appeared and, in front of the battalion commander, opened a carton crammed full of money. He indicated that his whole van was full of such cartons.

'The bank is not functioning,' explained the battalion commander, 'and will not be functioning. I arrested your people here but later let them go. Those were my orders. I can't accept your money.'

The three men with pistols held a long consultation between themselves and then threw a heap of cartons from the van straight on to the steps of the bank. One of them shouted something which sounded very offensive and the van vanished round the corner, clearing its path through the crowd with an unpleasantly shrill hooting.

Zhuravlev swore viciously. Then he ordered the sentries to bring all the cartons inside.

Fifteen minutes later the saga of the cartons was repeated. This time, the battalion commander understood that it was useless to argue and he just pointed in silence at the bank's door. The collectors threw their precious cargo straight on to the floor and then left without saying a word. Zhuravlev merely noted the van's number and the quantity of packages.

Then a whole flurry of black vans with grilled windows drove up. The mountains of cases, cartons and leather bags containing money grew menacingly. The collectors generally did not ask for receipts, but when they did Major Zhuravlev resolutely sent them to the devil and told them to take their packages with them. After some hesitation they threw everything on to the common heap.

It was difficult to understand where so much money had come from. On the first day of the liberation, the country was totally paralysed. Probably the money now flowing into the bank was from the previous day or even earlier. Long after midnight, when the last vehicle arrived, the mountain in the central hall recalled a picture of an Egyptian pyramid taken from a children's history textbook.

Sensing the inherent risk in the present situation, Zhuravlev dismissed all his sentries from the bank; the guard remained outside, while he alone was inside. It was safer that way.

There was no possibility of sleeping. Throughout the night Zhuravlev wandered about with a big bunch of keys among the depositories, opening armoured doors and steel grilles and locking them again and placing his seals on them. At his express wish the whole alarm system had been switched off by the nightwatchmen before he let them go.

It is an astonishing thing to wander alone about the vaults of a large bank. Zhuravlev came across gold bars marked with the Soviet hammer and sickle and with Czech lions, and gold plates with long serial numbers and the inscription 999.9, and thousands of the most varied coins. But most interesting of all was the foreign paper money.

He was absolutely indifferent towards money as such, but the intricate designs and the unequalled colour range attracted him. He spent hours on end studying notes which depicted kings and presidents, women and flowers, and thoughts of some unknown civilisation rose up in his imagination.

During all his thirty-two years he had seen quite a bit of the world. He had been in Siberia and the Far East, in Kazakhstan and in Polar regions. He had also studied at the academy in Moscow; he had taken part in parades in Red Square and in many of the largest training exercises. When he was twenty and still only a sergeant, he had found himself in Hungary, right in the centre of Budapest, in the very centre of that hell of fighting for the liberation of that brotherly people. Later still, he had served all over the Soviet Union. He served well: he went to Germany, and now finally he was in Czechoslovakia. During his lifetime, he had seen quite a number of those 245 million inhabitants. How often would you meet a man who had been in two foreign countries? And Zhuravlev had now visited his third country.

Once again he studied the designs on the crinkly notes and he felt a vague unease. These notes bore witness to some other completely unknown and unusual life. Every one of them had travelled a long way and lived a long life before landing in the vaults of a Prague bank and into the hands of a Soviet officer-liberator called Aleksandr Zhuravlev. Very soon all of them would be scattered abroad, and they would again return to their own mysterious world, while Major Zhuravlev would still be guarding all the honest people in his world. He would become a lieutenant-colonel and maybe even a colonel and then he would be retired from the army and tell colourful stories of his career to anyone who cared to listen.

Zhuravlev was awakened by a distant, regular and heavy knocking sound. Brought back to reality, he rubbed his eyes and ran down to open the heavy door. In came Lieutenant-Colonel Voronchuk, the chief of divisional reconnaissance. The sky was already clearing in the east and a pleasant coolness pervaded the air.

'Come in, come in.'

Quite recently, Voronchuk had been the reconnaissance battalion commander while Zhuravlev was his first deputy. Before this particular operation, during the shake-ups and rearrangements and replacements, both men had advanced one step higher on the service ladder. But this promotion did not interfere with their long-standing friendship.

'Well, banker, how's the battalion? It hasn't run away yet?'

'The ones with me haven't, but the ones with the political deputy, God knows what they're doing.'

'There's no political deputy any more. He's been taken to hospital. They smashed his head in with a brick this morning.'

'Was he busy agitating?'

'He was busy doing it himself and also urging all the other soldiers and officers to do the same, which is why quite a few of our people were beaten up on the bridges.'

'And who was shooting over there this morning? I'm cut off here and know absolutely nothing about what's happened to my companies.'

'The Czechs started the shooting and then two reconnaissance battalions were shooting at each other. The 35th Division hadn't got enough white paint, so some of your falcons had a go at them. Fortunately, the tanks were not at the head of the column. Still, your fellows shot two of the reconnaissance scouts: one of them slightly, but the other's seriously wounded.'

'Like to moisten your throat a little to keep me company?'

'No, Sasha, thanks. I have to see the divisional commander in an hour to put in my report.'

'When am I to be relieved?'

'Who knows? The tank regiment lost its way and we haven't made contact with it. Two motor-rifle regiments are jammed on the road. The artillery and rear column have dropped far behind. Only one motor-rifle regiment in the whole of our division made it into town properly. But you know yourself how chaotic it all is. Generally speaking, too many units entered Prague by mistake and there's nothing for them to do here. They came in by mistake and now they don't know what to do. They can't leave the city for the time being either, since all contact's been lost. It's like a fire in a brothel!'

'Well, let's have a drink. I've got some things to suck to kill the smell.'

'Pour it out then, and let's drink to the devil!'

'After all that training, just look at the shambles. There you are, you see!'

'If the Czechs had really started shooting, it would have been worse than Hungary.'

'But our people knew beforehand that the Czechs would never shoot. They're ready to submit to anyone and they'll lie down under anybody. They're not like the Hungarians. The Czechs won't lift a finger for the sake of their own freedom. Did you notice that, when the tanks just stand about not doing anything, the Czechs consider it quite natural and even behave themselves. Only when we embark on our propaganda and mind-bending, do the disorders seem to break out.'

'Of course I noticed it. I told my men to get it into their heads not to have any truck with that kind of talk. What the hell's it all for anyway?'

'You'd better be careful, Sasha. If the political deputies find out, you won't be able to lie your way out of it or to fight your way out of it.'

'I'm doing it while he's not around my neck. When the battalion was split into two, I sent him off to the bridges.'

'In any case, be careful. Their ears are just as long as their tongues. Sometime this morning have a few chats with the Czechs just in case the soldiers sneak on you.'

'Okay, I'll do that.'

'The tankmen of the 35th Division are keeping an eye on you. They may do the dirty on you, and the political creeps aren't asleep either.'

'Who do you mean?'

'Fomin, from the second long-range reconnaissance group, and Zhebrak who's with the tankmen.'

178

'I had my suspicions about them. I think Fomin's in contact with the "specials", and Zhebrak's the political deputy's lapdog.'

'Then there's Gareyev from radio reconnaissance.'

'Oh, him, I know about him.'

'Then there's Kurakin and Akhmadulin from the BRDM Company. Kurakin for sure and Akhmadulin looks very like it.'

'I did think about them, but I wasn't sure.'

'And your personal driver, of course.'

'Oh, go on!'

'He's absolutely typical!'

'Have you got anything concrete to go on?'

'No, I just feel it in my bones. I've a special eye. I've never been mistaken yet. Do be careful, Sasha, the reconnaissance battalions are filled to overflowing with political spies. It's quite normal of course: how could it be otherwise?'

'One more for the road?'

'Okay, but this'll be the last one.'

'Your health, Kolya.'

Next day, the flood of money cartons noticeably subsided and the day after it stopped altogether. But the oppressive feeling of heavy responsibility did not pass. Zhuravlev knew how difficult it is sometimes to give an account of even one rouble, and here were all the vaults filled with gold, currency and various kinds of paper money. If some commission or other arrived, and all this had to be accounted for, a whole year would not be enough to do the job. And suppose something was missing? How could he account for all these cartons? Who knew how many millions there were? A lot of them were not even sealed. The future possibilities of all this deprived him of his sleep for nights. Zhuravlev lost his appetite, became pale, thin and pinched. The town continued to seethe. All his friends were being assaulted by volleys of stones and insults, the tanks were busy dispersing the dissident elements and trying to locate underground radio stations. They were also continuing their agitation work and preaching and defending themselves against all comers. All those who knew where Zhuravlev was were extremely envious. The nickname 'Banker' stuck firmly. But, all the time, he was getting thinner, paler and more envious of those who were out on the streets.

Three times a day, a driver brought him food: unheard-of American tinned food, fragrant bread, delicious French butter.

'You'd better eat something, Comrade Major.'

'Okay. Off you go.'

'Comrade Major, you just tell me what you'd like and I can provide you with anything you want! We've never seen anything like it.'

'Okay, okay. Off you go!'

'Comrade Major, may I just ask you one thing?'

'What's that?'

'Comrade Major, allow me to go just two blocks down the road in a tank.'

'What for?'

'There's a chemist's shop. But if I don't go in a tank our patrols will stop me or else the Czechs will bash my head in.'

'Why do you want a chemist's shop? Have you got a dose of the clap?'

'No, Comrade Major. I want some contraceptives. I'll get some for both of us.'

'I don't need them, and what the hell do you need them for?'

The driver smirked and motioned towards the bulging paper cartons.

'My right fuel tank is empty. No one has counted the money. We could invest a couple of million in contraceptives and put them into the fuel tank. Nobody would guess! Do you know how much money you can stuff into one contraceptive? It stretches . . .'

'You dirty scum!' Zhuravlev grabbed his pistol. 'Throw your automatic on the floor! Face the wall! Escort, come here!'

'I was only joking, comrade.'

'Shut your mouth, you scum!'

Late that same evening, the divisional chief of staff and three others dressed in civilian clothes, plus an escort, forced their way towards the bank in a tracked personnel carrier.

'What's going on here Zhuravlev?' mumbled the chief of staff in dissatisfied tones.

'Comrade Lieutenant-Colonel, I have arrested driver Malekhin for attempted looting.'

'The comrades will investigate the matter. Where is he?'

Zhuravlev led them along a corridor towards the central hall. All three stopped dead in their tracks.

'We urgently need a radio station!'

'The driver is locked in that room.'

'We need a radio and not a driver!' the young shaven-headed 'comrade' interrupted rudely.

Zhuravlev was relieved of his duties quite suddenly and without any trouble whatsoever.

Half an hour after the 'comrades' had managed to contact their leadership, another two BTR-50Ps, packed full of officers and civilians, arrived at the bank. Zhuravlev spent the rest of the night on external guard duty at the bank. He was never allowed inside again not even to go to the lavatory.

Early the following morning, a tank battalion from the 14th Motor-Rifle Division, which was part of the army commander's reserve, approached the bank.

The tank battalion commander gave Zhuravlev an order personally signed by the 20th Guards Army commander, which instructed Zhuravlev to take his reconnaissance battalion out of the town immediately.

Zhuravlev sighed with relief. The order also mentioned that the part of his battalion at present guarding the bridges was also temporarily removed from his command, so he had nothing to worry about at all. And, merely to remove one long-range reconnaissance company and one tank platoon, was not a difficult task.

It took only ten minutes to get ready. Zhuravlev formed up his scouts and then checked their number, armament and ammunition. The tank engines began to roar . . . but at that very moment the tall crew-cut 'comrade' appeared on the bank's steep steps.

'Hey, Major! Wait!'

The insolence shown by the 'comrades', especially in the presence of soldiers and sergeants, always irritates the army officers, but of course they never show it.

'What's the matter?'

'Sign this Major.' Whereupon, he handed over a sheet of paper covered in columns of figures. 'Don't be in any doubt, everything's in order. Our chaps were checking it all throughout the entire night.'

Zhuravlev signed without even reading or examining it. How on earth, anyway, could he have known how much of everything there was in the bank?

The young fellow smiled.

'Here you are, Major, keep it as a souvenir' – and he put his hand into his sagging pocket and held out to Zhuravlev a big gold coin with the profile of some elderly woman wearing a crown.

The Reconnaissance Battalion of the 6th Guards Motor-Rifle Division of the 20th Guards Army, to the north of Prague. First days of September 1968.

Counter-Revolution

The motor-cycle was burnt out during a drinking bout. While the platoon was cleaning its weapons, somebody brought a bottle of Czech plum-brandy, which was quickly dealt with. The cleaning session promptly became much more cheerful. After a long march, weapons were always cleaned by washing them in petrol. This method is forbidden but it is the most effective. After cleaning, there was a short break for a smoke which took place close to the bucket containing the petrol. The first section's gunner threw his cigarette-butt into the bucket and the petrol flared up gaily. The platoon commander's deputy, Sergeant Mel'nik, kicked the burning bucket, while the scouts happily laughed. But the bucket turned a somersault in the air and fell back on to the motor-cycle, whose tank was open, as the petrol used for cleaning had been taken from it. The rest happened in a single second. Only the black charred frame of the motor-cycle remained.

Their state of intoxication had been very superficial, and it evaporated at once. The whole affair started to smell not only of burning rubber and paint, but also of a military tribunal and even of a penal battalion for the culprits.

The platoon commander's deputy became very gloomy, then moved away and sat down under a birch tree, clenching his head in his hands.

The first section commander came to his senses before anyone else. Looking round, and making sure that there were no officers or soldiers about who did not belong to the platoon, he gave a firm order: 'Platoon, get into formation! In two lines! Level up! Attention. Now pay attention!'

The accident had frightened the platoon, and feeling a strong hand they formed up in quicker time than normal. Only the platoon commander's deputy stayed under his tree not paying attention to anything.

'Now pay attention!' repeated the sergeant. 'A Czech car, a Skoda, dark blue in colour with three Czechs inside it, was approaching us. They threw an incendiary bottle at us. We were cleaning our weapons and therefore couldn't shoot back. The platoon commander's deputy did not lose his head, and hit one of them over the head with part of his dismantled machine-gun. The attacker was a fair-haired fellow. They immediately made off. Is that clear? The deputy commander is one of us, we're not going to sell him up the river. He's going to be demobilised soon and he's only been carrying out his international duty.'

The platoon murmured approvingly.

'I repeat, a Skoda, dark blue in colour, three men inside, they threw the bottle. The deputy commander hit one with part of his machine-gun. One more thing! The car number-plate had been intentionally obscured with mud. And, one last thing, a commission will come to investigate; they'll try to catch us out on details. No one should invent anything; repeat only what I have said. As for the rest: I don't remember, I didn't see, I don't know, I didn't pay attention! Clear?'

'Yes!'

'Dismissed!'

'Kolya, Kolya, don't get depressed. Maybe everything will still be all right. Listen, Kolya – better send a scout to the company commander and let him report about the Czechs. There's a conference going on there now at the commander's place. Meanwhile, tell the platoon to get ready to defend itself, as if we are expecting a second attack.'

An hour later all the company officers, including the commander himself, arrived at the platoon. After examining the terrain, the company commander ordered all the soldiers to come and see him one at a time. He was standing about eighty metres away from the others and, as each soldier approached him, he asked him three or four questions. The conversation with every soldier was tête-à-tête and no one could hear either the questions or the answers.

Then the commander summoned the first section sergeant.

'Not very bad weather, Sergeant is it?'

'No, Comrade Captain.'

'Only it'll probably rain towards evening.'

'Most probably, Comrade Captain' – the sergeant still could not understand what the captain was driving at. 'It's so boring, all this blasted rain.'

'Yes, it is boring,' agreed the captain. 'So you say they came in a Skoda?'

'Yes!'

'But where are the tyre marks? The earth is still wet.'

The captain was also a reconnaissance scout and to deceive him was not easy. But he did not want to have a blot on his company's record.

'Look here, Sergeant, where that bucket burned and where it flew into the motor-cycle, the earth must be dug over as if dirty oil rags had been buried there after cleaning. And all the ground round must be trampled down. In all other matters, stand your ground!'

'Yes! Stand our ground!'

'And tell the senior sergeant not to hang his head. If he did hit a counter-revolutionary on the head – why worry!'

Neither commission nor special investigator ever appeared at the platoon. Apparently they already had enough to do. Meanwhile the company commander wrote a report about battle losses during a clash with armed counter-revolutionaries in the pay of imperialistic intelligence services.

The battalion commander turned the report over in his hands and smiled.

'Well, I'll sign everything for you, but you must re-write all this, add that there was an anti-tank grenade-launcher, an RPG-7B, as well as the motor-cycle. You'll find its number in the 2nd Company. While we were still in Poland, those scoundrels sank it in a swamp and couldn't get it out.' The captain was prepared to object but, having caught the look in the eye of the battalion commander, he only growled sullenly.

'Yes, re-write it then!'

The report went on its way through the normal channels returning every now and then for another re-write.

When the report reached the rear commander of the Carpathian Front, who signed all reports concerning battle losses, he visualised a wonder machine which had been created on the base of a reconnaissance motor-cycle, the M-72. This miraculous machine was armed with a machine-gun and an anti-tank grenade-launcher; it had two active infra-red sights, a range-finder sight and an R-123 radio transmitter. The machine was also apparently intended for work in polar conditions as two bright new sheep-skin coats were on top of it at the time of the accident; and behind it, probably being towed, there was a 200-litre barrel of pure spirit. Unfortunately, it was all burned during the clash with the counter-revolutionaries.

The general turned the report over in his hands.

'Return the report, let them re-write it, add . . . Let's see.'

'In the 128th Division a BTR fell off the bridge.'

'As the result of an incident with counter-revolutionaries?'

'Yes.'

'That's better. Give me the report.'

And the platoon commander's deputy, Senior Sergeant Mel'nik, received a medal for his bold, decisive action while repelling an attack. There was even a newspaper report about him!

The outskirts of Koshitse. Early September 1968.

Flight

During the very first days of liberation, when troops were almost constantly on the move, our battalion stopped one night near a small town where there was a small factory. We spent the night in a field close to the town, after first taking all precautionary measures and putting forward guard posts and mobile patrols.

Next morning a very unpleasant circumstance came to light. The small factory proved to be not just any old factory but an alcohol plant. The previous evening I had smelt that special aroma all round us in the air: the other officers also could not possibly have missed it. But, at the end of the day, everybody was so tired that we all fell fast asleep at the first opportunity.

But our little soldiers did not sleep, nor did they waste any time either. The spirit plant like all other Czechoslovak factories at the time was not operating. But at night, the town's inhabitants, not without evil intent of course, pointed out to our soldiers the way to the factory, hospitably opened the factory gates and showed them how to open the appropriate taps.

Towards morning every single soldier in the battalion was a bit drunk. But we must do them justice, no one was really stoned. Everyone understood full well that it was only one step to the field disciplinary tribunal, and that the field tribunal would operate on a war footing. So all the soldiers were not really drunk, only slightly inebriated, very merry – tipsy.

The battalion commander immediately removed the whole column from that damned place and informed the higher command about the spirit factory, which was promptly taken under special guard. At the very first halt a thorough search was undertaken. It was found that all containers, all objects capable of holding liquid, were filled to capacity with spirits: flasks, canisters, mess tins, even hot water bottles belonging to the battalion's first-aid equipment. Any alcohol thus discovered was religiously emptied out on to the road. All officers of the battalion became drivers and the column started on its way. Of course there were not enough officers to replace all the drivers, and as a result many of the armoured troop transport carriers moved over the liberated country in a slightly zig-zag manner.

Towards lunchtime, all the soldiers had sobered up. The battalion spent the next night in a field far removed from any habitation. By early morning, we began to feel that again something was wrong. The eyes of most of the soldiers were glistening like oil. None of them was drunk, but each was definitely tipsy. We carried out yet another careful search, but found nothing. There was nothing wrong in principle with the fact that the soldiers were drinking a little from time to time. You won't find any kind of prohibition in any Soviet Army manual. Under battle conditions, soldiers are entitled to have a little to drink to give them courage.

The real problem was the fact that the present situation approximated to battle conditions, but we were to fulfil a purely diplomatic function, that is to say we were to disperse people who did not wish to be liberated. And it was not really proper on our part to carry out this task smelling of drink. If the enemy propaganda machine were to find out that 400 Soviet soldiers were carrying out their noble mission under the strong influence of Bacchus, it could lead to a world scandal.

The next morning, the story was the same, and the next also. What happened was that the KGB and Party agencies found themselves drawn into the common scheme of things and did not give away the location of the miraculous alcoholic spring. In Czechoslovakia, incidentally, all these KGB and Party servants immediately put their tails between their legs and were not at all in a hurry to write reports. It was all quite understandable as everybody was armed and it would be so easy to get killed by accident, or to be run over, by mistake, by a tank at night. This kind of thing went on everywhere. The business of settling accounts was swift, regardless of the differences in language and interests.

Nor was the battalion commander in any great hurry to report what was going on as, by doing so, he would call down a mass of trouble on his head. He preferred to discover the alcohol himself, with the help of all the other officers of the battalion.

It was clear that the stocks of spirits in the battalion were huge: enough for at least one soldier's mug every day, for each of the 400 soldiers. The battalion was constantly on the move, which meant that the spirit was not in the forest and not buried underground, but was moving along with us. It was somewhere in our vehicles. But where? We examined everything millimetre by millimetre. We even checked whether the spirit was inside the armoured troop carriers' tyres. But it wasn't there.

If this regular drinking had been going on in my company alone, I might have been in very serious trouble, but it was going on in other companies as well, so I relaxed. The question of the alcohol disturbed me only theoretically: where the hell could it be hidden? I firmly decided to locate that alcohol, by all possible means, regardless of what sacrifice it might cost. But I had only one thing to offer as a sacrifice and that was my gold 'Flight' watch. It was the only thing I possessed. And what, except a watch and a comb, can any Soviet lieutenant be expected to possess?

The watch was a splendid one and I had noticed for a long time that one of the radio men from the signals platoon always looked at it with very considerable interest. I don't know why, but I always had the impression that this man was very greedy, although I really hardly knew him.

At lunchtime, when there was absolutely no one around the field signals office and when I knew that the radio man was on duty alone inside, I entered the office. A visit by a company commander to the battalion signals office is a most unusual event. Without saying a single word I took the watch off my wrist and held it out towards him. He looked at the watch without daring to take it and then waited to find out what I would demand in exchange. Being a signals man he did, of course, speak a little Russian.

'I need the alcohol.' Whereupon I threw back my head, imitating someone drinking. 'Do you understand? Spirits.' Then I gulped, showing how it gurgles as it passes down the throat. He nodded. Even though he was a Moslem he still understood me. And apparently he also consumed his medicinal drink along with the others every day.

'Ten litres, understand?' I showed him ten fingers. 'Ten.'

He gripped the watch and said curtly, 'This evening.'

'No,' I said. 'I want it now.'

He turned the watch over and over in his hand and reluctantly returned it to me. 'Now is impossible.'

I put the watch in my pocket and slowly went towards the door, but just before I reached it I turned round sharply. The soldier was watching me leave with great sorrow in his eyes. Quickly, I took my watch and put it in his hand.

'I will take it myself.'

He nodded, seized it in a flash, wrapped it up in a handkerchief and put it in the top of his boot. At the same time he whispered a single word in my ear which I could not quite make out.

I hated the man; and yet, before coming to see him at the signals office I had sworn to tell nobody, not even the battalion commander, how I had discovered the alcohol. And so, in order not to give it all away, I did not run at once to the battalion staff, of course, but waited several hours. Only towards evening did I tap the commander's vehicle. The commander was sitting inside in complete dejection.

187

'Comrade Lieutenant-Colonel, would you like to take a mug of spirits with me?' It was the purest impertinence. But he, of course, forgave me.

'Where?' he roared, and, jumping up from his chair, knocked his head on the armoured roof. 'Where you son of a bitch?'

I smiled: 'Inside the radiators.'

Every armoured troop carrier has two engines and, since they both operate in extremely arduous conditions, every one of them has a very well-developed water-cooling system with capacious radiators, which in summer are filled with clear water. The soldiers had poured out all the water and filled them up with spirits. They drank it every evening by getting under the engines, and pretending to carry out maintenance.

The commander immediately formed up the whole battalion and personally went along the column opening the drainage cock in each machine. The autumnal forest was soon filled with a wonderful aroma.

And, one day later, the signals man, who had given away the secret, was found beaten nearly to death in the bushes near the signals office. He was taken urgently to hospital, and the doctors there pronounced that he was suffering from a result of an encounter with counter-revolutionaries.

After a few more days, when the other events had overtaken the signal man's case, another signals man approached me and held out to me my gold 'Flight' watch.

'Isn't this yours, Comrade Lieutenant?'

'As a matter of fact it is mine,' I said. 'Thank you – but where did you find it?'

'Apparently one of the men stole it from you.'

'Is that why you beat him so brutally?'

He looked intently at me.

'For that, among other things!'

Koshitse—Prague. September 1968.

Farewell to the Liberators

The alarm sounded at about five o'clock in the morning. It was beastly cold in the forest. Just the time to sleep and sleep, with your nose buried in the collar of your greatcoat. Slowly, I emerged from underneath my warm greatcoat – there were noises in my head after the previous day's jollifications. Not a single living soul paid the slightest attention to the alarm signal. During one short month, discipline had fallen catastrophically low.

From the depths of my memory I extracted a tirade especially prepared for just such an occasion as this, and in a low voice without any particular anger, I spoke it into the ear of the company sergeant-major, who was pretending to be asleep. The sergeant-major jumped up, not because he was frightened by my threats but only because the tirade was much too ingenious and interesting.

The sergeant-major went along the rows of sleeping men and sergeants kicking them with the tip of his boot and enveloping them in well-chosen abuse. Whenever I am awakened at dawn after a night spent in a cold forest, I always become very angry, I don't know why. The foulest curses accumulate in my throat, and now I was looking around choosing upon whose head I could pour them all out. But when I came eye to eye with the first of the soldiers, I controlled myself: there was probably even more anger in his eyes than in mine. He was dirty, unshaven, long-haired, and had not even seen hot water for many weeks. He had an automatic rifle over his shoulder and his cartridge pouches were full. You just go and provoke him now and he'll kill you without a moment's hesitation.

The officers were gathered together for a meeting. The chief of the regimental staff read out the battle orders, according to which our division was to be transferred urgently from the 38th Army of the Carpathian Front to the 20th Guards Army of the Central Front. We had to go many hundred kilometres across country and then towards evening form up to the north of Prague, in order to cover the troops of the 20th Guards Army. All tracked vehicles, tanks, tractors, and heavy armoured troop carriers were to be left behind and we were to move without baggage, using only wheeled vehicles.

The order was completely incomprehensible, even to our own chief of staff, who had received it from the top. But there was no time for discussion. The columns were quickly formed up and the signs of readiness – small white flags – started to emerge above the commanders' hatches (while troops were moving, radio signals are forbidden). In the end, white flags were displayed over every machine. The signals man of the first machine twirled his white flag above his head, clearly pointing to the west. Once more we set off into uncertainty.

There was enough food for anxious thought. If you take the power of one unit's tanks, then in comparison that of the motorised infantry is zero. Tanks in conjunction with motorised infantry can be indestructible. At the present moment we were rushing madly over the country in our 'wheeled coffins' having abandoned our tanks. Without them, we became a zero, though still a very big one. The question arose why, and for whom, all this was necessary. Particularly as we were moving without our tracked towing vehicles, in other words without our artillery. And, of course, all this tended to prove that we were not going to fight. So where were we going and what for? Were there really not enough troops in the Prague region already?

During the short halts, while the soldiers were checking the machines and topping them up, we officers gathered in little groups and shared our worst fears amongst ourselves. None of us could make up his mind to pronounce aloud the dreaded diagnosis, but the sinister words were nevertheless already hanging in the air. 'Demoralisation of the troops has begun.'

Oh, if only the Czechs would fire at us!

In our regiments, especially those from the Carpathians, at that time there were many officers who had been in Hungary in 1956. The Soviet Army paid with its blood for the liberation of Hungary. In Czechoslovakia the price was even higher. None of the Hungarian veterans ever witnessed the faintest hint of the demoralisation of the troops which was already starting here. The point is that, when you are shot at, the situation is simplified. There is no time to think: those who wait to think are shot first.

In the early days in Czechoslovakia everything went according to plan: they threw tomatoes at us, and we fired shots in the air. But very soon everything changed. I don't know whether it was a special tactic, or whether it was a spontaneous phenomenon, but the people changed their attitude towards us. They became kinder and this was exactly what our army, created in the hothouse of isolation from the world at large, was not prepared for. There was a mutual and extremely dangerous *rapprochement* between the local inhabitants and our soldiers. On the one hand the Czechs suddenly understood that the overwhelming majority of our soldiers had not the slightest idea where

190

they were or why they were there. And, among the local inhabitants, especially the country folk, there arose an incomprehensible feeling of compassion and pity towards us. The absence of hostility towards the ordinary soldiers created in the soldiers' minds a distrust of our own official propaganda, because something did not fit. Theory contradicted practice. On the other hand, among the soldiers, there appeared and began to develop with unprecedented speed the idea that a counter-revolution is a positive event which raises the people's standard of living. The soldiers could not understand why such a beautiful country had to be driven by force into the same state of poverty in which we lived. This feeling was especially strong among the Soviet soldiers who came to Czechoslovakia from the GDR. The fact of the matter is that these select units are made up mostly of Russian soldiers. And the Russian population in the USSR fares at least twice as badly as my Ukrainian people, and many times worse than the Central Asian and Caucasian peoples, where nearly every third family possesses its own motor car.

In our second echelon divisions, consisting basically of soldiers from the Caucasian and Asian republics, demoralisation was just starting, while in the first echelon divisions, which had arrived from the Group of Soviet Troops in Germany, it had bitten catastrophically deep. Because for these Russians, particularly, the contrast between the Czechoslovak and USSR standards of living was especially striking, and it was particularly hard for them to understand why this state of affairs had to be destroyed. A certain part was, of course, played by the community of Czech and Russian languages, as well as by the fact that in the first echelon divisions all the soldiers were able to talk to one another and to compare notes, while in the second echelon divisions all nationalities and languages were purposely mixed up, thus preventing any discussion and comparing of notes.

We reached our destination at dead of night. Our very worst suppositions were totally justified. Our task consisted neither of stopping the Western tanks, nor of dispersing the violent counter-revolutionaries, but of neutralising the Russian soldiers who were being withdrawn from Czechoslovakia.

The 20th Guards Army is permanently based in the GDR in the region of Bernau, close to Berlin but completely isolated, of course. Many of my friends from the Kharkov Tank School served in its divisions. This army is the best of all the Group of the Soviet troops in Germany. It had entered Prague first and here it was now, the first to leave Czechoslovakia. It was a strange exit. The regimental colours, the staff and the major part of the senior officers returned to the GDR. Part of the battle equipment was sent there too. And, immediately, tens of thousands of fresh soldiers and officers were sent from the Baltic Military District to the 20th Guards Army. And everything fell into place. It was as if the army had never left at all. But the majority of the soldiers and young officers from this army were sent from Czechoslovakia direct to the Chinese frontier for re-education. And the liberators were sent en masse, in whole echelons, as if they were prisoners and we their guards.

Meanwhile, new echelons with young soldiers destined to serve in Czechoslovakia were already coming in from the Soviet Union. From the very first day these soldiers were protected by high fences. The sad lesson of liberation had been learned: and all of us realised that, for the next ten years, regardless of what happened in the world, nobody would dare send us to liberate any country with a higher standard of living than our own.

The Soviet Army after the liberation.

Form and Content

Anyone who has studied at least the beginnings of Marxist–Leninist philosophy knows that a deep and indissoluble link exists between content and form. The Soviet Army more than any other army on earth is impregnated with Marxism–Leninism and, as a result, has had the opportunity of proving to itself every day that form is the very brightest and best expression of content.

Every new Defence Minister starts by changing the uniform of the whole army. During the sixty years of the army's existence there has been no exception to this rule. Every new minister has somehow to introduce himself to the army, to the Soviet people and to the whole world. Otherwise, how can he show his own dazzling individuality? For instance, when Stalin became Defence Minister, he introduced gold shoulder-straps for officers, which up to that time had been the symbol of White Guard counter-revolution. Marshal Zhukov preferred the Gestapo uniform, so he introduced it for all Defence Ministry personnel. Soviet officers in the Far East had just had time to receive the order notifying them of the new uniform and had just had their Gestapo uniforms made when the newly-appointed Defence Minister in Moscow, Comrade Malinovskiy, invented another new uniform, similar to that worn by the Americans.

Such a practice as this, especially on the scale of the world's largest army, works out extremely expensive. Tens of millions of sets of uniforms are needed for reservists in case of war. So, when uniforms are changed, not only the whole three million army uniforms have to be remade, but several millions of ready-made sets of uniform have to be thrown out from the stores and replaced by new ones. The wearing-out of old uniforms is expressly forbidden. If, in addition to a change in the cut of the uniform, the Minister also decides to alter its colour, this spells disaster for the whole sewing industry. Civilians go from shop to shop, swearing and cursing, and cannot understand why a good overcoat cannot be bought for love or money.

The situation was completely hopeless when the new Defence Minister, Marshal Grechko, came to power. This was no time for a change of uniform! It was simply a time for making both ends meet.

The country had hardly recovered from the 1964 revolution, and now it had to destroy Israel. Nasser had been fed and armed to the teeth, and all to no avail. We had to start again from the beginning. Then just when things with Nasser had more or less been straightened out, along came the fiftieth anniversary of Soviet power. To honour this jubilee there were so many ruinously expensive demonstrations of might, and so many records were established, that the country was brought to the verge of economic disaster. For instance, the meat production record was beaten in 1967, and in 1968 there wasn't a cow or a pig left throughout the whole country. And these very same records are still an anathema to this very day. Then came Czechoslovakia: so what talk could there possibly be about a change of uniform?

But the new Minister was adamant and he had a very weighty argument to back him up. What did our Soviet forces look like when they entered Czechoslovakia? They were dirty and bedraggled, dressed in greasy tunics and wearing canvas-topped boots. A liberator must be resplendent not only in deed, but also in dress. What if tomorrow we dare to liberate Rumania or Yugoslavia or even West Germany?

With such arguments as these the Political Bureau could not possibly disagree; and the decision was sanctioned on one condition. If the uniform was to be changed in the first place, then let it be the most beautiful in the whole world. Let everybody feast their eyes and be impressed, indeed astonished by it.

And the uniform really wasn't bad. It was a beautiful uniform but, as everyone knows only too well, beauty requires sacrifices, beauty has to be paid for.

The first victims of all this beauty were the junior officers.

The new caps for the new uniforms have extended peaks, which is why they were immediately christened 'SS caps'. The regimental commander looks good in his new cap and so do the staff clerks in theirs, but young officers of the line have to demonstrate to the soldiers all kinds of rifle drill on the parade ground in the self-same 'SS cap'. There is one manoeuvre when with one sharp movement you have to throw your automatic behind your back in such a way that the automatic's strap lies straight across your chest. During this operation neither your head nor your body should move, and only the hands have to do the work as if one's a juggler. It's easy for the soldiers – they've only got little caps on the sides of their heads. But the poor officer! Every time he demonstrates how to do this movement, his high 'SS cap' flies off into the dust, or into the mud, or into a puddle. Or just suppose there's a physical training run, over a distance of five to ten kilometres; platoon and company commanders have to be out in front, that's the commander's place. All the sergeants and soldiers can run unimpeded but it is much worse for the officers. The aerodynamics of their caps are not good and, even in a slight breeze, all the officers' caps cartwheel away across the fields. And you just try and catch them! That's why all young officers began to appoint their personal armour-bearers – if my cap rolls away, you run and catch it for me!

But the 'SS cap' is worst of all during exercises. If the command 'Gas' is given, all the soldiers put on their gasmasks, and their side-caps can fit into their pockets or in their tunics, or be tucked into their belts. But what can an officer do in such a situation? Where does he put his 'SS cap'? As it is, there are far more objects hanging off him than off any soldier. An infantry officer must have an automatic and 120 cartridges, a pistol, a two-way radio, a compass, a sack, a gasmask, anti-atomic boots, gloves and a cape and an extra cape, a supply of water and food, binoculars, a commander's bag with writing board, a steel helmet and a spade. So there is absolutely nowhere left to put his cap. During the cross-country run, it can be carried in the hand if the senior commander doesn't see it, but during exercises there is always an automatic in the officer's hand, or the radio, or the writing board. You have no time to turn round; but you are not allowed to be without a cap. The cap must always be on the officer's head or somewhere near by. That's an order! There have been many different suggestions for this cap, for instance to wear it only on parade and for everyday use, but to replace it in the field with something like a beret or a side-cap. But Comrade Grechko was inflexible: beauty comes first.

Meanwhile autumn came and our soldiers felt the effects of the changes which had been introduced into the army for the sake of beauty.

Formerly, a soldier's greatcoat was plain grey. With the new uniform, the greatcoat was preserved in its original form, as invented by Tzar Nicholas I 150 years previously. But the Soviet designers decided to freshen it up with some new details. Instead of the green shoulder-straps, they put red ones for the infantry, and on the left sleeve they put a beautiful golden emblem stitched on red cloth, while on the right sleeve they placed golden chevrons, to indicate how long the soldier had served in the army, and on the chest they put six gold buttons. Of course, these were quite useless as soldiers' greatcoats are anyway fastened with hooks, and the shining buttons were sewn on top just to make it look beautiful. To wear greatcoats like these in battle was, of course, impossible. With red shoulder-straps and shining buttons, a soldier would be visible even in the bushes a whole kilometre away. To crawl through a field was equally impossible. Before, the soldier's belly was as smooth as a serpent's and he could crawl wherever you like, but now the buttons caught on the ground. Therefore, in the end, it was decided to leave the field uniform as it was before: no buttons and plain green shoulder-straps and no red patches.

The only thing was that a soldier has only one greatcoat. In any case he serves during only two winters, and one greatcoat is quite enough for him. So what to do? The problem was reported to the Minister.

'What is the problem?' enquired the astonished Minister of Defence. 'If war comes we will cut off the buttons and change the shoulder-straps. It's quite simple.'

But the real problem is that a soldier would need to do this far too often. When during the night a division is put on alert, no one, including the divisional commander himself, knows how it will all end. Is it just a check-up on battle readiness to be followed by retreat five minutes later, or are there going to be major exercises, or is it the beginning of the liberation of Western Europe? Who knows?

Before, when the uniform was plain, only four minutes and thirty seconds were needed to waken, silently, all 300 soldiers of the battalion, to let them dress in darkness, to get their armament and to leave the barracks. No noise, great speed, and no light. It was never easy to achieve such harmony, but every battalion somehow managed to achieve it and there were even some who could do it still more quickly.

With the new uniform everything was changed. Now, at the sound of the alarm, the light had to be switched on in all barracks, which meant that when it was sounded a soldier had to run over to each window and black it out before the light could be switched on. Then, having dressed, everyone had to run to the wardrobe, find his greatcoat and return to his place, where he had to cut off all the buttons, shoulder-straps and chevrons with a razor and afterwards sew on new green shoulder-straps. Only after all that performance could he run to fetch his weapons.

Previously, after the alarm had been sounded, the commander looked round and saw that everything was normal, everybody had got up, dressed and silently taken their weapons. It was all okay. Not bad. Retreat! At this point there was no need to hurry him. The Soviet soldier values sleep more than anyone else. He knows that there will be no compensation for all these night alerts, and five minutes after retreat has sounded the whole battalion is sleeping soundly.

Things became much worse with the beautiful new uniforms. After retreat, every soldier must now sew six gold buttons on to his greatcoat, and in a special way, so that all of them have Soviet power facing in the right direction: the little hammer with the end of the sickle must be facing precisely upwards. Then he has to sew the stripes on the sleeves and then the shoulder-straps. But, in the morning at six o'clock, a new day starts and a soldier must be ready in his beautiful everyday uniform and not in his field uniform. So there he sits, a whole hour before reveille, changing his shoulder-straps. And if he lies down for half an hour before reveille there may suddenly be a new alert and this time it could be a real battle alert and everything starts anew. Cut off the buttons and stripes and change the shoulder-straps.

A rumour reached the ear of Comrade Grechko that this uniform did not allow enough time for the alert, even if it was the smartest uniform in the whole world. Maybe something could be changed.

'Well,' said Comrade Grechko 'it's a pity of course, but something will have to be changed!'

And what was changed was the time allowed for the alert from four minutes thirty seconds to twenty-four minutes. This, needless to say, lowers the battle preparedness of troops in time of war and raises the possibility of their being caught when still in their camps, as happened in 1941. All of which is not, of course, a very good thing, though it does mean that all that beauty can be preserved intact.

The Western Ukraine, near Mukachevo. 12 October, 1968.

Our Native Land

As they left Czechoslovakia, our divisions reminded one of the remnants of a defeated army, fleeing from the hot pursuit after a shattering defeat. What officer could look without pain at the endless columns of dirty tanks mutilated by barbarous treatment and deprived for many months of human care and attention? Our regiment had also been thinned out. While still in Czechoslovakia, many of the platoons and companies had been completely reformed into draft reinforcement battalions and sent straight to the Chinese frontier. Many of those whose term of service was shortly to expire were packed off home. Often there was only one driver left out of a whole tank crew and no one else at all.

Our native land greeted us with brass bands blaring and then promptly despatched us, whole regiments at a time, into field camps behind barbed wire. Some unknown engineer quickly examined the battle equipment, determining on the march then and there whether it needed a complete overhaul, dismantling or normal repair.

And we were examined by doctors with the same speed: fit – fit – fit. Others rummaged convulsively in our files and passed rapid resolutions: the Chinese frontier – the Chinese frontier – the Chinese frontier.

But, quite suddenly, the habitual rhythm was broken. Our sparse regiment was formed up along that broad forest clearing which represented the central road of our military prison camp. The chief of the regimental staff tediously read aloud various orders of the Defence Minister, the Military District Commander and the Army Commander.

Then, suddenly, an escort arrived and deposited a fellow out there in front of the formation. He looked about twenty years old. From the very beginning, I was astonished by the fact that, for some strange reason, he was barefoot. It was an unusually warm autumn in the Carpathians: but it was autumn all the same.

It was difficult to say by looking at him whether he was a soldier or not. He wore soldier's trousers, but instead of a soldier's field shirt he had on a peasant's shirt. He stood at right angles to the regimental line and peered myopically away somewhere far off at the blue summits of the Carpathians. He had a soldier's mess-tin in his left hand, and with his right hand he clasped to his breast some kind of parcel wrapped in cloth, which was apparently very dear to him.

Clearly and distinctly, the chief of regimental staff read aloud from a paper concerning the adventures of our hero. One year ago he had been called up for service. During preparations for the liberation he had decided to exploit the situation to escape to the West. But, during all those re-shuffles, he found himself in one of the 'wild' divisions, which did not go into Czechoslovakia. Then, brandishing his automatic, he went up into the mountains and several times tried to break out across the frontier. For three months he remained in the mountains, then hunger forced him to return to so-called civilisation, and he surrendered himself freely of his own accord. Now he must be punished. During peacetime, fellows like him are punished somewhere out of sight. But we were on a war footing and, since his 'wild' division had long since been dispersed, he was to be punished in front of our regiment.

While the chief of staff completed reading the sentence, the executioner – a shortish, very thick-set major of the KGB in soft bo ts, slowly approached the deserter from behind.

Never in my life had I witnessed with my own eyes the carrying out of the death penalty and imagined it somehow quite differently: a dark cellar, a layer of sawdust on the floor, gloomy archways, a small beam of light. In life, everything turns out differently; here was a forest clearing covered with a luxurious carpet of crimson leaves, golden spiders' webs, the crystal sound of a mountain waterfall and a boundless woodland space flooded with the farewell warmth of the autumn sun.

The action unfolded in front of us as if on a stage during a performance, with the whole audience biting their lips and digging their nails deep into the arms of their chairs, watching silently as death, stepping slowly, slowly approached a man from behind. Everybody saw it clearly except the one who was destined to die. Those who say that one always senses the approach of death are probably wrong. Our soldier did not sense anything. He stood there as silently as before and listened, or maybe he did not even listen to the words of the sentence. One thing was obvious, he did not even suspect that he was to be sentenced to death. And, of course, he could not possibly suspect that the sentence would be carried out the very instant it was pronounced.

Now, after many years, I could invent some noble feelings which I experienced then, but at the time I felt nothing. I stood and, like hundreds of others, I looked at the soldier and the stealthy executioner and I wondered if the soldier would turn round or not, and whether he would see the executioner with the pistol, and whether the executioner would shoot at once or not. The soldier was not tied up and, if he had seen the executioner behind him, he might have tried to run away, or shouted or knelt down.

The chief of staff filled his lungs with air and, clearly and solemnly, as if it was a government bulletin about the launching of the first cosmonaut, he uttered the final phrase.

'IN THE NAME OF THE UNION . . .'

The executioner smoothly cocked his pistol without a click.

'OF SOVIET . . .'

The executioner, moving as softly as a cat, took another two steps forward and placed his legs apart for steadiness. Now he stood one metre away from the hapless fellow, and one felt sure that the prisoner could hear the executioner's breathing. But he still seemed to sense nothing.

'SOCIALIST . . .'

The executioner stretched his right hand forward, holding the pistol so that its muzzle nearly touched the soldier's neck.

'REPUBLICS . . .'

With his left hand, the executioner squeezed the wrist of his right hand, so as to keep the pistol steady.

'SENTENCED . . .'

The sinister crack of a solitary shot whipped like a lash across my back. I hunched myself up and screwed up my eyes as if I was in unbearable pain, but I opened them immediately again.

The dead soldier hurled both hands over his head, and as he performed the last upwards jump of his short life, as if trying to seize hold of the clouds, he threw back his head in a way which would have been impossible for a live man. Probably at this very last moment, his eyes already dead met the executioner's calm, piercing blue gaze. And the echo of the shot rolled slowly away towards a distant wooded ridge and fell and subsided in an odd barking noise.

The soldier's body fell very very slowly, just like a maple leaf on a balmy autumn's day. Equally slowly, the executioner stepped aside to make room for the falling body.

'TO PAY THE SUPREME PENALTY.'

And so the chief of staff finished pronouncing sentence.

The executioner adroitly extracted the magazine from the pistol and, with a jerk, jettisoned from the chamber the unnecessary second cartridge.

A burial party consisting of five soldiers, carrying spades and a piece of tarpaulin, ran towards the dead soldier. And there he was, lying at our feet, gazing with his unwinking eyes into the endless depths of the sky.

Postscript

Have you ever been acquainted with a man during that period of his life between the pronouncement of the death penalty upon him and its execution? If not, it is high time that you and I met, for I am such a man.

I am no longer a liberator. Not for me that role, nor for my country either. For it is my own firm conviction that only a country, to which people flock by the thousand from all corners of the world, has the right to advise others how to live. And the country, from which so many others break out, across its frontiers, in tanks, or fly away in home-made balloons or in the latest supersonic fighter, or escape across mine-fields and through machine-gun ambushes, or give the slip to packs of guard-dogs, that country certainly has no right to teach anyone anything – at least not for the time being.

First of all, put your own house in order. Try to create there such a society that people will not dig underground passages in order to escape. Only then shall we earn the right to teach others. And not with our tanks, but with good advice and our own personal example. Observe, admire, then go and imitate our example, if it pleases you.

These thoughts first came into my mind long ago. Perhaps they are silly or hackneyed – it does not matter, at least they are my own. The very first I have ever had.

I was most anxious that they should not perish with my life, and therefore I needed to share them with at least two other people.

But in my position that was totally impossible. We professional liberators are shot for such ideas – in the back of the head.

Of course, one can always share such an idea with one other liberator, but there would be no time left to share it with a second.

So that is why I left. I carried my ideas away with my brains intact. I prepared my escape for several years but I never really believed that the outcome would be successful. Under communist law, I am a turncoat and a traitor, a criminal guilty of the most serious crime.

I was sentenced to death in absentia by the Military Collegium of the Supreme Court of the USSR. In such cases, the method by which the sentence is to be carried out is never specified. The executioners are given a wide choice. They may execute the sentence by means of a car accident, a suicide, or a heart attack, etcetera, etcetera.

But first they have to find me! And, in the meantime, I am living out that last slice of my life. I am between the death sentence and its execution. It is the happiest time of my life.

DATE DUE

355
CLASS

53
ACC

SUVOROV
(LAST NAME OF AUTHOR)

The "liberators"
(BOOK TITLE)

DATE DUE | ISSUED TO

355
CLASS

53
ACC.

SUVOROV
(LAST NAME OF AUTHOR)

The "liberators"
(BOOK TITLE)